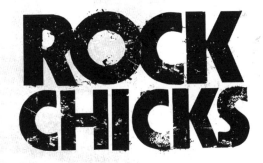

Published by Rockpool Publishing

24 Constitution Road

Dulwich Hill NSW 2203

AUSTRALIA

www.markbyrne.com.au

First published in 2007, updated edition 2010

Rock chicks : the hottest female rockers from the 1960s to
              now / Alison Stieven-Taylor ;
              photographs by Tony Mott.

2nd ed.

9781921295355 (pbk.)

Women rock musicians--Biography.
              Rock musicians--Biography.
              Rock music--History and criticism.
              Rock music.

              Mott, Tony.

781.66082

Cover and internal design by Debaser

Typesetting J&M Typesetting and Nicholson Design

Picture research by Lisa Perry

Printed and bound by I Book Printing Limited, China

10 9 8 7 6 5 4 3 2 1

ROCK CHICKS

The Hottest Female Rockers from the 1960s to Now

Alison Stieven-Taylor

ROCKPOOL
PUBLISHING

Contents

The 1990s

The 2000s

Note from the Author

Everyone of the rock chicks in this book have sung songs that are etched into my personal history. Such is the power of music that I only need to hear a few lines or the beginning of the tune and I'm immediately transported to the moment connected to that particular song — breaking up with my boyfriend, the birth of my sons, my first trip to Europe.

Suzi Quatro's *Can the Can* was one of the first albums I bought. I danced the heels off my stilettos to Tina Turner's 'Nutbush City Limits' at the disco end of the 1970s and tried to emulate Debbie Harry's two-tone hair while listening to *Parallel Lines*. Heart's rock anthems used to blare from my car stereo and I played Stevie Nicks' 'Rhiannon' and 'Edge of Seventeen' until the tape became so stretched it was cobbled up by the cassette player.

In the early 1980s I drank black coffee, wore black leather and lycra and smoked gold-tipped Russian cigarettes. I listened to Marianne Faithfull's *Broken English* as if it were the new religion. Marianne had taken tales of suicide, love, drugs, sex and hate and wrapped them in a vice-like grip with her tobacco-ravished voice and acid phrasing. It was an album of pure genius — and malice. I bought a bootleg copy from a friend who worked for Gaslight Records because it was banned in Australia for its use of profanity.

By 1983 I was working in Los Angeles as a publicist on the Men at Work North American and Canadian tour. Australian culture was having its fifteen minutes of fame in the USA — being an Aussie made you flavour of the day. I shared a house with two sound engineers who worked with Prince and bands like Motley Crue. When I returned to Australia the following year I moved from publicist to writer, interviewing artists for various music magazines including *Rolling Stone* and *Australian Musician*. Although today we are not allowed to accept gifts and freebies, journalists used to get great perks and I enjoyed my fair share of backstage parties and industry events. In 1998 I covered the New Zealand Music Awards for *Rolling Stone*, the year a tiny woman named Bic Runga swept the pool and alternate rock band Shihad were gods.

Even though trends shift, and what you were listening to in the 1970s is different to what you may enjoy today, the permanency of music and its ability to move you is constant. Music's ability to interpret, reflect, celebrate and commiserate the human condition is fundamental to how we communicate. For the average Jane on the street, music is a part of her everyday life. Through radio, CDs, films, video, TV and online, our senses — and imaginations — are constantly stimulated.

Music is also a business. Record companies advance money to bands to record, tour and make videos. All these funds have to be repaid through record sales. The musicians make money out of song royalties and those who are also songwriters — like Stevie Nicks, Pink and Madonna — can become seriously wealthy from song rights alone.

Rock Chicks celebrates the women musicians and singers who have given us some of the most stimulating and evocative songs by which our lives keep tempo. Rock on.

What is a Rock Chick?

A rock chick is a female musician, usually a lead singer, who rocks with real musicians. She has successfully defied the contemporary stereotypical image of women singers to rail against the pop princesses, girl groups and manufactured dolly music. She's high energy, in-your-face, daring anyone to challenge her right to be up there on stage rocking the audience.

The women in this book are unique in their interpretation of rock. Many have broken down barriers for generations to come — Janis Joplin, Stevie Nicks and Debbie Harry are three of the most influential women in rock and the most frequently cited as influences by other female musicians.

My list of rock chicks came together after I hounded around thirty music and entertainment industry experts who willingly lent me their collective brain and allowed me to pick through it. My list may not be their list — or yours. But it's the one I think best represents the essence of the rock chick.

Some puzzled over the fact that today the rock chick has almost disappeared.

Others questioned the inclusion of artists like Madonna. I don't think she meets the criteria musically, but her impact on popular culture — not just music, but film, literature, fashion, sexuality and even religion — cannot be ignored. She is a rock phenomenon who just happens to be a chick.

Courtney Love, too, is a controversial pick. In my opinion she barely scrapes in as a musician. She may have the pretences to rock, but she doesn't have the heart. She is more obsessed with fame than with the craft of music and if it weren't for the Nirvana-ish *Live Through This* album she wouldn't be worthy of more than a passing comment.

There are of course, other great women singers and musicians in so many different genres, but when it comes to rock — hard, gritty, spill your soul and don't apologise for it kind of rock — these women encapsulate it.

That *Indefinable* Rock Chick Thing

by Tony Mott

When I was first told about *Rock Chicks* I had two reactions. One was excitement — my career has been blessed with working with people I would define as rock chicks. The second reaction was — wow, what a task to compile the list without missing somebody out or upsetting other people. I was excited because rock chicks are fantastic to photograph. And I know it is impossible to make a perfect list because everybody has a different view of what defines a rock chick.

For me it's a combination of qualities. A rock chick is sassy, sexy and has loads of charisma — and, above all, is empowering both to herself and her audience.

The first rock chick I remember was Suzi Quatro. You just didn't see a bass player clad in a leather jumpsuit strutting her stuff with one of the qualities I believe is essential —attitude and in abundance. The first rock chick I photographed was Chrissy Amphlett from Divinyls. She was unbelievable on stage, ranging from banshee to an escapee from the local asylum. You never quite knew what she was going to do next. Unpredictable but she was always engaging and always believable and, yes, a contradiction. I couldn't keep my eyes — actually my lens — off her. For me, she still stands as one of the greatest performers I've had the pleasure to photograph.

A few other rock chicks have left a lasting impression on me. Kim Gordon from Sonic Youth was the queen of the rock grunge revolution — I think her single 'Cool Thing' epitomises that time. Alanis Morrisette's stage presence is unique, prowling the stage not unlike a caged lion. Meeting and photographing Marianne Faithfull — whose album *Broken English* still has the power to shock — was daunting in the extreme. Johnette Napolitano from Concrete Blonde was very much her own person and took no nonsense from her record company — after the label asked her not to wear too much black, she arrived in nothing but black, including black lipstick. Patti Smith was most unsociable but totally engaging on stage, screaming her poems and songs at a bewildered young audience at the Big Day Out. And from Geelong, Adilta from Magic Dirt is everything a rock chick should be.

Like anyone who picks up this book, my rock chicks list is my own. Here are some photographs of some of my favourites. I've included a few who aren't profiled. Although they may not have had the commercial success and/or influence of some of the other woman in the book, they are true rock chicks in my book.

1960s

The birth of the rock band

The cultural revolution that was the 1960s actually began the decade before with the rise of the Beats, a group of American writers who composed riffs challenging the mores of the stuffy Western society of the post-Second World War years. On the surface everything appeared sunny and civil. But there was an undercurrent of fear and oppression darkened by the shadows of the A-bomb and the Cold War and stirred by the increasingly potent black rights movement led by Martin Luther King. And the tidy society of suburbs and

17

wifely submission was about to be shaken by the introduction of the contraceptive pill and women's sexual 'liberation'.

The work of the Beats — most notably Jack Kerouac, William Burroughs, Lawrence Ferlinghetti and Allen Ginsberg — described the alienation of youth, was influenced by jazz and subjected to censorship. They lived on the fringe, experimenting with drugs and writing about subjects not discussed by polite society. Along with Marlon Brando and James Dean, they were 'rebels without a cause'. The Beats hung out in the North Beach area of San Francisco, smoking weed and chewing speed in open defiance of the authorities. Many of the rock chicks — including Janis Joplin, Marianne Faithfull and Chrissie Hynde — cite the writers of the Beat Generation as major influences.

In August 1961 Berliners awoke to find their city divided by an ugly barbed wire wall. Overnight the Soviets had erected a wall dividing East and West Berlin. Protests against racial segregation were splitting America and folk singers were beginning to top the charts with political protest songs. Two years later, John F Kennedy was assassinated, Martin Luther King gave his landmark 'I have a dream' speech and the US Congress held the first hearings into the fair treatment of women where terms like the 'glass ceiling' were heard. There had been a seismic shift in society.

Rock music was born into this world in turmoil. Whether it was a case of life imitating art or vice versa, the artists of the 1960s, and musicians in particular, were central to change. The music of the 1950s — the choreographed girl groups like the Chantels and the Chordettes, female singers Connie Francis, Rosemary Clooney, Patti Page, Petula Clark, Doris Day and Peggy Lee, and the male jivers Elvis Presley, Jerry Lee Lewis, Chuck Berry, Little Richard and Bobby Darin — began to look like crooning, left behind in the wake of a new genre in music.

The Beatles are acknowledged as the instigators of the revolutionary sound that became known as rock. It was a musical genre that morphed into new forms with a rapidity that was as mind-blowing as the psychedelic drugs that fuelled much of the creativity. It embraced a new culture based on personal freedom and experimentation, and endorsing psychedelic drugs, protest, 'free' love and 'free' living.

Within a space of only two years, popular music went from Chubby Checker and doing the twist in 1961 to the Beatles, who started to hit the big time in 1963. The British embraced the new sound with fervor, just as they took to Mary Quant's mini-skirt and other 'Swinging London' fashions. In the first half of the 1960s, the Brits gave the world the Rolling Stones, the Who, the Yardbirds, the Pretty Things, the Kinks and the Small Faces, many of whom took their inspiration from rhythm'n'blues. And soaring above the crowds were the stunning voices of Dusty Springfield and her American counterpart Aretha Franklin.

Beatlemania soon swept the States and almost all corners of the globe. In the

USA bands formed at the speed in which rabbits procreate. Live venues sprung up across the country and bands played in city parks, theatres, cafes, clubs and halls. Crosby, Stills and Nash were sharing the billing with the likes of the Lovin' Spoonful, the Mamas and the Papas, Simon and Garfunkel, Peter, Paul and Mary and Ian and Sylvia. Considered more folk rock than folk were Jefferson Airplane, the Grateful Dead, Moby Grape, Three Dog Night and Janis Joplin's Big Brother and the Holding Company. To crown it all, Bob Dylan, the golden boy of folk scandalised the Newport Folk Festival crowd by going 'electric' in 1965.

The fashionista were encased in velvet, leather, short skirts, high boots and sex and sizzle. Style was everything, and the Beatles and the Stones were widely imitated, particularly Mick Jagger. His partner Marianne Faithfull had a hit with 'As Tears Go By' and was the poster girl for teenagers. Everyone wanted to be Marianne — or Twiggy, the wraith-like model who introduced a look later known as heroin chic.

Like other female singers of the time, Marianne Faithfull didn't threaten anyone (that came later). The big stars of the day — Joni Mitchell, Judy Collins and Joan Baez — were folk singers. One exception was Grace Slick, whose deep voice was ideally suited to the psychedelic folk rock that made Jefferson Airplane famous. But it took Janis Joplin to really

1960s

shake things up, just as the women's liberation movement was becoming a force for political and social change.

The psychedelic drug, lysergic acid (LSD), had entered the collective consciousness by 1965 and advocates such as the Harvard professor Timothy Leary gave it celebrity status. Art, music and literature were under the influence, most famously the Beatles' 1967 groundbreaking *Sgt. Pepper* album, which introduced a new acid rock sound influenced by mind-altering drugs and Eastern mysticism.

The Haight-Ashbury area of San Francisco was taken over by stoned hippies who were 'dropping out' of conventional society and embracing a 'holistic' attitude to life, in which spirit, earth and self come together. The hippie movement spread, fuelled by music, acid and disillusionment with the politics of war and discrimination. The young were leaving behind the beliefs and values of their parents' generation. Song lyrics shifted from love to environmentalism, consumerism, politics, war, drugs and personal freedom. There were anti-war songs, songs against segregation and songs like Jefferson Airplane's 'White Rabbit' about the effects of psychedelic drugs.

By 1967 — the 'summer of love' — the hard-edged London fashions had morphed into frills and flowers, and the hippie movement had blossomed into a community of tens of thousands, many of whom congregated in San Francisco. At the world's first large-scale rock festival, at Monterey in California, Janis Joplin gave the landmark performance of her career. Less blossom, more grunge, Warhol darling Nico was recording her first album with the Velvet Underground in New York.

It wasn't all peace, love and sex. By 1968, when Martin Luther King was assassinated, crime rates in the USA had increased nearly tenfold on the decade before, anti-Vietnam demonstrations were daily events and race riots were causing havoc. In some American cities the atmosphere was close to that of civil war. Musically, one of the positives was the rise in prominence of African-American singers such as Tina Turner. For the first time, black artists were being ranked in the mainstream charts and rock artists like Janis Joplin and the Rolling Stones continued to cover songs by old blues artists.

Joplin was a headliner at 1969's Woodstock, a festival held on a farm in upstate New York. For three days, over 400,000 people grooved — to Jefferson Airplane, the Grateful Dead, Jimi Hendrix, Santana, Canned Heat, Sly and the Family Stone — as the heavens opened and rivers of rain turned the ground into a bog. Hippies got stoned, danced, rolled naked in the mud, made babies and freaked out on bad acid.

But the peace and love turned sour at the Stones' free concert at Altamont in California when a concertgoer was stabbed to death by one of the Hell's Angels, who were acting as security guards.

As the 1960s came to a close, man [*sic*] walked on the moon with a greater certainty than he was treading the earth.

JANIS JOPLIN

Queen of the Dionysian Rock Age

The Janis Joplin camp is split into two factions.

She's a
misunderstood
genius

who broke down
rock music barriers
for women.

Or a vulgar,
drug-addicted

exhibitionist

whose excesses were greater
than her talents.

But few can deny her impact. Her on-stage flamboyance, bravado, raw vocal style and drug-ravished rock-star behaviour shocked a society used to women being compliant and polite.

Janis could sing like an African-American blues singer then pick it up a tempo and roll her voice around the new hard-core rock sound. She was the first real rock chick, shaking up the music scene with her powerful performance and strong personality. Her influence extends far beyond her musical output — she only recorded four albums. She was a role model for young women who were inspired by her apparent

she had disastrous relationships with cruel men and emotionally dysfunctional women. She got stoned and beaten up on the street

fearlessness at being herself, of embracing the times. Some thought her hard. But Janis was struggling, caught up in the moral dilemmas of eschewing the established social mores.

David Dalton, one of the founding editors of *Rolling Stone* magazine, interviewed Janis numerous times. 'It is really important the way she is represented because she was a wonderful person,' he told me. 'I did a lot of the *Rolling Stone* interviews and I love a lot of the people I interviewed, but Janis absolutely was my favourite person.'

Port Arthur, Texas, where Janis was born in 1943, was an oil town, a bastion of redneck conservatism. The American South was still segregated and racial tensions were high. Janis was the black sheep of a conventional, church-going family, always questioning the status quo, but she excelled at school. As a child she loved to perform. At high school, she was always singing or starring in plays she wrote. She developed a talent for drawing and instead of painting landscapes, as expected, she specialised in voluptuous sexy nudes — and delighted in the scandalised reactions.

Bill Haley and the Comets and Elvis Presley were dominating the radio waves, but Janis gravitated towards the rawness of the blues, preferring Bessie Smith and Big Mama Thornton. She sang in the church choir and in glee club as a child, but never thought of being a singer until she was in her late teens.

An avid reader, Janis devoured the Beat writers, in particular Jack Kerouac whose seditious take on the world appealed to her. Adopting the rebellious idiosyncrasies of Kerouac's characters, she took on mannerisms that were masculine and concealed her insecurities. She felt unattractive. She began dressing in a mannish manner, with trousers and long shirts, her unbrushed hair pulled back into a rough ponytail. Her face was pock-marked with acne scars, her skin dry and patchy. She never wore make-up. Janis attached herself to a group of male musicians and writers who fancied themselves the ultimate rebels. But her outrageous antics rattled her male companions, who were bemused and horrified at the same time. Her 'unladylike' manner and penchant for profanity landed her in hot water wherever she went.

In 1961 she enrolled to study arts at Lamar State College in Port Arthur, but she barely lasted the year. That summer she took off for Los Angeles. It didn't take her long to gravitate to Venice Beach, then a seedy suburb where dealers, pimps and con artists littered the boardwalk. Grass, benzedrine, heroin and codeine-based cough syrup were readily available. Janis began a wild ride of drugs and indiscriminate sex with men and women. She exuded confidence, but her bravado concealed her anguish. Janis just wanted to be loved and accepted.

Whatever she was looking for in LA didn't materialise. The following year she was back in Port Arthur to resume her arts studies. She started singing at a club in Austin, Threadgill's, every Wednesday night as part of the Waller Creek Boys, a trio with Powell St John on harmonica and Lanny Wiggins on bass. They played the club circuit around Austin and on campus at the University of Texas, where Janis was now studying and where she was named 'ugliest man on campus' — an incident that reportedly drove her to despair and haunted her for years to come.

By 1963 Janis was back in California, living in North Beach, San Francisco, where the Beats had hung out in the 1950s. The area swarmed with artists, poets, writers, musicians, painters and actors, the accepted lifestyle was dionysian and LSD was becoming the favourite party drug. For the first time, Janis felt she belonged.

She began singing at small venues like The Coffee Gallery, sometimes alone playing her autoharp or with guitarist Jorma Kaukonen, who would turn up later in Jefferson Airplane. On the personal front she was turning from one disastrous relationship to another with cruel men and emotionally dysfunctional women. She got stoned, beaten up on the street and ended up in hospital after a motorbike accident.

The next year Janis was in New York, singing in Slug's and other East Village clubs. Her outfit had morphed into black pants and a V-neck jumper. She cut a slender figure, thanks to an increasing flirtation with the city's newest drug craze. Janis hung with the speed freaks. But it wasn't long before she returned to the more mellow vibes of San Francisco and the nascent Haight-Ashbury scene. The city was rocking along with Dylan and the Stones and overloading on grass and acid.

Chet Helms, an old Texas friend who was managing and promoting bands, suggested she hook up with Big Brother and the Holding Company, who were looking for a female singer. Janis was her usual unkempt self when she arrived to meet Big Brother but wowed the band with her deeply drawn blues voice.

Big Brother — Sam Andrew, Peter Albin and James Gurley on guitars and Dave Getz on drums — was transformed by Janis's powerful stage presence. Within months the band, along with the Grateful Dead, Country Joe McDonald and the Fish and Jefferson Airplane, had a big following. They became an instant attraction on the touring circuit, spending much of the year on the road playing halls, theatres and campuses around

She was raw, emotional, sexy and at times agonisingly ugly in her pain

America. Through it all, Janis was consuming vast quantities of pills, powders and heroin. She was loving recklessly, often with strangers, and drowning her sorrows with hard liquor. The first album, *Big Brother and the Holding Company*, was released on Mainstream Records. Then it was into the studio to record *Cheap Thrills*, which was released in 1968 and reached number one. The album features one track written by Janis, 'Turtle Blues'.

But it wasn't the record that catapulted Janis into rock stardom — it was her live performance which rocked in a way no white woman had ever done. She was raw, emotional, sexy and at times agonisingly ugly in her pain. Her stage performance — fuelled by the copious quantities of Southern Comfort that she slugged before, during and after a concert — lifted the audience to great heights and spun them around with the emotional urgency of her voice. When Janis and Big Brother performed at the first Human Be-In Festival in Golden Gate Park in 1967 — on the bill with Jefferson Airplane and the Grateful Dead — each performance was more dramatic and flamboyant than the last.

The turning point was at the Monterey Festival later that year. Taking to the stage in a silver lurex pant suit, Janis mesmerised the audience, crews and other performers with her electrified performance. She sang Big Mama Thornton's 'Ball and Chain', one of the songs she'd listened to as a child, and Bessie Smith covers. The press

Rolling Stone compared her to Judy Garland: a tragic artist hell bent on self-destruction

went overboard in their praises and began to seek Janis out for interviews. She was featured in *Newsweek* and *Time* as the woman who had infiltrated the male rock world. Her Monterey performance made Janis an instant celebrity and the media swarmed, delighting in her bad behaviour. Soon she was signing a deal with Albert Grossman, Bob Dylan's manager. Grossman had the reputation of behaving like a pit bull, but with Janis he was caring and understanding.

Her dependency on Southern Comfort was growing to such an extent that she wrote to the distiller pointing out how much free publicity she was giving its product, making her one of the first artists to leverage product endorsement. The company responded by sending her a fur coat.

Photos of Janis were appearing in journals like *New York* magazine, the *Village Voice* and *Vogue* and the rock sections of the major dailies such as the *New York Times*. The rash of new music titles led by *Rolling Stone*, the first issue of which was published in San Francisco in November 1967, were fighting to feature the wild woman of rock. The Janis of Big Brother jangled with jewels, bangles, rings and bright swirling scarves. She often wore pants, lots of black and lots of bling. The press loved her flamboyance and theatricality, her multi-coloured hair and the layers of fabric. She rarely disappointed in her raw emotional crudeness. Reviewers raved about her as if she were a new species.

But Janis was more than the performing, partying animal, although few had the opportunity to know the real person. She was intelligent and outspoken, her rebellious statements stabbing at the heart of conservatism. Janis topped the list of rock stars not permitted to perform in Texas because of their liberal views.

Janis and Big Brother played to thunderous applause at the opening of the new Fillmore theatre in San Francisco in 1968. The Fillmore became one of the central venues to watch psychedelic light shows enhanced by LSD. Mirroring theatrical gatherings, the men dressed in tail coats with velvet pants and leather top hats and women wore layers of colours, flowing pants and handkerchief skirts. There were high heels and sandals. Boots and suede. Bangles and bells.

With the money starting to flow in, Janis bought herself a Porsche and an apartment. She paid for a headstone for Bessie Smith who had died impoverished. But most of her money went on partying and drugs, and she footed the bill for a considerable entourage.

Despite her commercial successes and the adoration of fans and media, Janis wasn't happy. She was constantly brought down by the drugs and booze hangovers. The emptiness didn't evaporate with the endless procession of lovers and the ever-increasing substance abuse. Janis was consumed with self-loathing and doubt.

Grossman started telling Janis she needed a more professional band, a view repeated in reviews. Although she felt guilty about it, she recognised Grossman was right. Janis didn't want to be seen just as the

when Kristofferson arrived at Janis's house to discuss the song with her, 'he was terrified because Janis is overwhelming'

queen of the Haight-Ashbury sound. She wanted to be a big star. A new band was one way of getting the professional acclaim she was seeking. Before the year was out Janis had left Big Brother, taking Sam Andrew with her.

Her new backing band, Kozmic Blues, included horn and saxophone session players and Andrew on guitar. Janis appeared with her new line-up at the annual concert held by Stax-Volt, one of the leading R&B recording companies, in Memphis in late 1968. Her performance was atrocious. Clearly inebriated, she wailed and screamed and was her usual unruly self. The crowd were used to choreographed routines and booed her off stage. Although she loved R&B artists' music, the compliment wasn't returned.

S till rattled by her performance at Stax-Volt, Janis took the stage with her new band at the opening of the Fillmore East in New York a few months later. She was obviously nervous and throughout the performance sought approval from the audience, prompting one *Rolling Stone* journalist to compare her to Judy Garland: a tragic artist hell bent on self-destruction.

Janis toured Europe in 1969, the only time she performed outside North America, playing to capacity crowds at such venues as the Albert Hall in London. She was on the bill for the massive Woodstock Festival, but her performance didn't come near the brilliance of her Monterey act two years earlier. Complaining she couldn't connect with the 400,000 crowd, Janis spent the day drunk, surly and antagonistic, snapping at everyone and refusing to do interviews.

In between touring Janis went back into the studio to record *I Got Dem Ol' Kozmic Blues Again Mama!* The album featured eight tracks, with a re-recording of 'Piece of My Heart', one of her Big Brother hits, the Bee Gee's 'To Love Somebody', her own 'One Good Man', 'Try (Just A Little Bit Harder)' and Hart and Rogers' 'Little Girl Blue'. The album reached number five on the Billboard charts, but her move further into blues didn't sit well with fans. They wanted the rocking Janis back.

As the next decade dawned, Janis left Kozmic Blues behind, taking two of her band mates with her: bass player Brad Campbell and guitarist John Till. The new ensemble, Full-Tilt Boogie Band, also featured drummer Clark Pierson, organist Ken Pearson and pianist Rick Bell.

Around this time Janis embarked on a brief affair with Kris Kristofferson, who gave her 'Me and Bobby McGee' to record, one of her most memorable songs. It appears on the posthumously released album *Pearl*. Her association with Kristofferson was erratic, like all her relationships. David Dalton tells of Kristofferson arriving at Janis's house to discuss the song with her. 'He was like terrified because Janis is an overwhelming person you know. Incredibly endlessly needy and wanting and this is not the kind of thing that guys are especially attracted to … poor Janis. She was always pursuing guys who weren't likely to really be life-long mates. … it was always said as part of the Janis Joplin persona, but if I would hit on a waitress or an airline steward, Janis would say, "well, what about me honey?" … I think that a lot of people were probably intimated by her.'

By the time she was on the Festival Express railroad tour of Toronto, Winnipeg and Calgary in early 1970, she was no longer shooting heroin, but was feeding herself plenty of booze, powder, pills and dope. Dalton joined Janis on the tour, spending days with her, recording interviews and random conversations. 'Festival Express was very innocent,' Dalton said. 'People always imagined all this wild stuff, but really it was just people having a good time and getting together and recreating the whole situation on the Haight-Ashbury before they became famous. It was wonderful in that way, there was no real monstrous behaviour.'

The Festival Express tour featured the Band, the Grateful Dead, Delaney and Bonnie and Friends, Ian and Sylvia, New Riders of the Purple Sage, Tom Rush, Buddy Guy, Eric Andersen, Ten Years After, Traffic, Seatrain, Cat, Mashmakan and the Modern Rock Quartet. As there were no washing amenities on the train, in each town the musicians and crew would descend upon the local swimming pool. Janis threw modesty to the wind, stripping naked and plunging into the pool to the horror of authorities and amusement of her fellow musicians, many of whom followed suit.

she loved to party, but she was very introspective — she was a beatnik and intellectual. She was very philosophical, had a very, very serious side to her

'She loved to party, but she was very introspective,' said Dalton. 'A lot of the time on tours she would be in her room reading; she was a beatnik and intellectual, someone who pondered. She was very philosophical, had a very, very serious side to her. I think this created a dilemma with her desire to present the Janis Joplin character twenty-four hours a day. She felt she had to go out and be this person,'

When the Festival Express tour ended Janis sunk into a depression. She had enjoyed the camaraderie and getting stoned, singing, drinking and playing with the other musicians.

Dabbling in heroin again, Janis flew to New York that year to perform at the Peace Festival at Shea Stadium. She was electric on stage and it was one of her best performances, the crowd spinning and jumping wildly. The band played numerous dates in New York and Janis befriended the young Patti Smith, who was starting to put words to music. She gravitated towards Greenwich Village and hung out at Max's

she exuded
confidence
but her
bravado
concealed
her anguish.
Janis just
wanted
to be
loved and
accepted

Kansas City, where Debbie Harry waited on her. Feted by the artistic elite, including Warhol and Ginsberg, Janis became entrenched in the celebrity culture.

After New York she paid her family a visit in Port Arthur, which might as well have been on another planet. Her parents were at wits' end and were no longer prepared to tolerate her bizarre lifestyle. Her desire to be different drove her poor, staid mother Dorothy to distraction. Her father Seth was a stern man who didn't understand his unruly daughter. Rock music was as foreign to him as casual sex and drugs. Sparks flew. Janis left the house disgruntled and emotionally shaken.

Returning to her home in Larkspur in San Francisco, Janis threw herself back into the social fray, trying to shake off her anger and hurt. There she met Seth Morgan who was twenty-one, six years younger than Janis. They became inseparable. For a few short weeks she played house, shopping, cooking, going to the movies, eating out — doing all the normal things you do when in a new relationship. She enjoyed the semblance of normality but knew it wouldn't last. She was scheduled to go to LA to lay down tracks for *Pearl*.

According to Dalton, 'Fame is one of the huge paradoxes of Janis's life because in a way she started out wanting to find a good guy who would love her and care for her, but her fame created a situation where that was going to be impossible. The sort of guys she claimed she wanted — log-splitting guys who lived in Alaska and fucked bears — are not going to turn up back stage. The kind of people she met were more like the sexy lounge-lizard character who was always there on tour, like her fiancé Seth Morgan. A good-looking hustler and ex-drug dealer. They were going to have an open marriage. I don't think Janis realised quite how open that was going to be, you know.'

Janis was planning a whole domestic package with Morgan: marriage and perhaps even a baby. She began talking about winding down her career and touring less, much to the chagrin of Albert Grossman, who was

after she'd shot up the smack, she ventured into the hotel lobby to buy cigarettes

battling an increasing number of promoters reluctant to take on Janis. Her reputation for blowing off gigs and her manic on- and off-stage antics preceded her. Her arrest for using profanity on stage did not help Grossman's attempts to book her. Promoters were playing hardball and local governments banned certain performers and musical genres. Janis incited audiences to frenzy, her calls to 'fuck not fight' infusing an already-electric atmosphere. For those lucky enough to have seen Janis perform live the memories are unforgettable.

Tearing herself away from Morgan, Janis headed off to the Landmark Hotel, a Los Angeles establishment as popular with celebrities then as Chateau Marmont. In the studio under the direction of the Doors producer Paul A Rothchild, work on *Pearl* was progressing. Janis recorded 'Me and Bobby McGee', which would become her greatest hit. The album also included 'Mercedes Benz', which she co-wrote with Michael McClure.

Also at the Landmark was her old mate Peggy Caserta, a lesbian she knew from her San Francisco heroin days. Caserta is infamous for penning the bestseller *Going Down with Janis Joplin*, which opens with a description of Janis giving Caserta head while stoned on heroin.

By 1970 she had overdosed five times on heroin. But on 4 October she didn't recover from the super-pure heroin she shot up around one in the morning alone in her hotel room. That day she'd been in the studio listening to the tracks already put down. Then she went with the band to eat at Barney's Beanery before retiring around 12.30 am.

Apparently, after she'd shot up the smack delivered to her earlier by her dealer, she ventured into the hotel lobby to buy cigarettes before returning to her room. There she fell and died at 1.40 am that night.

Her death, aged twenty-seven, became one of the most celebrated events of the era, along with those of Jimi Hendrix, Otis Redding and Jim Morrison. Perhaps the one person who would have been most surprised is Janis herself, who had often imagined herself as an eccentric old lady making music well into her twilight years.

Janis Joplin's place in history is secured. While she continues to inspire a new generation, the rock chick will live on.

MARIANNE FAITHFULL

Marianne Faithfull once described

herself

to the *Observer* newspaper as

'a fabulous

beast.

I should only be glimpsed very rarely through the forest running away for dear life.' Never was there a more apt description for this enigma from the 1960s.

Tales of her drug addiction and life on the streets of London as a heroin junkie have kept Marianne in the media for the past forty years, relegating her considerable artistic achievements to second place, much the same way as her relationship with Mick Jagger did in the early days.

Before her landmark album *Broken English* was released in 1979, Marianne enjoyed a string of hit singles in the 1960s. A whisper of a girl with a slightly husky voice, large eyes framed by thick lashes, blonde hair and 'big tits', as her first manager so charmingly described her, she was the quintessential 1960s waif — all sex, pout and attitude. Singing for her was just a hobby.

Marianne Faithfull was born in 1946, the only child of Eva, a headstrong, feisty Austro-Hungarian baroness, and Major Glynn Faithfull. They were not a wealthy family and there was little love between her parents. Her father, a somewhat eccentric inventor, was off on tangents that her mother couldn't fathom. When Marianne was about four her parents split and she didn't see her father for years.

Under the care of her mother and grandmother, Marianne grew up in Reading in southern England. Sent to the local Catholic convent as a charity boarder, she was not allowed to forget her lowly status. She didn't like the confines of the convent, its cloisters feeling more like a prison, its staid thinking stifling her adventurous spirit.

As a teenager in the early 1960s she sang folk songs at coffee shops and performed in amateur theatre. She didn't know what she wanted to do, but thought it might involve performance. Artistic and articulate, Marianne was a compulsive reader interested in existentialism, Nietzsche

> Marianne was artistic and articulate, interested in existentialism, Nietzsche and de Beauvoir, jazz and poetry, Bardot and Greco

and de Beauvoir, jazz and poetry, and Brigitte Bardot and Juliette Greco. She visited London often, going to the ballet and theatre, attending art gallery openings and revelling in the excitement of pop culture. London was a creative melting pot. Fashion designer Mary Quant, artists like David Hockney and Lucian Freud, the Beatles and the Rolling Stones were among those pushing the boundaries, placing London at the heart of the swinging 1960s.

Marianne was 'discovered' at a party in London. Within minutes of seeing her, Andrew Loog Oldham, the Rolling Stones' manager, decided to sign her. He didn't know if she could sing, but that was immaterial. She had the right look — a virginal waif with a glint of confidence in her eyes — that promised an exciting mix of innocence and sex.

When her first single 'As Tears Go By' was released in 1964 she was in her final year at school. One semester to go and she bailed. The lure of London and the status of pop star were calling. The song, the first written by Mick Jagger and Keith Richards, wasn't written for Marianne, despite folklore. But the cachet of it being penned by the new rock'n'roll aristocracy wasn't lost on Marianne or on the record-buying public. It reached the top ten.

Within weeks of the single being released Marianne appeared on *Top of the Pops*, *Ready Steady Go!* and *Juke Box Jury*, the three big music shows on British television, along with the likes of Dusty Springfield and Sandie Shaw.

she had the right look — a virginal waif with a glint of confidence in her eyes — that promised an exciting mix of innocence and sex

To promote the single Marianne hit the road on one of the multi-bill shows that were popular at the time. Performing in draughty halls to punters who wanted her to either get her gear off or get off — they hadn't come to see her — she quickly discovered that touring wasn't all it was cracked up to be. The lesser known act on a bill that included the Hollies, Freddy and the Dreamers and Gerry and the Pacemakers, Marianne was far down the pecking list. Stiff and sore from sleeping in crammed spaces, jostled about by the rickety old bus, and suffocated by the testosterone in the air, her bright-eyed enthusiasm was eroded by the endless loneliness and monotony of being on the road. Falling ill, Marianne left the tour early.

Another two singles followed in quick succession: a cover of Bob Dylan's 'Blowin' In The Wind' failed to chart, but the February 1965 release of 'Come and Stay With Me', written by Jackie De Shannon, shot Marianne back into the top ten. Then there were tours with Gene Pitney and Roy Orbison.

On the surface, she was living a life that made her the envy of tens of thousands of young girls. But behind the hip bravado and the on-tour affairs, Marianne was longing for love. Despite the loose love ethos of the 1960s, she wanted to belong to someone.

That someone was her longtime boyfriend, poet John Dunbar. He ran an art gallery and was the epitome of the cool intellectual. Such were the circles Dunbar moved in it wasn't uncommon to find Paul McCartney or John Lennon at one of his gallery's glittering parties. In 1965 she married Dunbar and later that year gave birth to her only child, Nicholas.

But Marianne quickly learned that being married wasn't all it was cracked up to be. Before they'd tied the knot, the two had happily co-existed, Marianne doing her thing and coming back to Dunbar when she was ready. Once Nicholas arrived, the playing field changed. She had intended to play wife and mother, but the novelty soon wore off. She was only nineteen and felt hemmed in by the confines of married life and motherhood. Through it all Marianne kept working, recording four singles and two albums, and performing at the Uxbridge Blues and Folk Festival with the Who. *Come My Way*, her first album, reached number twelve on the British charts. It didn't make any impact in

Anita Pallenberg introduced her to a whole new level of hedonism

America but her second, *Marianne Faithfull*, made it into the top twenty on both sides of the Atlantic.

She started going to parties and events without Dunbar, whose flirtation with heroin was beginning to escalate — much to the disapproval of his wife, who was a lightweight in the drugs stakes. Around this time German model Anita Pallenberg entered Marianne's life, introducing her to a whole new level of hedonism. Pallenberg was muse and lover to Brian Jones, one of the original Rolling Stones. Pallenberg and Jones dressed in theatrical garb and were stoned to the eyeballs morning till night. Marianne worshipped the glamorous, intimidating Pallenberg and started to feel her stay-at-home life was dull in comparison.

Of course Marianne was much more than a housewife, being the main breadwinner in the family. Her royalty cheques paid for their lifestyle and fed Dunbar's smack habit. Resentment began to creep into the relationship, from both sides, and soon baby Nicholas was the only glue keeping them together. Marianne grew tired of stepping over Dunbar's drugged-out mates, who would crash at their flat. Litter was everywhere, cigarette butts, syringes, empty booze bottles. She began to spend an increasing amount of time at Anita and Brian's apartment in Kensington, where life was much more scintillating.

Mick Jagger was fun, rich, young, famous and he pursued her relentlessly — he was her knight in shining armour

In 1966 there were three singles, 'Go Away From My World', 'Tomorrow's Calling' and 'Counting', and two albums, *North Country Maid* and *Faithfull Forever* (released in Britain as *Love in a Mist*), none of which came near the success of her previous works.

The writing was on the wall for her marriage. While still married to John, she took up with Mick Jagger. He was fun, rich, young, famous and he had pursued her relentlessly, making him her knight in shining armour. Moving into Jagger's house in Cheyne Walk with baby Nicholas, Marianne found herself in a world of excess — it was a constant cocktail of drugs and alcohol on hand, shopping sprees and a nanny to look after the baby.

Decadence ruled the day. It was astonishing there was only one major drug bust, which ended in suspended sentences for Richards and Jagger and the famous 'Who Breaks a Butterfly on a Wheel?' editorial from *The Times*, arguing that the two were being persecuted because of who they were. The media coverage was phenomenal. Not only because it was the first incident of its kind to involve the rock'n'roll hierarchy, but because of the naked girl found wrapped in a fur rug, reportedly with a Mars bar between her legs.

That girl was of course Marianne. She thrived on the notoriety. If she were going to be famous for something, a beautiful, sexy, naughty rebel was the perfect fantasy, although the addition of the Mars bar was a pure fabrication that incensed her for years.

In 1967 Marianne released only one single, a cover of the Ronettes hit 'Is This What I Get For Loving You?', but it failed to make it into the top forty in either Britain or the States.

More interested in pursuing a career in acting, Marianne made her film debut in the forgettable *I'll Never Forget What's 'Isname* with Orson Wells and Oliver Reed and she played Irina in Chekhov's *Three Sisters* at the Royal Court. The next year she appeared in *Girl on a Motorcycle* with Alain Delon (known as *Naked Under Leather* in the US), a film better known for Marianne reportedly being naked under her bikkie leathers than for its quality.

She and Jagger were blissfully happy during the early years together but he didn't share her enthusiasm for heroin. Acid, pot and pills were his general fodder. He was too focused on the main game. Only the dedicated ventured into cocaine and heroin territory — and Marianne was fast on her way there. Her body was already suffering from the constant abuse. She was rail thin, and anaemic, the reason given for a 1968 miscarriage.

her experience in Australia was uncannily similar to that of the character in 'Sister Morphine', the song she'd written with Jagger and Richards

She played Ophelia in the film version of *Hamlet*, directed by Tony Richardson and starring Nicol Williamson. The next year, 1969, it was off to Sydney where Jagger and Marianne had been cast in Richardson's next film *Ned Kelly*, but she was dropped after a botched suicide attempt that left her in a coma for six days. The Australian media pronounced her dead. Marianne's experience in Australia was uncannily similar to that of the character in a song she had written earlier with Jagger and Richards, 'Sister Morphine', which documented the demise of a young woman, the morphine taking her away from her pain. It must have been a spin for Jagger to see its lyrics come to life.

When Marianne and Jagger returned to London they presented a vision of togetherness in public. But behind closed doors it was a different story. Marianne had started her affair with heroin in earnest. There was clearly no room in her life for anything other than drugs. She has said she was greatly influenced by William Burroughs' *The Naked Lunch*, which motivated her to seek out the life of a drug addict. Marianne threw herself headlong into the world of heroin, twisting the novelist's words to suit herself — Burroughs had not set out to glorify the life of a junkie, quite the opposite.

41

Marianne and Jagger presented a vision of togetherness in public. But behind closed doors it was a different story

Her relationship with Jagger ended in the same year that her divorce to a very bitter and twisted John Dunbar was ratified. Still smarting from the years when Jagger had played daddy to his son, John wanted custody of Nicholas and was prepared to battle an already beleaguered Marianne in court. When he was granted custody, Marianne's mother Eva, who had been caring for her grandson, was driven to attempt suicide. Unlike her daughter, she was furious she had failed.

Without Jagger to give her protection and status, and her music career for all intents and purposes over, Marianne plummeted headlong into self-pity and self-medication.

It is at this point that the Marianne Faithfull tale takes a turn that in fiction wouldn't seem plausible. Leaving behind a life of glamour and fame, she opted to become a full-time junkie, moving out of her mother's home, where she'd been living after her split with Jagger, to take up her station on the street at St Anne's Court in Soho along with the other desperate souls — winos, junkies and prostitutes. It was this location that became her stomping ground, a piece of wall marked as her territory, where she slept and sat in stoned silence almost every day for two years. Marianne was a registered heroin user on the National Health Service. She fronted up with her prescription each day, got her fix and returned to the wall to shoot up and stay stoned. She never ran out and she never had a reason to stop.

Seemingly able to live on nothing, occasionally spotting a fiver from doormen or accepting the charity of passers-by, Marianne was a virtual beggar on the streets of London. She has denied the accusation she resorted to prostitution.

without Jagger to give her protection, Marianne plummeted headlong into self-pity and self-medication

And she didn't take welfare. One British newspaper described her as 'far too hoity-toity to do anything as common as signing on.'

Marianne must have had one hell of a guardian angel. In all the time she lived on the streets she was never attacked or harassed or even arrested. Everyone left the strange, skinny, blonde girl whose beauty was still evident, if spectral, alone. She was only in her early twenties and her 165-centimetre frame was a pitiful forty-one kilograms. She was in mortal peril. It is some kind of miracle that she didn't go the way of Morrison, Hendrix or Joplin.

It seems incongruous, but even during this time she was still making records, if unremarkable ones. In 1971 Mike Leander, the producer she'd worked with in the 1960s, took Marianne under his wing and back into the studio to record *Rich Kid Blues*, an album that wasn't released until 1985. It features cover songs from the hit-makers of the day, including George Harrison, Bob Dylan, James Taylor and Cat Stevens. You can hear the weariness of life on the streets in Marianne's voice. Once the recording was over, she went back to her spot on the wall.

Just as she was at her lowest ebb there came another knight in shining armour. Oliver Musker, an academic, rescued her. As only Marianne could, she entered an unorthodox rehab program based on the premise that if you can have as much of anything you will eventually cease to want it. It took her eight months to get bored, during which time she shot a lot of smack.

After rehab she took off to India in 1973 to film *Ghost Story*, a B-grade horror flick. Musker was by her side. But the stronger she became, the less she needed him. He wanted to marry her and she wanted freedom. She was back to her old self, before the heroin — although that drug would prove harder to banish than the men in her life.

With Musker behind her, Marianne took up with her old manager Tony Calder to try and reignite her singing career. Her first comeback album *Dreamin' My Dreams* was a collection of pop and country-influenced songs released in 1977. The album didn't chart, but it did send a message to the rock fraternity that Marianne Faithfull wasn't dead after all. The record was re-released early the following year with slight variations, including a name change to *Faithless*. Again Marianne had included a Dylan song, 'I'll Be Your Baby Tonight', along with Chuck Berry's 'Sweet Little Sixteen' and the self-penned 'That Was The Day (Nashville)'.

After *Faithless* came more years of drugs and a new partner in crime, Ben Brierly, a punk bass player whose edict to live on the edge appealed to the rebel inside Marianne. They lived in London squats with no electricity or running water, making ends meet on Marianne's royalty payments until her record company set her up in a decent flat in the hope that she'd get her act together and fulfill her contract.

Drugs, drugs and more. Marianne moved like an automaton. Days were

filled with one hit after another, visits to and from dealers, and mad shopping sprees — clothes and furniture — that gobbled up money meant to last months.

The record company's faith in its wayward charge was finally rewarded with the mature work that Marianne delivered with *Broken English* in 1979. The album was confronting on all levels — a fabulous, punk-oriented effort that saved her life. *Broken English* was 'a lifeline so crucial to my very being that I think had I not made it I would surely have gone raving mad or cut my throat,' she says in her autobiography.

The furore that followed the release of *Broken English*, and in particular the song 'Why'D Ya Do It' with lyrics by poet Heathcote Williams, took Marianne by surprise. The album included a cover of John Lennon's 'Working Class Hero', 'Brain Drain' penned by Brierly, and the enduring 'The Ballad of Lucy Jordan'. Critics raved. Her rasping, smoky voice was captivating. No one but Marianne could have pulled off an album that seethed with such malice and narcissism. It was brilliant.

Always one for drama, to add to her already complicated life, she married Brierly in 1979, not long after the album was released. Despite its success, the money trickled in very slowly and once again Marianne was living on the poverty line. But that didn't stop them hopping back on to the drug roundabout. *Broken English* eventually earned her tens of thousands of pounds, which she blew in a staggeringly short time.

The lacklustre *Dangerous Acquaintances* followed eighteen months later. Marianne

Broken English was confronting on all levels — a fabulous, punk-oriented effort that saved her life. It was brilliant

had procrastinated over it and it received a lukewarm response. Whatever magic she had conjured for *Broken English* seemed to have been lost.

Arriving in New York to promote the new album, Brierly and Marianne indulged in all the goodies of the Big Apple. It was like two kids being let loose in a candy store, but in this case it might as well have been a shooting gallery. As his wife's notoriety escalated, Brierly's drug-fuelled paranoia resulted in ugly scenes and venomous exchanges. Marianne grew bored. He had become dead baggage. Finding Brierly in bed with another woman, she showed him the door.

A Child's Adventure was released in 1983. Marianne co-wrote a number of tracks on the album with producer Wally Badarou, who had worked with M on the hit 'Pop Music' and Joe Cocker, and musician Barry Reynolds who played on *Broken English*. The album made its way into the Billboard top 200, peaking at 107.

It wasn't until she fell, stoned to the eyeballs, and broke her jaw that she decided

for a woman
who traded
on her beauty,
growing old
can be difficult
to swallow. 'It's
very hard having
been so beautiful
when young,'
she lamented

to seek help for her addictions again. This time she checked into Hazelden in Minnesota, a no-nonsense rehab centre where many celebrities have gone to get their act together. There Marianne was subjected to a rigourous detox program that shook her to the marrow.

During the sober years that followed, Marianne released *Strange Weather*, her 1987 Dietrich-esque album that featured a selection of songs sung with a haunting blues ambience, including 'Boulevard of Broken Dreams', 'I Ain't Goin' Down to the Well No More' and 'Penthouse Serenade'. It also featured a re-worked version of her first hit 'As Tears Go By', which benefitted from the maturity of the delivery and the world-weariness of her voice.

In the late 1980s she took off to Ireland where she holed up in a beautiful, somewhat decrepit cottage on a country estate in County Wicklow and had problems with the landlord and rats. In 1988 she had married Giorgio della Terza, a writer she'd met at Narcotics Anonymous, but Marianne reportedly spent much of the marriage away on tour. By 1991 it was over and she was back to living alone. She stayed sober for five years before she dipped into the drug pool again. This time she stayed clear of heroin, but thought it her duty to try ecstasy.

The quiet of the Irish countryside was obviously conducive to creativity. Marianne had sung Kurt Weill on the Hal Wilner 1985 tribute album *Lost in the Stars*, recording 'The Ballad of The Soldier's Wife' accompanied by Chris Spedding on guitar. In 1989

> ## she holed up in a beautiful, decrepit cottage on a country estate in County Wicklow and had problems with the landlord and rats

she performed two concerts of the sung ballet, *Seven Deadly Sins*, composed by Weill with Bertolt Brecht's lyrics. The performances, at the Church of St Ann and the Holy Trinity in Brooklyn Heights, New York, were acclaimed as masterful interpretations of Weill's work, planting the seed for a Weill album of her own.

The 1990 live album *Blazing Away*, recorded at St Ann's, included songs that spanned her career, from 'As Tears Go By' to 'Broken English', 'Guilt' and 'Sister Morphine'. Hal Wilner was producer along with Barry Reynolds.

For her next album Marianne chose to work with composer Angelo Badalamenti on 1995's *A Secret Life*. Badalamenti, best known for his work on David Lynch's *Twin Peaks* soundtrack, co-wrote most of the tracks with Marianne. Some reviewers felt the orchestral arrangements swamped the work. But there was no question about Marianne's voice and its ability to handle the material.

In 1992 she had played Pirate Jenny in the Gate Theatre production of the Brecht/Weill *Threepenny Opera* in Dublin. Now, three years later, with pianist Paul Trueblood she performed *An Evening in the Weimar Republic*, her Kurt Weill tribute concert, at New York's Brooklyn Academy of Music. The resoundingly positive reception prompted Marianne and Trueblood to tour the show down the American West Coast and to Europe, where she performed at the Berliner Ensemble Theatre in what had been East Berlin. Recordings from the performance feature on 1997's *20th Century Blues*.

A recording of *Seven Deadly Sins*, released in 1998 featured the Vienna Radio Orchestra conducted by Dennis Russell Davies. Marianne's cigarette-ravaged

Marianne's cigarette-ravaged voice conveyed the intellectual and emotional depths and intimacy of the work — reviewers compared her with Kurt Weill's wife Lotte Lenya

voice was an ideal vehicle to convey the intellectual and emotional depths and intimacy of the work. Many reviewers compared her with Kurt Weill's wife Lotte Lenya.

In 1999 Marianne returned to a more contemporary sound. *Vagabond Ways* may not have been a chart success but it was a critical triumph. Barry Reynolds was in the studio again with Emmylou Harris on back-up vocals and Roger Waters playing synthesiser. The album contained mostly original material co-written by Marianne with a number of her close associates.

Marianne was back in front of the camera in Patrice Chereau's *Intimacy,* voted best film at the Berlin Film Festival in 2001, followed the next year by an independent cinematic release *Far From China.* Marianne hooked up with French filmmaker Francois Ravard, who became her manager and lover, and moved to Paris where the pair currently reside.

When she came to record her 2002 album *Kissin' Time*, Ravard suggested she make up a wish list of those she'd like to work with. This album, she has said, was the first in which she committed to being an active participant in the creation of her work. She was 'beginning' to take it into her own hands, she said. *Kissin' Time* again proved that Marianne was the mother of reinvention. She collaborated with a younger group of artists to give the record a pop music feel that hadn't been present in her work in the 1990s.

In 2003 she was back in the studio to record *Before the Poison*, which featured another who's who of contemporary artists, including PJ Harvey who wrote five songs for the record (two with Marianne) and Damon Albarn. Nick Cave was also on board, writing three songs with Marianne, and his Bad Seeds played on these collaborations, which were tailor-made for her rasping vocals. One reviewer described *Before the Poison* as 'poetic and unnerving'.

Marianne appeared in the 2004 production of *The Black Rider*, the William Burroughs' play with songs by Tom Waits, in London and San Francisco. The following year she toured through Britain, Europe and the United States. However, then fifty-seven, she had to pull out of her final European dates, and also a planned performance of *The Black Rider* at the Sydney Festival in Australia early the next year, due to exhaustion.

For a woman who has traded on her beauty, growing old can be difficult to swallow. The creeping decrepitude drove her into therapy in 2005. 'It's very hard having been so beautiful when young,' she lamented to the *Sunday Times*.

Kissin' Time again proved that Marianne was the mother of reinvention

Marianne took the role of the young queen's mother, Marie Theresa of Austria, in Sophia Coppola's *Marie Antoinette*, released in 2006. Her next cinematic outing was in *Irina Palm*, in which she played a grandmother who resorted to working as a prostitute in order to save her ill grandson.

In stoic French style, Ravard has stood by his grand dame through her recent health scares: a minor heart attack in 2005, which finally prompted her to give up her sixty-a-day cigarette habit, and diagnosis of breast cancer in 2006 (from which she has made a rapid recovery).

The Marianne Faithfull story is an extraordinary one — one that isn't over yet. We can anticipate more work from one of the most enduring female performers in rock 'n' roll. As Hal Wilner said, 'she's among the royalty now' — where she has always wanted to be.

TINA TURNER

Shake that Thang

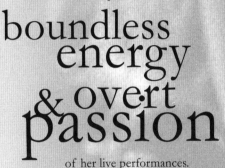

From the outset, Tina Turner's on-stage presence set her apart from other performers.

And no one else has captured the

boundless energy & over·t passion

of her live performances.

She is *exotic, erotic* and the fastest woman in a pair of heels. As she gyrated across the stage in the late 1950s as a member of Ike Turner's Kings of Rhythm band, her movements were reminiscent of something **wild uncontrolled and untamed.**

Ann took the
microphone
and sang for
Ike Turner.
In that
instant, her
life changed
forever

Of course the reality was quite different. Tina on the tight leash of Ike Turner, who she met when she was sixteen, was anything but free. Ike was a dominating bully and kept Tina wrapped in a cocoon of subservience, violence and fear.

It took Tina sixteen years to break free. When she finally did it was the act of a desperate woman, fleeing for her life, her sanity, her self-respect.

Tina Turner was born Anna Mae Bullock in 1939. She grew up in the cotton country of the American South in and around the township of Brownsville, Tennessee. By the time Ann, as she was called, was born her parents' relationship was on the rocks. Zelma Bullock always resented Ann, whose birth had not revived the marriage as hoped, and she showed her daughter no affection even as an infant. Ann's memories of early childhood include wandering in the fields, sitting under the trees on hot summer days and the warming smells of cornbread and beans in winter. Her father was caretaker of a cotton plantation and the family lived comfortably. She and her elder sister Alline had their own rooms, a luxury in many African-American families.

Her parents split up when she was around ten years of age, her father moving to Chicago and her mother to St Louis. The sisters were separated. Ann was shunted off to live with her father's folk, who were unemotional and disciplinarian. Forced to go to church every Sunday, Ann soon joined the choir. She was a natural performer and would often break into song, singing tunes she heard on the radio. In the 1940s the radio waves were humming with the sounds of the big bands of Glenn Miller, Duke Ellington and Tommy Dorsey, and the likes of Billie Holiday, Ella Fitzgerald, Charlie

it appeared to be one big, happy family. In reality it was a cauldron of clashing egos, adultery, domineering men and conniving women

Parker and Dizzie Gillespie. By the time she was in high school, she was holding down a job as a live-in house maid for a middle-class white family. The Hendersons were generous and Ann was made to feel one of the family.

When she was around sixteen, she sought out the big city lights of St Louis, moving in with her mother and Alline. It wasn't long before Ann, who looked older than her years, got into the club scene, tagging along with her sister. One of East St Louis's jumping night spots was Club Manhattan, where the Kings of Rhythm played. Alline was dating the drummer and the girls spent every weekend at the club. One night Ann took the microphone and sang for Ike Turner. In that instant, her life changed forever.

A singer by night and schoolgirl by day, Ann began living a dream. But once her mother got wind of what was going on reality came crashing down. Zelma put a stop to the singing.

Ike had been in the music game for years. Hailing from Clarksdale, Mississippi, he was an accomplished pianist and guitarist who had played on records for Howlin' Wolf, Otis Rush and Elmore James. He'd been with the Kings of Rhythm, an R&B ensemble, since 1951. But his real talent lay in being a bandleader and he had a firm grip on the Kings' musical and business direction. Convinced that Ann's powerful vocals were the key to his band's future success, Ike wasn't going to let anyone stand in his way. He sweet-talked Mother Bullock and within days Ann was back on stage.

To Ann, the Kings of Rhythm seemed more like a family than a band. All the members and their partners and kids used to congregate in a house in St Louis. There was always music in the air, food on the stove and people everywhere. It appeared to be one big, happy family. In reality it was a cauldron of clashing egos, adultery, domineering men and conniving women.

Ann fell for saxophone player Raymond Hill. Still in her last year of high school, she discovered she was pregnant. For a time Ann lived with Hill in the band's house, but it wasn't long before he shot through and she moved back in with her mother. In 1958, at the age of eighteen, she gave birth to a son, Raymond Craig. No longer welcome in her mother's house, Ann found herself living on her own, looking after her newborn baby, working as a nurse's aide in the local maternity hospital and singing at night in order to pay the rent. It was a hard slog.

> cocaine fuelled Ike's already skewed perspective on reality. He didn't just slap Tina or punch her, he used twisted wire coat hangers for maximum impact

Ike could see the pace was wearing her out. He gave her a pay rise and Ann ditched the nursing job. She was now a full-time singer. For a time she was swept away with the glamour of the life Ike promised. Initially they were like brother and sister, but one thing led to another and Ike, nine years her senior and a chronic womaniser, seduced the young singer. Ann didn't want a sexual relationship but, thinking that without Ike she had nothing, she acquiesced.

It wasn't long before she was pregnant again. Ike's response was to go back to his common-law wife Lorraine. For a time the three of them lived in the same house along with the other band members, Ann sleeping in a room down the hall from Ike and Lorraine. Ann became one of his other women, a silent player in Ike's world of deception and violence.

she moved and sang in a way no other woman dared. She was uninhibited and intoxicating

She may have been compliant in her private life, but on stage Ann was a different person. Her powerful voice was as arresting as her wild antics. She gave the Kings of Rhythm the edge on other bands playing the club scene. She moved and sang in a way no other woman dared. She was uninhibited and intoxicating. When she was on stage all eyes were glued on her.

Ann sang backing vocals on the 1958 single 'Box Top'. On the strength of her performance on the record, which was released by an independent St Louis label, industry insiders recommended that Ike put Ann up front of the band.

'A Fool in Love', released in 1960, was her first single as lead singer and her first as Tina Turner, another Ike masterstroke. There had been no consultation about changing her name. 'A Fool in Love' got to number three on the Billboard R&B charts and, more significantly, made it on to the pop charts, reaching the top thirty.

Ike had an extraordinary grip on Tina. She was pregnant, in hospital with hepatitis, a young son to care for and Ike's wife back on the scene, and he still convinced her to defy doctor's orders and leave the hospital so he could promote 'A Fool in Love'. They hit the road. At their first gig as the Ike and Tina Turner Revue, in Cincinnati, Tina concealed her pregnancy in a flowing, micro-short dress. Soon the duo, now complete with three backing singers known as the Ikettes, were performing on the smash-hit

it took Tina sixteen years to break free. When she finally did it was the act of a desperate woman, fleeing for her life, her sanity, her self-respect

TV show *American Bandstand*. This was a level of success Ike had never experienced before — and it was clearly due to Tina. Then in October Tina gave birth to a second son, Ronald. Five days later she was on stage again. Ike had allowed her two weeks off from touring.

The following year another single, 'It's Gonna Work Out Fine', made it into the top thirty pop charts. It was quickly followed by two more singles, 'Poor Fool' and 'Tra La La La La', which both made it into the charts but not with quite the same success.

In 1962 Tina sealed her fate, marrying Ike in Mexico. Another top twenty hit was released that year, 'I'm Blue (The Gong-Gong Song)'. Professionally the Turners were on fire, but their personal life left a lot to be desired.

The pair moved to LA and set up house in the up-market, predominantly white suburb of View Park. Now Tina was the wife expected to put up with Ike's other women. He didn't bother to conceal his philandering and even bedded other women in their marital home. His control over Tina reached into every corner of her life. The only thing she did without him was to go shopping. It became her escape. As the money rolled in, Tina took the allowance Ike gave her and bought expensive clothes and accessories, filling her wardrobes with designer labels and developing a habit that would last a lifetime. She was the original shop-till-you-drop girl.

Paralleling their success was the escalating abuse that Tina suffered at the hands of her husband. At any moment Ike would fly into a rage. Make-up covered the bruises and Tina learned to perform with cracked ribs and bloodied mouth. Everyone around them knew what was going on. Ike didn't save his fists for his wife alone. His other women also knew the sting of his temper. Band line-ups changed frequently as did the members of the Ikettes. No one wanted to be around Ike for too long once they'd seen his true colours.

The Ike and Tina Turner Revue performed fifty-one weeks a year, usually multiple shows each night. They played the LA club circuit for half the year and hit the road for the rest of the time. Tina's children spent weeks away from their mother in the care of nannies. Despite the constant touring, the chart successes began to dry up and in 1964 the Revue had only one hit, 'I Can't Believe What You Say'.

Phil Spector was eager to work with Tina. In 1965 the boy-wonder producer — of the Ronettes, Connie Francis, the Righteous Brothers, Darlene Love and Bobby Sheen — negotiated a deal with Ike, who was less than thrilled that the producer only wanted Tina. Still, Ike was a shrewd businessman and he could see the sense in hooking up with the quirky little producer who had orchestrated a string of hits.

Spector wanted Tina to record 'River Deep, Mountain High', a song he'd written with husband-and-wife team Jeff Barry and Ellie Greenwich, one of the most successful songwriting duos of the time. Spector produced the song in his wall-of-sound style using multiples of the same instruments — guitars, keyboards, horns, percussion, strings — to create a musical storm that engulfed the listener with its orchestral majesty. It was a masterpiece. Some of the hottest musicians of the day — Glenn Campbell, Leon Russell, Hal Blaine and Jim Horn — worked on the record. But it bombed in the States, sending the eccentric producer into semi-retirement. In Britain it was a different story and it became a top ten hit. Years later *Rolling Stone* magazine would list 'River Deep, Mountain High' at number thirty-three in the 500 Greatest Songs of All Time.

The Revue toured Britain in 1966 supporting the Rolling Stones, playing to predominantly white audiences who were fascinated by American black music. On

in Dallas in 1976 Ike lost his temper with Tina for the last time. She walked, despite the fact they were in the middle of a tour

stage, Tina transformed from subservient wife into a screaming, shaking, kicking, fast-moving powerhouse of limbs, lips, wild hair (she wore a variety of wigs), micro mini-skirts and nosebleed heels. The way she moved on stage was breathtaking, keeping the audience constantly in her grip. Comparisons with Mick Jagger were obvious.

Touring with the Stones, Tina's 'rock' spirit was awakened. She knew the kind of music she really wanted to perform and it wasn't R&B. Jagger and Richards became close friends and often dropped into her dressing room after the show. Ike was close at hand of course, watching over his wife and the Ikettes. He didn't like those boys sniffing around his women.

After two years without a song in the charts, Ike and Tina Turner came up trumps once again in 1968 with 'I've Been Loving You Too Long', a classic by Otis Redding. The album *Outta Season* was released at the same time, featuring songs by BB King and Elmore James. Tina was co-producer of the record with Bob Krasnow, best known for his work with James Brown.

When the Rolling Stones toured the US in 1969, Ike and Tina Turner were on the bill along with BB King. The tour introduced the Turners to white America en masse and the audience went wild for Tina. That year saw the release of another album, *The Hunter*, again produced by Krasnow.

The Turners signed to United Artists on its new Minit Records label in 1970. Their version of Creedence Clearwater Revival's 'Proud Mary' hit the airwaves in 1971 and became their biggest success, reaching the top five of the pop charts and giving them their first Grammy award, for best R&B vocal performance by a duo.

The gruelling work pace finally began to take its toll on Tina, who had not had a break in more than a decade. She ended up in hospital with tuberculosis. It would take her the best part of the 1970s to recover. Despite the lingering malady, she continued to adhere to Ike's relentless touring schedule.

The money was flowing freely and with it came cocaine, which fuelled Ike's already skewed perspective on reality and gave him an even greater sense of his own import and power. And as the hits began to dwindle, the beatings grew more violent. He didn't just slap Tina or punch her, he used twisted wire coat hangers for

59

> make-up covered the bruises and Tina learned to perform with cracked ribs and bloodied mouth. Everyone around them knew what was going on

maximum impact. Twice she tried to leave and both times he found her and beat the living daylights out of her and then went back to business as usual. Tina patched herself up and took to the stage, the audiences oblivious to the horror she was living.

After a couple of slow years on the charts, the Turners had a surprise hit in 1973 with 'Nutbush City Limits', a disco-dance song written by Tina, which reached the American top thirty and number two on the British charts. Nutbush was a small Southern town where Tina and her sister had lived for a short time as children and the lyrics captured the essence of life in that part of the country in the 1950s.

The following year Tina was offered a role in the Who's rock-opera *Tommy*, a film featuring Elton John, Eric Clapton, Roger Daltrey, Keith Moon, Pete Townshend, and actors Oliver Reed, Jack Nicholson and Ann-Margret, who had befriended Tina when they were both performing in Vegas. Tina played the Acid Queen.

Tina was enjoying the projects she was undertaking without Ike. When the shoot for *Tommy* wrapped, she stayed on in London to appear on Ann-Margret's TV special. The pair sang a number of duets, including 'Proud Mary' and the Stone's 'Honky Tonk Woman'. She made an odd decision to record a solo country album, *Tina Turns the Country On*, which didn't sell well. The following year there was another solo album, *Acid Queen*, a more rock-oriented effort, but it didn't have the cut-through Tina was looking for.

In Dallas in 1976 Ike lost his temper with Tina for the last time. She walked, despite the fact they were in the middle of a tour.

Now she was breadwinner, homemaker and sole parent of four teenagers (Michael and Ike Junior, the sons Ike and Lorraine had together, also lived with her). For a time Tina and her sons lived in a rented house in LA and got by on food stamps and the generosity of friends. Debt weighed her down as promoters looked to her to compensate for the cancelled tour dates.

The battle to separate herself from Ike on many levels — financial, professional, emotional — was the greatest fight of her life. But she'd lived through the nightmare of Ike's bashings, through a failed suicide attempt (for which he beat her almost to the point of killing her) and the humiliation of his other women. She

on stage, Tina became a screaming, shaking, kicking, fast-moving powerhouse of limbs, lips, wild hair, micro mini skirts and nosebleed heels

would come through this stronger than before. Tina had embraced Buddhism in 1974. In the years following her separation, she would turn to chanting to get her through the most torrid times.

She took any work she could get, making guest appearances on various TV shows, including *The Osmonds*, *Cher* and *Laugh-In*, but the debts continued to mount. She left Ike the money and property accumulated over the years they had been together. Her not wanting anything drove Ike insane. He went through five lawyers during the divorce, but Tina wouldn't step into the fray. At last she was in control. She wanted her freedom, her dignity, her sanity. Ike could keep the possessions — they didn't mean anything to her.

Ike waged a terror campaign and many who helped Tina felt his wrath. Cars were blasted with gunshots, houses burned and people threatened. Tina carried a gun and at one point had to hire bodyguards. Her eldest son Craig stuck with his mother, but eventually the madness drove him away and he joined the Navy. Tina's second son

Ronnie got caught up with drugs and then later Scientology. Michael and Ike Junior went to live with their father after the divorce.

Less than eighteen months after her break from Ike, Tina mounted a cabaret-style show, *The Tina Turner Show,* mixing R&B tunes with disco and rock'n'roll. Fashion designer Bob Mackie helped her with costumes and the stage show glittered with the pomp and pizzazz of a true Las Vegas spectacle. The high-energy theatrics and smouldering sexuality of the show, complete with male and female dancers, drew the crowds. She took her new show out for a run in Canada before bringing it to the States, where she played hotel ballrooms like the Fairmont in San Francisco.

In 1978 she released her first album without Ike, *Rough.* It was aptly named. The album bombed as did 1979's follow-up *Love Explosion,* a disco-oriented record that missed the disco boom. Suddenly Tina was without a recording contract in America, although United Artists, through their British label EMI, kept the faith across the Atlantic.

An invitation from Olivia Newton-John to appear on her TV special *Hollywood Nights* in 1979 led Tina to Roger Davies, an Australian who would become her manager and orchestrate one of the greatest comebacks in showbiz. Davies was working for Lee Kramer, Newton-John's lover and manager at the time. He caught Tina's show in San Francisco and was blown away. She had the audience eating out of her hand. Davies was convinced Tina should be singing mainstream rock. That meant throwing out the cabaret-style performances and starting again. Tina put her trust in Davies and the pair began to work on bringing out the rock chick within. To make ends meet Tina took her Vegas cabaret-style show on the road, touring to South Africa, Australia and Asia.

The major turning point of Tina's career came in the summer of 1981. Davies booked her into the Ritz in New York. Word was out that Tina Turner was on the comeback trail, and everyone who was anyone wanted to be there, including her old buddy Mick Jagger. The new show featured Tina on stage with a band only, a first for her. The show went off and Tina, exhilarated by the experience and the genuine adoration of the crowd, was buoyed with a new confidence.

After New York came a quick succession of opportunities: a duet with Rod Stewart on *Saturday Night Live* and an invitation to join the Stones US tour. During the tour she and Jagger performed a spirited rendition of 'Honky Tonk Woman', much to the audience's delight. Tina Turner was on her way.

Part of Davies' strategy was to get out a single as quickly as possible. When Tina's cover of the Al Green song 'Let's Stay Together' was released in 1983, it rose to number five in the British charts. But in the States, Capitol Records refused to pick it up until imported copies of the single made their way into the dance clubs. 'Let's Stay Together' was officially released in the USA in early 1984 and made it into the Billboard top thirty. To support its release, Tina hit the road as the opening act for Lionel Ritchie. Then she landed the starring role of Aunty Entity in *Mad Max: Beyond Thunderdome* with Mel Gibson and sang two songs for the film's soundtrack — 'We Don't Need Another Hero' (another top five hit) and 'One of the Living'.

Davies was amassing a range of songs that became the playlist for the pinnacle of her career, *Private Dancer*. The album was recorded in Britain with a number of different producers, among them percussionist Ndugu Chancler and Englishman Rupert Hine. The first single from the album, 'What's Love Got to Do with It', written for Tina by the Australians Terry Britten and Graham Lyle, became a number one smash hit, topping the Billboard chart in September 1984. Tina was ecstatic. Not long after she made the cover of *Rolling Stone*. She was forty-five and her star status was confirmed. Another massive hit from the album was 'Better Be Good to Me', which made it into the top five. The title song, which was later released as a single, was written by Mark Knopfler of Dire Straits and featured Jeff Beck on guitar. The album reached number two on the Billboard top 100 for 1984, going multi-platinum.

Private Dancer earned Tina three Grammys, two American Music Awards and the MTV award for best female video for 'What's Love Got to Do with It'. To promote the record, Tina spent twenty-one months on the road playing over 170 shows — her first world tour as a solo artist. *Private Dancer* sold in excess of twenty million albums. As a grand finale to the year, Tina was one of forty-five artists in the USA for Africa's 'We are the World' single, sang a duet with Mick Jagger for the Live Aid concert at Wembley Stadium — and was given a star on the Hollywood Boulevard Walk of Fame.

In 1986 *Break Every Rule* was released. Once again Tina worked with an impressive line up of producers, including Rupert Hine, Bryan Adams, Mark Knopfler and Bob Clearmountain. Terry Britten, who also co-produced,

Tina made the cover of *Rolling Stone*. She was forty-five and her star status was confirmed

contributed five tracks, including 'Typical Male', another number one hit, and 'What You Get is What You See', which reached the top twenty — both co-written with Graham Lyle. The album sold millions of copies around the world and Tina picked up another Grammy.

While promoting *Break Every Rule*, Tina met Erwin Bach, an executive with EMI Europe. Tina enjoyed the company of the young German — he is eighteen years her junior — and the two became an item. She had dated infrequently in the decade since she'd left Ike and this was her first serious relationship.

a wealth of musicians were keen to work with her — Mick Jagger, Keith Richards, David Bowie, Rod Stewart

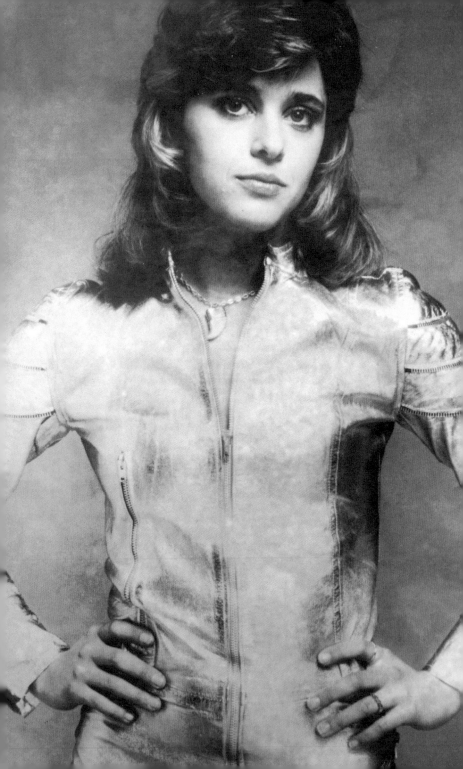

In the late 1980s she moved to Europe to live. The decision behind the move wasn't only to be closer to Bach. She'd captured the hearts of fans on the Continent way back in the 1960s. And it wasn't only fans who were eager to see her. A wealth of musicians and producers were keen to work with her — the likes of Mick Jagger, Keith Richards, David Bowie and Rod Stewart. Tina set up home in Notting Hill, London, moving into a six-floor townhouse, quite a change from her sprawling San Fernando Valley house in LA.

Tina was inducted to the Rock and Roll Hall of Fame along with Ike in 1991. There followed more awards and other milestones, including the release in 1993 of the movie *What's Love Got to Do with It,* an epic about her life starring Angela Bassett and Laurence Fishburne. Bassett was nominated for an Oscar for her performance. Tina shot back into the Billboard top forty with the single from the film's sound track, 'I Don't Wanna Fight'.

In 1999 Tina was awarded the lifetime achievement award at the Black Music Awards in Britain. The album *Twenty Four Seven*, released that year, featured Bryan Adams on 'Without You' and the single 'When the Heartache is Over', which was the album's only top forty hit. Even at sixty, Tina's voice easily managed the different styles on the album, from rock to ballads. That same year her mother Zelma died. Her mother had never supported or given her comfort in the years she suffered at Ike's hands. Ike turned up at the funeral and played the dutiful son-in-law, weeping openly. Tina did not attend. She preferred to say a very private goodbye to the woman who dealt her the cruellest blow — the withholding of a mother's love.

The new millennium saw Tina relaxing and enjoying the spoils of her success. She officially retired from the road after a tour of Europe and the States, made a guest appearance on the *Ally McBeal* television show and sang 'Great Spirits' for the soundtrack of the Disney animation film *Brother Bear*. In 2004 a double compilation CD *All the Best*, which included hits from her days with Ike, as well as duets with David Bowie, Bryan Adams and Italian star Eros Ramazzotti, made the US top five and British top ten.

Tina made a rare appearance in February 2008 performing with Beyoncé at the fiftieth Grammy Awards. The reception was overwhelming and fanned the fire in Tina. It took little coaxing to get her to announce a tour, which she did in April on the Oprah Winfrey Show. The fifty-three date tour, spanning the USA and Europe, kicked off in Kansas City in October that year. After four frenetic months, the sold-out Tina Turner Live tour was over. It was one of the highest grossing tours of the year. In 2010 Tina was in Zurich to receive a Swiss Award. She has lived in Switzerland with Bach for nearly twenty years. And at the time of writing Tina, now in her seventies, was considering another world tour.

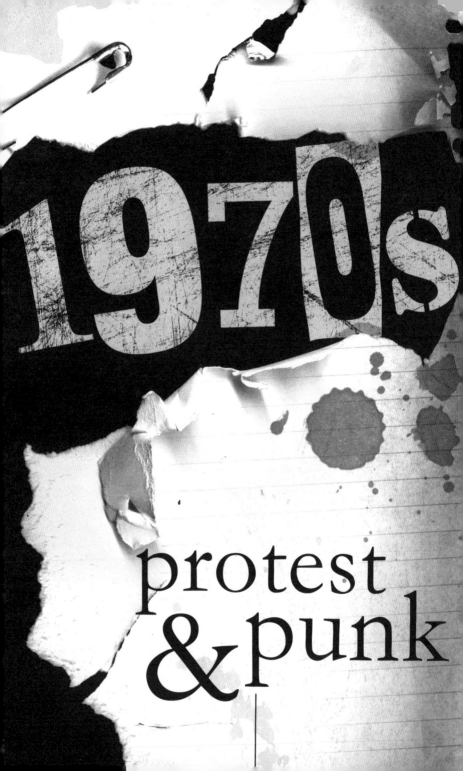

1970s

protest & punk

Peace and love were becoming distant memories by 1970. Every night the graphic horrors of the Vietnam War were played out on television screens in the world's living rooms. Anti-war protests were heated. At one of the most notorious, in 1970 troopers open fired on students at Kent State University in Ohio, killing four. Janis Joplin lost her life to heroin the same year. In 1971 the largest anti-war protest was held in Washington DC. Actress Jane Fonda flew to North Vietnam and Janis Joplin's 'Me and Bobby McGee', released posthumously, topped the US charts. Scandalously, at a White House dinner for the *Reader's Digest* founder, Carole Feraci, one of the wholesome Ray Conniff Singers, held up a sign saying 'Stop the Killing'.

While the slaughter of soldiers and civilians continued unabated in Southeast Asia, the world was rocked by the killing of eleven members of the Israeli team at the 1972 Munich Olympics. Each of the Beatles had songs in the British charts, as did Rod Stewart, Elton John and the Bee Gees. The musical landscape was changing once again. The glam rock bands — Gary Glitter, the Sweet and Mud — were out in force too. The Jackson Five dominated the American charts along with the Temptations, Stevie Wonder and soft-listening groups like the Carpenters.

Watkins Glen Grand Prix Raceway in New York in 1973 was the venue for the largest rock concert to date, with 600,000 fans dancing to the Band, the Allman Brothers and the Grateful Dead. The sweet sounds of the Caribbean became hits for the joint-toting Rastafarian Bob Marley, who turned a generation on to everything Jamaican.

Swedish band Abba won the 1974 Eurovision song contest singing sweet harmonies in shock-jock hair and skintight whites. In fantastic contrast, the punk movement was gaining momentum in England and in New York musicians like the New York Dolls, the Ramones, Patti Smith and Television were developing a new wave sound. Bruce Springsteen — 'rock and roll's future', as one critic called him — had begun to make waves, and so had Billy Joel, Jackson Browne and heavier styled rock anthem bands, aka stadium bands, including Aerosmith, KISS and Heart led by the Wilson sisters.

Then America pulled out of Vietnam, President Nixon resigned in disgrace and abortion was legalised. The first African-Americans were elected mayors in major cities such as LA and Detroit. The number of women in politics trebled — about time too — propelled by the feminist movement and inspired in part by the 1970 publication of Germaine Greer's landmark *The Female Eunuch* and Kate Millett's *Sexual Politics*. Gay Pride marches were held and women were ordained priests. Hippies were turning into spivs, going for moustaches, tailored denim suits, flares and platform shoes. A heavier, guitar-driven rock emerged along with a trend toward theatrical approaches. David Bowie's *Ziggy Stardust*, Alice Cooper's *Welcome to My Nightmare* and Pink Floyd's *Dark Side of the Moon* all pushed rock's creative boundaries.

Tina Turner was still with Ike and the women creeping up the charts included Joni Mitchell, Helen Reddy, Aretha Franklin, Roberta Flack, Cher, Olivia Newton-John, Linda Ronstadt, Carly Simon and the super-smooth Pointer Sisters.

But a new rock chick was emerging. Suzi Quatro carved up the British charts — but failed to make any impression on the other side of the Atlantic. Patti Smith, Debbie Harry and Tina Weymouth of Talking Heads conquered with New York's punk-art new wave, and the Runaways were heating the blood of adolescent males.

It was getting very grungy, particularly in Britain. By the second half of the 1970s, punk groups — the Sex Pistols, the Damned, Siouxsie and the Banshees, the Clash, Elvis Costello, Joy Division — had taken the anti-establishment messages of the 1960s and made them their own. Punks pierced their skin, put safety pins in their cheeks, ripped their black clothes and wore chains and military issue boots.

Disco — the antithesis of punk — reached its highpoint with the 1977 release of the soundtrack from *Saturday Night Fever*, the John Travolta movie which made the Bee Gees its biggest stars along with Donna Summer and Gloria Gaynor. Skirts were short and flouncy, shirts satin and there was lots of lycra and spandex even as Diane Keaton's prissy, preppy look in Woody Allen's *Annie Hall* was widely copied. But then so too were the bizarre costumes of *The Rocky Horror Picture Show*, which gained cult status all around the world.

At the close of 1979 Marianne Faithfull shook up the world with *Broken English* and Debbie Harry, Stevie Nicks, the Wilson sisters and Joan Jett were going hard. A young Pat Benatar had just scored herself a record deal and was poised to take the rock chick to new heights. Eleven fans were crushed to death at the Who concert in Cincinnati. Once again music was being blamed for society's ills.

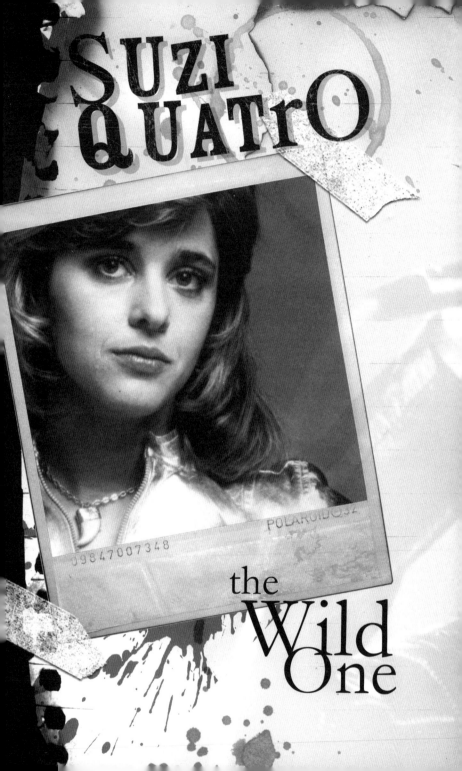

*Standing only 152 centimetres
with an equally tiny
— almost androgynous — frame,*

Suzi Quatro holds the lofty title as the
mother of guitar-
strumming
gals
who front the band.

Remember Joan Jett? She
was the spitting image of
Suzi when she fronted
the Runaways, a band
Suzi has said wouldn't
have existed if she hadn't
done the groundwork.

Suzi's path into rock'n'roll began in Detroit, Michigan, in the 1960s. But it wasn't until she moved to England in 1970 that her career kicked into gear. Suzi wasn't about trying to fit into some accepted female model. She wanted to do her own thing — and that was playing rock'n'roll, hard, fast and loud, just like it should be.

She was as tough as she looked. Her signature outfit was a leather catsuit under which she was naked, much to the delight of her fans. Heavy boots, chains, tattoos (on wrist and shoulder) and a slap of lipstick (sometimes) completed the look. Suzi was a straight shooter with no feminine wiles. Her manner at times was described as brash. Many journalists branded her a tomboy, rough and ready. And that's exactly what she was. For those who complained she lacked finesse, Suzi just laughed. 'You can have class and … excitement, but you can't have them both together,' she said. And Suzi was nothing if not excitement.

On stage she was a ball of frenetic energy, thrashing her bass and screaming into the microphone in a gruff, yet girly voice, backed by an all-male band. Other stars of the day — Marc Bolan, the Sweet, Gary Glitter, Mud — resorted to high heels, make-up and glamour costumes. But Suzi and her boys were hard-core rock: 'I could play my instrument … nobody has ever … said you play OK for a girl.'

Susan Kay Quatro was born on 3 June 1950. The second youngest of five children of Art and Helen Quatro, Suzi spent her childhood in the affluent Detroit suburb of Grosse Point on the shores of Lake St Clair. The Quatro — originally Quatrocchio — family were a musical bunch,

when, at age seven, she first saw Elvis on TV she knew rock'n'roll was the life she wanted

Art playing jazz when he wasn't working in management at General Motors. Suzi was a huge Elvis Presley fan. From age seven, when she first saw him on TV, she knew rock'n'roll was the life she wanted.

Suzi made her professional debut with her father's band when she was eight, putting in a spirited performance on the bongos. Trained in classical piano, by the time she hit her teens Suzi was losing interest in tinkling the ivories. She wanted a more active instrument.

The Quatro sisters put together the Pleasure Seekers, Detroit's first all-girl rock group, in 1964. Suzi was designated bass player because no one else wanted the role. Once she started there was no looking back.

The bass, Suzi thought, was the most important instrument in any rock band, laying the foundation, along with the drums, on which the rest of the music was layered. Not only did she enjoy the thumping beat, but the weight of the instrument and the way she held its power between her legs was a real turn on. On stage in Detroit one night she had a sexual encounter with her guitar. 'I was playing really low … I felt this feeling come up and I had an orgasm right … there.'

Suzi was more at home in jeans and T-shirt — even at the age of fourteen she was reluctant to play the stereotypical female role — but she was a realist. No one was interested in watching girls in trousers. So, along with her sisters, she put on a dress in order to get the band hired. But they were not demure or compliant. The Pleasure Seekers were loud, wild and showed that girls could rock as hard as the guys.

> the reality of Vietnam was like a horror movie. Suzi and the band were encouraged to visit the hospital wards. 'I saw … horrific things,' she said

Detroit was a hive of rock'n'roll activity. Iggy Pop and Alice Cooper were earning their stripes in the motor city. The Pleasure Seekers got their start at the Hideout, a club run by music promoter David Leone. Hideout Records, an offshoot of the club, gave young hopefuls a shot at the big time — artists including Ted Nugent, Glen Frey and Bob Seger recorded their first songs on the label.

The Pleasure Seekers released their first single, 'What a Way to Die'/'Never Thought You'd Leave Me', in 1967. This led to an invitation from the American government to perform for the troops in Vietnam. Suzi and the gang were looking forward to the adventure, but the reality was like a horror movie. They were encouraged to visit the hospital wards. 'I saw … horrific things. I went out the … door and fainted,' she said. She was only seventeen.

Mercury Records picked them up and another single, 'Good Kind of Hurt'/'Light of Love', was released in 1968 and received national airplay.

The Pleasure Seekers had various line-ups, but the core was Suzi on bass and lead vocals, her sisters Patti on lead guitar and Arlene playing keyboards, with drummer Nancy Ball. They spent nearly three years touring bars, clubs and some truly sleazy dives, singing everything from the Stones to Motown. It was hard going, performing multiple sets every night.

It was obvious that the Pleasure Seekers was never going to amount to anything but a club act. The band made a line-up change and reformed as Cradle. Arlene left to marry Leo Fenn, who had been the band's manager and would later handle Alice Cooper — actress Sherilyn Fenn is their daughter. Suzi's other sister Nancy joined as a vocalist. They began performing more of their own material and heavier rock, including Hendrix and Cream covers. But Cradle wasn't destined for success anymore than its predecessor was. The girls began to lose interest.

The man who would change Suzi's musical fortunes was at one of the last Cradle gigs in 1970. British record producer Mickie Most was in Detroit to work with Jeff Beck. Most had made his mark with the great Animals' track 'House of the Rising Sun' and had formed RAK Records in London. When he caught Cradle at

Mickie Most offered Suzi the chance to go to London to record a single. She didn't hesitate. Those she left behind were furious

a local club, the band itself didn't interest him. But the twenty-year-old bass player sparked his imagination. Mickie Most offered Suzi the chance to go to London to record a single. She didn't hesitate. Those she left behind were furious.

The first long, lonely months in London were some of the blackest days of Suzi's young life. Her first single was released in 1972. 'Rolling Stone', co-written by Suzi with Phil Dennys and the frontman of Hot Chocolate Errol Brown, was off the mark and didn't take advantage of her rocking qualities. It didn't make any impression on the charts, except in Portugal, where it went to number one.

To support the release of the single, and to earn her keep, she hit the road as a support act for British glam-rockers Slade with her newly formed band. The line-up featured Len Tuckey on guitar, Alastair McKenzie on keyboards and Keith Hodge on drums. Being on the road with one of the hottest acts in the country was a quantum leap from the days of touring with the Pleasure Seekers. At last, Suzi was getting a taste of the rock'n'roll life she was certain she'd been born to.

Suzi thought the bass was the most important instrument in a rock band. And the weight of the instrument, the way she held its power between her legs, was a real turn on

The lacklustre performance of the 'Rolling Stone' single prompted Mickey Most to call on the songwriting genius of Australian Mike Chapman and partner Londoner Nicky Chinn, the talent behind hits for the Sweet and Mud. They came up with the catchy 'Can the Can' and the public gobbled it up. Released in 1973, 'Can the Can'

became a solid gold hit for Suzi, making number one in Britain, Europe, Japan and Australia — a country that embraced Quatro and where one of her biggest and most loyal fan bases remains.

With 'Can the Can' came a new image. Gone was the soft-lens portrait of Suzi in blue jeans sitting in a field and looking dreamy — the photo used for the cover of 'Rolling Stone'. The Suzi of 'Can the Can' was poured into a leather jumpsuit that showed every ripple of her athletic body. Soon critics were describing her as if she were a porn star. 'Underwear is what Suzi Quatro doesn't wear anymore,' raved one reporter in 1974. 'No bras or panties, just lots of chains and big boots … and [her] bass thrust between her legs.' Very British tabloid.

she declined Elvis's invitation to Graceland. She couldn't imagine being in the same room as the King

Another described listening to 'Can the Can' as a sexual experience: Suzi 'rips your clothes off, licks your spine with her hot tongue, and then slices into your back with razor blades.' Her uni-sexuality, as she described it — the word 'androgynous' would only enter the rock'n'roll vocabulary later, with Annie Lennox — was confusing, tantalising, mysterious and it was seriously sexy.

In the 1970s usually an artist released one single after another in quick succession before putting down a first album. 'Can the Can' was followed by '48 Crash' and 'Daytona Demon', all written by Chapman and Chinn. Some reviewers dismissed Suzi as a lightweight. But the record-buying public disagreed. The second two singles both made it into the British top twenty, with '48 Crash' reaching the top five. They were also chart hits across Europe and in Japan and Australia.

Her first album, *Suzi Quatro*, released in 1973, featured Suzi in leathers on the cover together with the boys in her band, including new drummer Dave Neal, in singlet tops. It was an image of a woman who was tough, played the game just like a man and was the undisputed leader of her gang. For once the publicity hype was true. Rumour has it that Hodge left the band because Tuckey won the heart of the lead singer. Neal was brought in to fill the gap left by Hodge's departure. The album was a hit. Suzi and Tuckey collaborated on a number of songs on the album, including 'Glycerine Queen', which became a favourite.

In the space of twelve months Suzi had gone from virtual obscurity to sought-after chart-topper. She appeared on a number of European TV music shows and performed on German TV no less than three times that year. During the band's choreographed routines Suzi would hold her guitar high above her head and dance in unison with her band mates, driving the teenage audiences wild. Soon Suzi Q clones began to spring up across Europe as young girls picked up guitars and squeezed into leather.

At times the attention was overwhelming. When Elvis Presley heard her cover of 'All Shook Up' on her debut album he invited her to Graceland. She declined. She couldn't imagine being in the same room as the King. 'I didn't feel worthy to meet my absolute hero.'

Despite her growing notoriety, she was incredibly grounded. In the early days of the Pleasure Seekers her father had counselled his daughters that playing music professionally needed to be treated like any other business.

At a time when female stars in Britain were in the mould of Olivia Newton-John, Brenda Lee and Lulu — and Marianne Faithfull's true self was still submerged — Suzi stood out like a wicked fox in among the chickens. The titillation factor inflated her status to pin-up girl and she was asked to pose as the centrefold in one of the girlie magazines. She accepted with one stipulation — she keep her clothes on. 'It doesn't take any talent to take off your clothes,' she said. Suzi became the first woman to do a centre spread fully clothed. As one male reviewer said later, who needs clothes when you're wearing liquid leather. Rock'n'roll may have been dominated by men but Suzi was changing the rules of engagement.

Suzi Q clones began to spring up across Europe as young girls picked up guitars and squeezed into leather

The 1974 'Devil Gate Drive', penned by Chapman and Chinn, went straight to the top of the British charts — although back home in the USA Quatro was virtually unknown. The single was followed by 'The Wild One', which also made it into the top ten. 'Too Big', a single from her second Chapman and Chinn produced album, *Quatro*, became her third top twenty hit for the year. She made two tours of the USA supporting Kiss and Grand Funk Railroad. And when she came to Australia for the first time that year, folklore has it that the Hells Angels met her at Melbourne airport and escorted her into the city. Suzi's third album in as many years, *Your Mamma Won't Like Me*, contained another two Chapman Chinn British chart successes.

As her profile rose, the media sought to label her. But the tough-talking Yank from Detroit wasn't going to let anyone tell her what or who she was or how she should act. She shot straight from the hip, leaving no room for her words to be misinterpreted. To complaints she was unladylike, she simply remarked, 'If I swear too much, tough shit.' Was she a lesbian? No. She drew criticism for her music, pundits suggesting Suzi Quatro was manufactured because she was from the Chapman Chinn stable. Suzi reminded them she had been rocking for nearly a decade before she came to London. She was a serious musician and if you wanted to see sparks fly all you had to do was challenge her on that point.

Having being labelled a 'pop tart' by rock bible *Rolling Stone* when she first hit the scene, Suzi made its cover in 1975. Her female contemporaries usually sang about love and wanting that man. Suzi was singing about male menopause, the shock value of wearing inappropriate clothing and what it feels like to discover another woman's lipstick on your boyfriend's mouth. She sang about the things people dealt with on an everyday basis, exposing the layers below the façade. She was interested in human emotions, not making political statements. 'Politics and music don't mix,' she said.

That year she and the boys hit the road as a support act to Suzi's old Detroit mate Alice Cooper on his six-month Welcome to My Nightmare tour of the USA. Cooper was riding the crest of a massive wave of popularity and he filled huge stadiums around the country. But even with this level of exposure, success stateside eluded Suzi. The Americans weren't ready for female rock'n'rollers.

Suzi was singing about male menopause, the shock value of inappropriate clothing and what it's like to discover another woman's lipstick on your boyfriend's mouth

Suzi lived to perform and motored through the monotonous days of travelling on buses and sleeping in a different bed every night with relative ease, armed with a bottle of gin, crosswords and a good sense of humour. But she had no interest in getting wasted.

Having determined not to return to the USA to live, Suzi bought a sixteenth-century manor house near Chelmsford in Essex, less than 100 kilometres east of London. It became her sanctuary where she could relax, write songs and chill out after months on the road. But Suzi spent more time on the road, in buses and on planes than she did in her adopted country.

Aggro-phobia, her fourth album, was released in 1977 and introduced a new member of the Suzi Quatro band, Mike Deacon, who replaced Alistair MacKenzie on keyboards. Produced by Mickie Most, the album was an eclectic mix, with the Elvis classic 'Heartbreak Hotel' included alongside Steve Harley's 'Make Me Smile' and an Everly Brothers cover, 'Wake Up Little Susie'. The one Chapman Chinn song, 'Tear Me Apart', became *Aggro-phobia*'s only single to make it into the

New Wave punk was gathering momentum and Suzi didn't fit the bill

British top thirty. Suzi also produced a live album which was recorded while she was on tour in Japan in 1977 in Tokyo and Osaka to feed the insatiable appetite of her Japanese fans.

Crossing the Atlantic again that year, Suzi tried her hand at acting. She appeared in the hugely popular American sitcom *Happy Days* playing Leather Tuscadero, the younger sister of Fonzie's girlfriend Pinky and a character not unlike herself. The sitcom was a perfect audience for Suzi's music. But mainstream American rock fans still weren't moved enough to buy her records. Years later she stated that Mickie Most could have done more to push her records in the American market, but he released them on small labels that didn't have much promotional power.

While Suzi was rocking her heart out in Britain and across Europe, rock chicks like Debbie Harry were slinking across New York stages taunting with a different kind of sexuality. New wave punk was gathering momentum and Suzi didn't fit the bill.

Suzi and guitarist Len Tuckey, who had been together for some time, married in 1978, twice — first in England and then in a traditional ceremony in Japan. Maybe marriage had an effect, but *If You Knew Suzi …* released that year introduced a new, softer edged rock chanteuse sans leather and tough-bitch attitude. Pictured on the album cover in jeans and a blouse, this Suzi was a heartbreaker not a ball-breaker. The album featured three new Chapman Chinn songs, including the top five hit 'If You Can't Give Me Love'. There were also covers of Ray Davies' 'Tired of Waiting', Tom Petty's 'Breakdown' and 'Evie' written by songwriting duo Vanda and Young.

Then at last, in 1979, Suzi had her first real chart success in America, hitting number four on the Billboard charts with the unlikely ballad, 'Stumblin' In', a duet with Chris Norman from British band Smokie. And *If You Knew Suzi …* became her highest charting US album, making it into the top forty.

at last, in 1979, Suzi had her first real chart success in America, hitting number four on the Billboard charts with the unlikely ballad, 'Stumblin' In', a duet with Chris Norman

Continuing her relentless recording schedule, *Suzi and Other Four Letter Words* followed the next year, the last album Suzi would record for RAK Records. In 1980 Chapman and Chinn left the company to start Dreamland, taking Suzi with them. Her first record on the new label, *Rock Hard*, became her worst performing album to date. Sales were slow in all markets except Australia, where her fans bought everything she produced. Suzi was left facing an uncertain future. Her brand of rock was well and truly left behind in the wake of the new music coming from Spandau Ballet, Joy Division and the Clash.

For the first time since her London-based career was launched, Suzi released an album without Chapman and Chinn, whose Dreamland label had already folded by

1982. *Main Attraction* was produced by Len Tuckey and keyboardist Chris Andrews. She was pregnant during its recording with her daughter Laura. Suzi didn't go back into the studio to put down another original album for nearly a decade.

Motherhood didn't slow Suzi down. With baby in tow she toured to Australia again in 1983. Another child, Richard, was born the next year. Suzi simply took her brood on the road, juggling her multiple roles of mother, wife and rock star with her usual pragmatism.

Celebrity status saw Suzi invited to appear on various British TV shows in the early 1980s, including *Television Scrabble* — scrabble is one of her favourite games. The opportunity to combine two things she loved, singing and acting, came in 1986. At the suggestion of Andrew Lloyd Webber, Suzi took the lead role in the musical *Annie Get Your Gun* to critical acclaim. The show ran for two years in London's West End, and when it ended Suzi picked up her bass again and hit the road. This time she was touring the perestroika-era Soviet Union, where she played to over half a million people over a six-week tour in 1989.

Her performance in *Annie Get Your Gun* opened the sluice gates to acting opportunities in Britain. She had her own midday chat show *Gas Street* in 1988, and played cameos as Suzi Quatro the rock star on television in *Minder* and *Absolutely*

at the suggestion of Andrew Lloyd Webber, Suzi took the lead role in the musical *Annie Get Your Gun* to critical acclaim

Fabulous. 'Suzi Quatro really is a character,' she has said. She is more a jeans and jumper kind of girl at home.

After clocking up more television successes, Suzi took time out to work on a pet project she'd been carrying around in her head for years. In 1991 *Tallulah Who?*, a musical written by Suzi with composer/lyricist Shirlie Roden, opened at the Queen's Theatre, East London. It was based on the life of Hollywood actress Tallulah Bankhead, a scandalous character whose bisexuality and drug abuse shocked Americans in the 1920s. Suzi played the role to rave reviews.

Signed to a new label, Suzi put out a new studio album in 1991, *Oh Suzi Q*.

Bolland & Bolland was run by the Dutch pop music brothers Rob and Ferdy Bolland, who had enjoyed success as performers and also as producers of bands like Status Quo.

Suzi and Tuckey were the only two left from the original band line-up and session musicians were used for the recording.

After fourteen years Suzi ended her marriage in 1992, a decision she said was the bravest thing she's ever done. She put the marriage's failure down to the fact that she and Tuckey had been drawing apart musically for some time. The same year her mother and mother-in-law died. Wanting to share what she had learned of the grieving process, she teamed with Shirlie Roden to produce a self-help album, *Free the Butterfly*. Subsequently Suzi was involved in the Festival of the Mind, Body and Spirit in Britain and Australia.

After a whirlwind romance, Suzi popped the question to Rainer Haas, a German concert promoter. They married in Las Vegas in 1993 and now split their time between homes in Essex and Hamburg.

In the mid-1990s Suzi produced *What Goes Around: The Latest and Greatest*, mostly a revamp of old hits designed to attract a new generation of rock'n'roll fans. The album went gold. It was followed in 1998 by *Unreleased Emotions*, a collection of unreleased songs that Suzi had written and recorded in 1982 when she was pregnant with Laura. As the decade came to a close, she hosted a phenomenally successful BBC radio series, *Rockin' With Suzi Q*, which ran for multiple seasons and led to a 2006 nomination in the Sony Radio Academy Awards.

When she turned fifty in 2000, Suzi celebrated in Berlin in front of more than 22,000 fans. She toasted the audience with champagne and was presented with a massive birthday cake on stage.

In 2004 Suzi appeared in *Edgeplay: A Film About the Runaways*, a documentary produced by former Runaway bass player Vicki Tischler Blue. In *Edgeplay* Suzi recalled touring to LA in the early 1970s and day after day seeing Joan Jett in the foyer of her hotel, a silent Suzi clone, flattering and somewhat un-nerving at the same time. The next year Joan was wielding her own bass guitar with the Runaways. *Back to the Drive*, Suzi's first original studio album in fifteen years, was released in 2006.

Suzi Q is a bit like Peter Pan. She's still thrashing about the stage, with a bass guitar, inciting the audience to rock out

In 2009 Suzi was back in the studio with producer Mike Chapman working on a new album slated for release the following year. The same year she also toured Australia and New Zealand and was a guest host on *Australian Idol*. Then in 2010 she was on the road again, performing limited dates in Germany, Britain, Norway and Denmark before making the finishing touches to her latest studio effort.

Suzi Q is a bit like Peter Pan, the wand of time seemingly passing her over. Now in her sixties she is still thrashing about the stage, wielding a bass guitar that has always looked too big for her, as she continues to incite the audience to rock out, no matter what their age.

JoAN JETT

the
Prodigal
Daughter

Clad in
Black Leather,
inches-thick
eyeliner
black close-cropped hair,
tattoos

and flat abs that would make most twenty-year-olds jealous, Joan Jett is still rocking hard after more than thirty years in the biz. And she's still playing the one song she is best known for — 'I Love Rock'n'Roll', one of the all-time great hits out of the 1980s, and one that has refused to die. **Even Britney Spears has covered it.**

The road to that number one hit — the success of which Joan has ridden ever since — was bumpy and full of the drama one would expect from a heavy-duty rock chick.

In the 1970s there were the manic highs of being rhythm guitarist, and later lead singer, of the Runaways, the first-ever manufactured girl group (we're not talking Spice Girls here), and then the sinking lows of the early 1980s when no one wanted to know about her. Joan was turned down by twenty-three record labels after the Runaways folded. There was no interest in this butch tomboy in the baseball cap who some in the industry asserted couldn't sing anyway.

Joan Marie Larkin was born in 1960 in Philadelphia. When she was about twelve the family moved to Los Angeles, to the San Fernando Valley. She got her first electric guitar at the age of thirteen, a Christmas present from her folks. Joan instantly became a songwriter and obsessive about music.

Her first guitar lesson was a bittersweet experience — the male teacher didn't think playing rock'n'roll was the right thing for a young lady. Instead he taught her 'On Top of Old Smokey'. It was her first and last lesson. She taught herself out of a 'how to play' book. Under the influence of the glam-rock bands like Gary Glitter and the New York Dolls and rock legends Led

no one had ever put teenage girls together in a rock band —the titillation factor alone would draw attention

Zeppelin, Black Sabbath, the Stones, Iggy Pop and Hendrix, she put all her energy into music.

Her parents divorced not long after the move to Cailfornia and she took her mother's maiden name, Jett. The fifteen-year-old Joan began jamming with drummer Sandy West who lived in Huntington Beach, about an hour's drive south of LA. The girls knew few songs, but were filled with teenage determination to play rock'n'roll. They hooked up with songwriter Kari Krome, another teenager, who led them to LA record producer Kim Fowley.

Fowley had been around the music scene since the early 1960s — he'd been a songwriter and producer for bubblegum pop bands like the Murmaids — and knew a good thing when he saw it. The Runaways was born. Fowley was more interested in the band as a social musical experiment. No one had ever put teenage girls together in a rock band — he was sure the titillation factor alone would draw attention.

The first Runaways line-up featured Michael (Micki) Steele, who would later turn up in the Bangles, on vocals together with Joan and West. But Fowley thought Steele was too old and she didn't last long in the role of lead singer. At the audition they played the one song they all knew, Kiss's 'Strutter', and by all accounts it was a woeful experience. Lita Ford came in on lead guitar and Jackie Fox was recruited on bass. The finishing touch to the line-up was Cherie Currie. A blonde bombshell, Cherie wore corset and suspenders, an outfit that screamed underage sex.

As all teenagers do, the girls thought they were tough and knew everything. In fact they were incredibly young, naïve and ill-prepared to cope with their rapid rise to fame. Signed to Mercury Records in 1976, their first single, 'Cherry Bomb', a song written on the spot by Joan and Fowley for Currie at her audition, threw them into the limelight. Promoted as jailbait rockers, every sleazebag on the planet came out to see the girls shake their stuff.

When their self-titled debut album was released later that year, they took off across the country playing clubs, including CBGB in New York where new wave punk groups like the Ramones and Blondie had got their start. They also supported Tom Petty and headlined shows in Scotland and England, where they played to testosterone-fuelled audiences. In Glasgow 'it took fire hoses' to force the mob away from the Runaways' cars. Their fans also made an assault on the hotel where the girls were staying.

While in Britain, the Runaways hung out with punk gods the Sex Pistols and the Damned. There were rumours that Joan and Rat Scabies, the Damned's drummer, were an item, a suggestion that Joan strongly refuted. Her association with the Pistols though would come in handy in the future.

The Runaways exposed Joan to all the good and bad things that rock'n'roll can offer — five teenagers with no experience of touring, the loneliness of being on the road with virtual strangers, and the constant verbal abuse from Fowley, who prefaced each barrage he delivered with 'hey, dog shit' or 'you, dog piss' or 'dog c--t'. The Runaways quickly deteriorated into a mire of sex, drugs, alcohol and misery.

The music press didn't help their self-esteem, labelling them tough-talking sluts or dykes, focusing on their behaviour — drinking, smoking, drug-taking and swearing — and treating their music as a footnote. Joan has said that if the

Runaways had been blokes, the media wouldn't have taken the same tack. But it wasn't only the press who wore the girls down. The bands they toured with treated them with little respect, as did the crews.

Unable to cope with the constant prying into their lives and the aggression that surrounded them, the band members descended into a drug-hazed hell. When Joan claimed she was 'the Keith Richards of the group' perhaps she wasn't just alluding to her stage presence and hard rock attitude. Her substance abuse was paralleling the rise in popularity of the band. She was playing hard in every sense of the word.

Fowley manipulated the band, controlling their money and dishing out paltry sums as though he were their father giving them pocket money. But he was anything but a father figure, allowing the girls to run amok emotionally and physically. He and co-manager Scott Anderson constantly stirred the pot, keeping the band in a permanent state of jealousy, insecurity and virtual poverty. They didn't only abuse their roles as

promoted as jailbait rockers, every sleazebag on the planet came out to see the Runaways shake their stuff

managers, but also as adults in charge of teenagers. Fox was reportedly the only band member not to have slept with Anderson.

In 1977 the Runaways undertook a sell-out tour of Japan, their biggest fan base, and where Joan is still hailed as a superstar. On that tour Fox tried to commit suicide. After she was sent home alone, Joan picked up on bass and the girls went back to business as usual. On the tour they recorded *Live in Japan*, which was released later that year.

Back in LA Vicki Blue (now Vicky Tischler Blue) filled the breach as bass player. It would only take her a few days to realise she had stepped into a nightmare.

Recording the band's next album, 1977's *Queens of Noise*, Currie missed a couple of days in the studio recovering from an abortion. Joan took over on lead vocals and sang the album's title track, a song Currie had brought to the band. That one act caused the existing animosity between the two to reach

the press labelled them tough-talking sluts or dykes, focusing on their behaviour and treating their music as a footnote

a crescendo. Currie quit on the spot. She thought she was a 'goddamn queen', Joan said, and wanted the Runaways 'to be Cherie Currie and her back-up band'. Joan became lead singer.

The unraveling of the Runaways continued at a rapid pace. In 1978 Fowley produced the third album, *Waitin' for the Night*, but it didn't rate on the charts and many suspected it was because fans didn't like Joan's voice as much as they had Currie's. Whatever, it was a voice destined to become one of the most recognised in rock'n'roll — harsh, gravely and drawn from deep in her gut. Joan was born to roar.

Shortly after the release of the album, Fowley left and the band was taken on by Toby Mamis, Blondie's manager. But even Mamis had trouble convincing the record companies that Joan was a worthwhile substitute for Currie. They wanted a sexy blonde not a butch tomboy.

The band went back into the studio to record what was their final album, *And Now ... the Runaways*. Joan clashed head on with producer John Alcock, who didn't particularly like her or her choice of music. Alcock was keen to see the girls play heavier rock, not the glam-rock that appealed to Joan. West and Ford sided with him. Vicki Blue quit, citing her inability to work with Alcock. The hostilities within the band were fuelled by escalating drug and alcohol abuse. When the band finally broke up, Joan was devastated. It was 1979.

Her bitterness about the break-up ran deep. She was the only band member not to participate in the documentary *Edgeplay: A Film about the Runaways*, released in 2004, and withheld permission for the use of footage and the inclusion on the soundtrack of songs on which she held copyright. The story goes that Joan and her management didn't think the film featured her prominently enough, but her absence made a stronger statement.

Life after the Runaways was hard. Joan had no band and no recording contract. Refusing to be relegated to the rock'n'roll graveyard, she tried her hand at producing, working on *(G.I)*, which turned out to be the only album of LA punk band the Germs. Released in 1979, it was widely regarded as one of the most impressive American hardcore punk rock albums.

Later that year Joan headed to London, where she put down a couple of demo tracks with ex-Sex Pistols Steve Jones and Paul Cook. 'I Love Rock'n'Roll' was released along with 'You Don't Own Me' and 'Don't Abuse Me' as a single package in Holland.

Joan returned to LA in 1979 to complete filming and record the soundtrack

Joan took over on lead vocals and sang the album's title track. That caused the existing animosity to reach a crescendo. Currie quit on the spot

for a movie loosely based on the Runaways, *We're All Crazy Now*. Joan was the only one to play herself — actors were brought in to play the other band members. The movie wasn't released as originally intended, but in 1984 part of the footage featuring Joan was used in *Dubeat-E-O*.

On the surface doing the film might not have seemed a terrific career move. But it turned out to be a godsend, putting her in touch with songwriter and producer Kenny Laguna who would become her business partner, mentor and friend. Laguna, who had been keyboard player and back-up singer with Tommy James and the Shondels, had produced a number of bands on the Who's label in London. Hired to finish off the soundtrack on which Joan would sing and play guitar, Laguna expected a 'little girl in a baseball cap'. But, he said, 'she played … better than anyone on the tape.'

Soon Laguna and Joan were heading to London, where the Who let them use a studio gratis to put down tracks for Joan's first solo album. Laguna called in favours left, right and centre. Ritchie Cordell stepped in as co-producer. An impressive line-up of punk-rock musicians, including the Ramones' Marky and Dee Dee, Paul Cook and Steve Jones of the Pistols, and Clem Burke and Frank Infante from Blondie also pitched in.

Recording completed, Joan headed back to the US, to New York, and set about trying to get a record deal. She sent demo tapes to every label in the country. Turned down consistently by the majors and independents, Joan and Laguna pooled their resources, started Blackheart Records and pressed copies of the record, which they

sold at gigs out of the trunk of Laguna's 1976 Cadillac Coup
De Ville. Laguna enlisted industry heavyweights — Steve Leber,
whose management company looked after Aerosmith and Kiss,
came on board — but even with that kind of support behind her,
Joan still couldn't get signed.

Undeterred, in 1980 Joan put together the Blackhearts,
comprising Ricky Byrd on guitar, Gary Ryan on bass, and Lee
Crystal on drums — all three coming from an ad Laguna placed in
the music press. Joan and the boys hit the road, touring for the best
part of twelve months and playing wherever they could get a spot.

The breakthrough was a performance at the Ritz in New York
filmed as part of the documentary *Urgh-A Rock War*, which
featured the Police, Toyah Wilcox, Wall of Voodoo and a host of
other bands filmed at various venues. It got Joan on to the music
industry's radar. Finally in 1981 independent label Boardwalk Records
re-released Joan's debut album as *Bad Reputation*. It didn't do any great
shakes, but the title song is still played today and was included in the
animated film *Shrek*.

A second album followed quickly in February 1982. The album's title

doing *We're All Crazy Now* might not
have seemed a terrific career move.
But it put her in touch with songwriter
and producer Kenny Laguna

song 'I Love Rock'n'Roll' is now part of rock history. A cover of a B-side
single by British band the Arrows, it held the number one position on the US
charts for eight weeks and catapulted Joan into the rock'n'roll stratosphere.
The album, produced by Laguna and Cordell, featured a number of original
tracks written by Joan and Laguna as well as covers of Dave Clark Five's 'Bits
and Pieces' and Eddie Cochrane's 'Summertime Blues'. It became Joan's highest
charting album, reaching second spot.

Joan Jett and the Blackhearts took to the road that year supporting the likes
of the Police and performing major stadium gigs in the USA before taking off
to Europe and Australia. Joan's cover of Gary Glitter's 'Do You Wanna Touch
Me', released in 1982, received significant pick-up on radio as did the album's other
single, 'Crimson and Clover', a cover of the Shondell's song. Suddenly Joan was a
multi-platinum selling artist and the major labels were taking her seriously.

Her success in the charts didn't end with *I Love Rock'n'Roll*, but the drug abuse that had hampered her in the days of the Runaways did. Laguna had strict rules for his 'Joanie' and the Blackheart boys. Drugs were off limits. He wasn't going to let pills and powder ruin the band's chances to ride the wave of success they'd worked so hard for. Anyway booze was a good enough substitute for numbing the boredom of being on the road.

After the release of *I Love Rock'n'Roll* Joan and the Blackhearts toured solidly for nearly three years, only coming off the road to put down tracks for another album before heading out again. They played long tours with a who's who of rock — Aerosmith, Deep Purple, Cheap Trick (who had opened for the Runaways in 1977), ZZ Top, the Who, Journey, Queen and Foreigner. Joan loved touring and what she called 'the physical element' of performing — getting 'all sweaty' — and the intimacy of the relationship with the audience.

Her next record, simply titled *Album*, was released in 1983. It featured covers of some of Joan's favourite songs, including Sly Stone's 'Everyday People' and the Rolling Stones' 'Star Star'. Reviewers likened *Album* to Joan's first solo offering, *Bad Reputation*, noting that there weren't any stand-out songs or chart toppers, but a good selection of solid rock'n'roll tunes. *Album* went gold.

Glorious Results of a Misspent Youth followed the next year. It included another

Laguna had strict rules for his 'Joanie' and the Blackheart boys. Drugs were off limits

Gary Glitter classic, 'I Love You Love Me Love', and also the song the Runaways are most remembered for, 'Cherry Bomb'.

But despite numerous albums and a relentless touring schedule that in the space of three years took Joan and her band around the world and back multiple times, things weren't all rosy in Blackhearts' financial camp.

Broadway Records, which had released *Bad Reputation* and *I Love Rock'n'Roll*, had folded in 1982 with the death of its founder. Joan and Laguna never received what would have been massive royalties for *I Love Rock'n'Roll*, although Joan did secure the radio rights to the title song, which in years to come would deliver handsome profits. Money was still tight and Laguna had to resort to paying for promotional necessities like video production on his credit card as he negotiated to move Joan from MCA, which had released *Album* and *Glorious Results*, to CBS Records.

In 1986 Joan turned her hand to acting, appearing with Michael J Fox and Gena

Rowlands in *Light of Day*. Directed by Paul Schrader, who wrote *Taxi Driver* and *Raging Bull* and directed *American Gigolo*, the film received a mixed reception from critics, although there was consensus that Joan's performance as a rock singer was exceptional.

It was unfortunate timing that Joan's next album with the Blackhearts, *Good Music*, was released around the same time as the movie's soundtrack — or that was the excuse her management offered for the album's lacklustre performance, particularly from a radio airplay perspective. There was little pick-up other than Joan's cover of 'Roadrunner' by Jonathan Richman.

In 1987 the band went out on the road for almost twelve months. On stage is where Joan really comes into her own. She's a powerhouse of energy, attitude, sweat and deafening guitar playing — you don't leave Joan's

Joan loved what she called 'the physical element' of performing — getting 'all sweaty' — and the intimacy with the audience

concerts without your ears ringing for days. By this time the Blackhearts line-up had changed. Kasim Sulton, who had worked with Mick Jagger, Bon Jovi and Patti Smith, was on bass and Thommy Price on drums. Price had played on previous Blackhearts albums in between touring with Mink de Ville. He toured with the Blackhearts in 1987 and returned in 1990 as a permanent member of the band. He's still hanging with Joan.

Joan was back in the top ten in 1988 with 'I Hate Myself for Loving You', the best performing single on that year's album, *Up Your Alley*. Songwriter Desmond Child and Ric Browde, who had worked with big-hair rock boys Poison, were

Joan and Laguna never received what would have been massive royalties for *I Love Rock'n'Roll*

brought in to add fresh ideas without losing Joan's three-chord rock sound. The album was recorded in classic Blackheart style with all the musicians in the one room as if they were playing live. *Up Your Alley* featured a cover of Iggy Pop's 'I Wanna Be Your Dog', which Joan had been playing live for years, and a little known Chuck Berry song 'Tulane'.

The Hit List of 1990 featured covers of some of Joan's favourite bands. It was an eclectic mix of songs that worked surprisingly well and kept diehard fans buying records. *Notorious* was released the next year and, as *Rolling Stone* magazine said, it gave Joan's fans exactly what they were hoping for: 'anthemic hard-rock ditties packed with gritty riffs, strong melodies and a touch of grunge, all topped off by Jett's wonderfully rasping voice.' The album was followed by

Flashback, a collection of lesser known songs and B-sides, which demonstrated the breadth of Joan's work since going solo in 1980.

In 1993 she worked with Bikini Kill, producing their 'New Radio'/'Rebel Girl'. Joan and Bikini Kill singer Kathleen Hanna co-wrote 'Spinster', 'Rubber & Glue', 'Go Home' and 'You Got a Problem' (with Desmond Child), all of which appear on Joan's 1994 album *Pure and Simple*. Now signed to Warner Brothers, this Joan was more in the vein of the 1990s riot grrrls — who had held her up as a model for female rockers. The album featured Kat Bjelland of Babes in Toyland and Donita Sparks and Jennifer Finch from L7.

Around this time Joan embarked on a new artistic pursuit, painting. On the rare occasions she was at home with her cats, she would set up her easel and let her mind wander while she daubed paint on to canvas. On tour she preferred reading, often books on philosophy.

In 1995 she recorded an album with Seattle band the Gits, whose lead singer Mia Zapata was raped and murdered in 1993 during the time Joan was in Seattle working with Bikini Kill. Proceeds from the album, *Evil Stig* (Gits Live backwards), were donated to the Mia Zapata investigative fund which paid for private detectives' work to solve the murder.

Zapata's death inspired Joan and Hanna to write *Pure and Simple*'s 'Go Home' about being stalked. The song also appears on the *Home Alive: The Art of Self Defense* benefit album for Home Alive, a Seattle anti-violence organisation co-founded by Valerie Agnew of 7 Year Bitch. The album features Pearl Jam, Nirvana, the Wilsons from Heart and Soundgarden.

Joan has said numerous times that rock'n'roll is her life. In 1996 she was able to combine the two true loves of her life, sports and music. For an advertisement for US sports network ESPN promoting women's basketball, she recorded the theme song from the *Mary Tyler Moore Show*, 'Love is All Around', giving it a decided rock edge. The reaction was phenomenal, sending Joan back into the studio to record a full-length version of the song.

Back on the touring circuit in 1997, a new-look Joan had short cropped bleached blonde hair, reminiscent of Billy Idol's 1980 cut, and a tank top replacing her bodysuit and showing off finely honed abs. It proved that being a non-drinking, non-smoking, yoga-practising vegetarian is good for your body.

The title song of the album *Fetish*, released in 1999, was Joan's raunchiest song to date with blatant references to sadomasochism delivered with a brutality and profanity that hadn't been part of her repertoire. The song gave new life to

what many had thought was a career in its twilight and delivered Joan a younger audience.

To celebrate the new millennium Joan shaved off her bleached locks and then appeared as Columbia in a New York production

the burkha stomping made it on to CNN, much to the chagrin of the military honchos

of *The Rocky Horror Picture Show*. Wielding her screaming guitar, her powerful stage presence, enhanced by her shining bald head and the ethereal lighting, was well received.

When she performed for the troops in Afghanistan in 2001 she took to the stage in a burkha, which she threw off and stomped on. Underneath she wore a see-through top, camouflage pants and what looked like army issue boots. It made it on to CNN, much to the chagrin of the military honchos. She rallied for women's health too, recording the Beatles song 'The Word' for *It's All About Eve*, an album to raise funds for breast cancer awareness.

In 2004 Joan and the Blackhearts released *Naked*, which was available only in Japan. On the *Naked* cover was a black-haired Joan topless, the word 'naked' scrawled across her nipples. After spending considerable time writing songs, re-recording tracks from *Naked* and laying down unreleased material with the latest incarnation of the Blackhearts — Dougie Needles on lead guitar, Thommy Price on drums and Enzo Pennizzotto on bass — the long-awaited new album came out in 2006. *Sinner* was released on her Blackhearts record label.

Sinner was a work of true maturity that showed Joan could still rock as hard, and better, as she ever had. But it is somewhat of a shift into a more politicised rock, eschewing the loves-lost-and-found themes of her previous work. *Sinner* reveals an older, more introspective person. The single 'Riddles' is a political anthem.

When in New York Joan hosts a weekly program on Sirius Satellite Radio, *Radio Revolution*. She and Laguna have signed more alternate bands to Blackheart Records, including the Vacancies, whose album *A Beat Missing or a Silence Added* picked up a 2007 Independent Music Award.

The teenage Joan Jett wanted to be a rock star. She's rocked hard for more than thirty years now and there's no sign of her losing her love of rock'n'roll.

We come from
a musical
family...

there was always music
and singing around the house,'
Nancy Wilson has said.
Playing guitar with sister Ann
in arena rock band Heart was
just an extension of what
they'd always done.

Ann was born in San Diego in 1950, and Nancy four years later when the Wilson family was living in San Francisco. Their father, a highly decorated officer in the US Marine Corp, moved from one posting to another, including Korea, Taiwan and Panama. He retired in the early 1960s, when Ann was around twelve, and the Wilsons put down roots in the middle-class suburb of Bellevue in Seattle. There their father went back to his great loves — English literature, poetry and music.

A tight-knit family, the Wilsons gave their daughters plenty of love as well as freedom. The three Wilson sisters — Lynn is the eldest — have strong voices and they sang all the time. When Ann was around thirteen her grandmother gave her a guitar to help pass the time while she recovered from illness. Nancy wanted a guitar like her big sister's. She began playing at the age of nine. Not long after, she was composing. 'She's a natural,' Ann said.

For Ann — who played the flute and was planning a classical career — the musical turning point came in 1963 when she got hooked on the Beatles. Three years later she saw them in concert and thought all her Christmases had come at once: 'that entire summer we lived on top of this mountain of ice cream and candy floss because we'd been in the same room with the Beatles.'

The Wilson girls had teenage flirtations with drugs — acid trips and pot smoking — but much of the excitement came from the thrill of scoring. Dabbling in a little contraband was rebellious. But they weren't into excess

> they were fired from one gig. Four days later they were supporting Rod Stewart in concert. That's how fast the game changed

and were rather scared by the antics of Janis Joplin, a big influence at the time.

Constantly struggling with her weight, Ann skulked around dressed in black, desperate to conceal her size. Being uncomfortable about her figure compounded the complexities of an already shy personality. But music was something she could lose herself in. By the time she was in her late teens she was playing around the traps in Seattle with various bands. She recorded a couple of singles, including 'Through Eyes and Glass' written with Nancy, with folk-rock group Daybreak and the two played in the Viewpoints, another folk-oriented band.

But it didn't last. Nancy was intent on going to college. And Ann wanted to be a rock chick.

Answering an ad in 1972, she auditioned for Roger Fisher and Steve Fossen, who had been playing together for years. Fisher remembers Ann 'busting loose' with a voice of 'incredible power' that just blew him away. She joined their band. It was heavily influenced by Led Zeppelin and named Hocus Pocus.

When Fisher's brother Mike, who had been playing with Roger before fleeing to Canada to avoid the Vietnam War draft, snuck down across the border, 'I fell in love with him instantly,' Ann confessed. It was a mutual attraction. Ann moved the 200 kilometres up the coast to Vancouver to be with her man. Fisher and Fossen followed. Mike worked with the band in various capacities, at one point as manager.

Ann wanted her sister to join Heart. It took until 1974 before Nancy, who was in college, acquiesced. But she only agreed after being assured she'd be able to use her acoustic talents — mandolin, keyboards and acoustic guitar — *and* play electric rock. Soon Nancy hooked up with Roger Fisher. Now both sisters were in relationships within the band.

After three years of playing every conceivable rock venue, the now-named Heart finally made its mark. It was hard going, doing the rounds of the clubs. They would play sets over five hours in as many nights as they could get bookings. Roger lost his temper at one lousy venue and set the band room on fire. They were fired. Four days later they were supporting Rod Stewart in concert. That's how fast the game changed.

Heart released its first album, *Dreamboat Annie*, in 1976 on the Canadian Mushroom label run by producer Mike Flicker, Howard Leese and Shelly Siegel. Before the band signed, Mushroom had offered Ann a solo deal. She wasn't interested. She was the dynamic vocalist in a bone fide rock'n'roll band — just where she wanted to be.

Leese, who'd met the Wilson sisters two years earlier and had worked with them on a demo tape, played keyboards on the album. Before long he officially became a member of Heart. Drummer Michael DeRosier completed the permanent line-up. And Ann and Nancy's big sister Lynn sang back-up vocals on the album.

Siegel knew Heart had to crack America. The Canadian market was just too small. He watched the success of other arena rock bands, like Foreigner and Boston, and wanted some of that magic for Heart. After all the major record

they were
a marketer's
dream —
an innocent
blonde and
a voluptuous
brunette. The
fact they were
sisters and
serious rock
chicks made it
even better

labels rejected the band's work, he set up an independent distribution network in the States and succeeded in getting radio time for *Dreamboat Annie*.

That was all it took. The record sold over a million copies and peaked at number seven on the US charts. Rumours were rife that the single Ann had written, 'Magic Man', was about Charles Manson (the real subject was an old boyfriend). That didn't hurt sales. The song was Heart's first top ten American hit. The album's two other singles written by Ann and Nancy, 'Crazy On You' and 'Dreamboat Annie', both reached the top fifty.

'Magic Man' was the band's mass-market breakthrough. Rock fans loved Ann's powerful, hypnotic, incredibly sexy voice and Nancy's classy guitar work. The press, with Mushroom Records' help, began to refer to Heart as Ann and Nancy

Ann's voice ranged from melodic to the animal howls of a true rocker. She was like a tornado, whipping everyone around her into a frenzy

Wilson. It infuriated the band. But Mushroom was only interested in selling records. These two were a marketer's dream — an innocent-looking blonde (Nancy) and a voluptuous brunette (Ann). The fact they were sisters *and* serious rock chicks made it even better.

They were bare shouldered on the cover of *Dreamboat Annie* but it looked as if they were naked. Mushroom used the picture with the tag line 'Heart's Wilson Sisters Confess: It Was Only Our First Time' in an ad — the implication being the sisters were lesbian lovers.

But there was a lot more to the Wilson sisters than sex appeal. They were almost obscenely talented. Ann's voice was her most impressive asset, but she was also a good musician (guitar, ukulele, flute) and a powerful lyricist. Nancy's true brilliance lay in arranging music to Ann's lyrics. She played a range of electric and acoustic instruments and could hold her own as a vocalist too.

The publicity machine spun and spun. Heart was new. And it was a band with women. Often the questions came back to how much cleavage they were showing. But once the band started playing, it was very obvious that these rock chicks could rock. 'We want people to know this is a real band, not one of those machines that turns out records and never tours,' Ann said. 'We love to get out and play … We're the most fulfilled when everybody gets off.'

Heart toured extensively, building its reputation as a potent live act.

Ann was mesmerising, a powerful singer who commanded the spotlight. Nancy was equally dynamic, her svelte body at one with the guitar as she rocked her way across stage. On tour they were one big happy family, the Wilson girls and the Fisher boys. But being in close proximity in a high-powered, ego-sensitive environment was courting disaster.

Mushroom offered Ann a solo deal. She wasn't interested. She was just where she wanted to be

They were losing faith with Mushroom Records, mainly because of the way the girls were being portrayed as rock'n'roll sex kittens. As Ann said, you can be both a heavy rocker and a woman — and not sell your soul in translation.

With the 1977 amnesty for American draft dodgers, Mike Fisher was able to return home. Heart pulled up stumps and went back to Seattle. Leaving Mushroom for CBS subsidiary Portrait, they found themselves in legal hot water. Their first CBS album *Little Queen* was released in the middle of that year and got strong reviews. It cemented Heart's position as rockers on a par with Led Zeppelin and Black Sabbath, bands the girls had idolised. But within months Mushroom released *Magazine*, an album that had been recorded in 1976. Heart didn't want it to see the light of day — when they did nothing to support it, *Magazine* quickly faded from view.

'Barracuda', the biggest hit from *Little Queen*, was written by the Wilsons with their old friend Sue Ennis and drummer DeRosier. It reached eleven on the Billboard charts and sent rock reviewers' hearts racing. Ann's voice ranged from melodic tones to the animal howls of a true rocker. She was like a tornado, whipping everyone around her into a frenzy, band and audience alike. *Little Queen* clocked up multi-platinum sales.

When *Dog & Butterfly*, was released in 1978 the band was awash with personal crises. Ann's relationship with Mike, who produced the album, was starting to fray and Nancy had broken up with Roger only to take up with DeRosier. During a show in Portland, Oregon, Roger snapped, smashing his guitar and storming off stage. Then Ann and Mike split.

No way were broken love affairs going to break up the band, although they screwed things up emotionally for a time. The press couldn't help comparing Heart's heartaches with those of other mega-1970s group Fleetwood Mac — but in this case the emotional fireworks were not sparked by drugs.

A nn moved into a house by the woods that Nancy and Ennis shared in Seattle and the three women worked on songs for the next album. *Bebe Le Strange* was released in 1980 to mixed reviews. It was a departure from the heavier arena rock style that had made them stars — more introspective and more feminine. Reviewers suggested the album suffered from Roger Fisher's absence. Its single 'Even It Up' made it to the top forty and the album peaked at number five, but it wasn't enough to stem the downturn in sales and the album only went gold — a poor performance compared with their previous efforts.

Commercially, it was the beginning of a downward slide. In the space of just three albums and three years — *Bebe Le Strange*, *Private Audition* and *Passionworks* — Heart had gone from superstar, multi-platinum artists to racking up a pathetic half-million sales for *Passionworks*, even though its single, 'How Can I Refuse', reached number one.

> broken love affairs screwed things up for a time. The press couldn't help comparing Heart's heartaches with those of Fleetwood Mac

P assionworks was the last of three albums contracted to Epic, with whom there was no love lost, and it may have suffered as a result. It was also the first with Denny Carmassi on drums, and Mark Andes on bass. DeRosier and Fossen had quit after the recording of *Private Audition* — although it was as if they had already split, such was the lack of input from either in the creative process.

By the time Heart started to record the self-titled album in 1984, the band had their backs to the wall and their own money on the line.

But they got a new deal with Capitol Records and they pulled against the musical tide that was sweeping arena rock bands away. *Heart* sold over five million copies, ending up at number one on the US charts. That was largely thanks to the producing genius of Ron Nevison. *Heart* was enriched by Grace Slick, who was now singing with Starship, singing back-up vocals.

The album included their first number one hit, 'These Dreams', which was written by Bernie Taupin and Martin Page, the first of numerous hits for Heart written by other songwriters. Its four singles — 'These Dreams', 'Never', 'What

having nearly gone to the wall financially, they were prepared to play the record company's game. But the constant preening was a chore

About Love' and 'Nothin' At All' — all made it into the top ten.

The release of *Heart* introduced a new image for the Wilson sisters — as sexy vamps. Lots of cleavage, cinched waists, high hair and thick make-up in classic 1980s style. Having nearly gone to the wall financially, they were prepared to play the game. Even though the endless preening was a chore.

When the band wasn't in the studio it was on the road playing to massive arena crowds around the world. They loved it. For Nancy, performing was 'beyond the physical'. It was like 'an all inclusive state of euphoria,' she said.

Heart and the subsequent *Bad Animals* album, issued in 1987, refilled the coffers.

The Wilsons were back on top, hailed as superstars of a supergroup. Success the second time round was that much sweeter.

In 1986 Nancy married *Rolling Stone* writer Cameron Crowe, who turned screenwriter/director with the film *Almost Famous*, based on his life on the road as a music journalist. Nancy was wrapped in a cocoon of romantic bliss.

But Ann was struggling with her personal demon — food. She'd battled to

the Wilsons were back on top, hailed as superstars of a supergroup. Success the second time round was that much sweeter

keep the kilos off all her life. As much as forty-five kilos overweight at times, she had managed to camouflage her weight problems in the early years. But when MTV came along in the 1980s the whole rock'n'roll game changed. Now it wasn't just about how you sounded. It was all about the video.

As Ann's weight escalated, the record label tried to disguise her size. Photos from the time never show her in full view. She is off to the side or behind Nancy. The super-confident singer was reduced to a bundle of anxiety. The one thing she loved more than anything, performing for an audience, became an agony. She was paralysed with fear. 'I'd sing my head off but all they would notice would be what I looked like in the review,' Ann told a journalist.

The inclusion of material by other songwriters continued with 1990's *Brigade*. Again it paid off. Its hit single, 'All I Wanna Do is Make Love to You', written by John 'Mutt' Lange, reached number two and the album got to three on the Billboard charts. This success was followed by *Rock the House Live* in 1991, recorded during the concert tour for *Brigade*.

In the early 1990s the Wilsons started to dabble in other projects. Ann recorded two duets that hit the top ten — 'Almost Paradise' with Mike Reno for the *Footloose* soundtrack and 'Surrender to Me' with Robin Zander from Cheap Trick, which featured in the movie *Tequila Sunrise*. Nancy began scoring films for husband Cameron Crowe, including the Tom Cruise–Renee Zellweger hit *Jerry Macguire*. Ann adopted her daughter Marie in 1991 and seven years later a boy, named Dustin, her mother's maiden name.

The 1993 *Desire Walks On* seemed to lack that Heart magic and only reached the top fifty. By 1995 the band — now consisting of the Wilsons and Howard Leese — had trouble finding a spot for *The Road Home* among hits by pop stars like Mariah Carey and rappers such as Coolio.

Ann and Nancy kept busy with a band they formed for the Support the Troops concert in Seattle during the first Gulf War. Reluctant to perform as a duo, they started the Lovemongers — a play on 'warmongers' — with Sue Ennis on keyboards, guitarist Frank Cox and Ben Smith on drums. A philanthropic vehicle, it allowed the Wilsons to support causes they believed in while playing music they loved. It was far removed from Heart. They performed concerts to benefit everything from breast cancer research to the environment. Ann described it as 'heavy harmonies and old folk rock, protest music like anti-war stuff'. It was family sing-along music — but political at the same time. Ennis believed the Lovemongers 'was a reclaiming of who Ann and Nancy were artistically'.

The Lovemongers played around Seattle in the 1990s, recorded a cover of Led Zeppelin's 'Battle of Evermore', which appeared on the soundtrack of Crowe's 1992 film *Singles* and released two albums, the 1997 *Whirlygig* and *Here is Christmas* the next year. And in 1997 Nancy made her first solo album, *Live at McCabe's*, recorded at the guitar shop in Santa Monica, California. It has a folk-rock edge with confessional, Joni Mitchell-esque lyrics.

Three years later, at the age of forty-six, Nancy gave birth to twin boys. As their families grew, so did the tour entourage. Both women took their children on the road as often as possible, along with nannies and support staff. Often tours would be scheduled around school holidays. At the height of Heart mania in the 1980s, touring was on private jets in superstar style. Now, on the Beatles tribute tour, Inside the Abbey Road with Todd Rundgren, Alan Parsons and John Entwistle, Ann was

108

the Lovemongers were far removed from Heart. They performed concerts to benefit everything from breast cancer research to the environment

travelling by bus. Her she-bus, as she called it, had 'cool music, great movies, candles, the whole back lounge for the kids … I love the tour bus thing, but it has to be done just right … boys will be boys on the road even the best of them. Leave them to it.'

By the age of fifty-one, Ann had tried every diet in the book. Now she made the decision to undergo lap-band surgery, which limits the amount of food you can eat. The operation had a miraculous effect on her health and wellbeing.

When Heart hit the road in 2002 the only original members were Ann and Nancy. They were joined by the Lovemongers'

Ben Smith on drums, Mike Inez from Alice in Chains on bass, Tom Kellock on keyboards and guitarist Scott Olsen. *Alive in Seattle*, recorded at a Heart show in Seattle, was released in 2003 and displayed the Wilsons' range and versatility over twenty-five years.

Jupiter's Darling, the first studio album from Heart in eleven years, was out the same year. As Nancy explained, 'we've been thinking about going back into the studio as Heart for a long time … we went back to our … dream … of giving Led Zeppelin a run for their money.' Nancy's first attempt at producing, it sounds more like the Heart of old. *Jupiter's Darling* put the Wilsons back on the rock'n'roll map. Reviews were largely united: Ann is 'powerful and dynamic', Nancy sings 'steamy vocals' and plays 'hard fast licks'.

Heart continues to rock without rehashing the hits of the 1980s — or the high hair and glam-rock. Their army of fans, known as Heartmongers, is evidence of their longevity as well as the relevance of their current songs. Nancy isn't convinced the path is any easier today for women than it was when the Wilsons were earning their stripes. 'What's allowed for women in rock culture is still very narrow … the pole dancer vibe is so strong now … I feel bad for a lot of the girls out there.'

PATTI SMITH

POLAROID@32

09847007348

Rock'n'roll's
Bard

Patti Smith was the

new wave punk
movement.

One of the most influential women in rock music, she has been described as the artist who led the movement on both sides of the Atlantic. Her Patti Smith Group was the first of the handful of New York underground bands to release an album — and she conquered the world with what began as an idiosyncratic metro sound.

A poet at heart, Patti had a clear rock agenda. She wanted to 'shake things up' and invigorate rock'n'roll, which she saw as losing its way. Her startling 1975 debut album *Horses* shifted the rock paradigm into a new realm. It was a bold experiment with musical form and sound. Critics were wowed by her audacity and intrigued by her manipulation of voice, words and music — all done without any slick embellishment. Scribes from *Rolling Stone* to the *New York Times* hailed *Horses* as one of the most original, thought-provoking, emotionally charged and important records of the time. Thirty years on, it has lost none of its potency.

Christened Patricia Lee Smith, the eldest of the four children of Beverley and Grant Smith, Patti was born in Chicago in 1946, and grew up in Woodbury, New Jersey, on a housing estate built on reclaimed swamp land. Money was very tight. Patti's mother worked as a waitress and her father in one of the local factories. A sickly child who suffered from bronchial troubles, including TB, Patti wore an eye patch to correct a stigma for several years. Her mother was Jehovah's Witness, a religion Patti followed until she was around twelve. She explored Catholicism and Buddhism in later years and religion was ever present in her art, particularly Christ, who regularly featured in her musings and whom she has nominated as one of her 'favourite guys'.

For much of her early childhood Patti identified with the male side of her nature. She was more comfortable hanging out with the boys. She hung out with her crew by the railway tracks, as many of the youths in

she was toying with words, jotting down random thoughts and scribbling rambling poems about love and death

South Jersey did. It was a rough place and Patti learned early on to look after herself. As she grew into teenagehood, she found it increasingly difficult to cope with being female.

Painfully thin, with long dark hair and sharply defined facial features, Patti was not considered pretty. That and her personality oddities set her apart. She began to feel social pressures to adopt a more feminine stance. But she just wanted the freedom to keep on wrestling and fighting with the neighbourhood boys.

On the exterior she may have seemed just another Jersey kid, but what was going on in Patti's head was another story. A compulsive daydreamer, she would drift off for vast spaces of time, her fantasies keeping her entertained and tuned out from the world around her. She was an avid reader and fell in love with the decadent nineteenth-century French poets, Arthur Rimbaud in particular. She also adored William Blake. Her musical tastes spanned everything from jazz, which her mother loved, to rock. She was a fan of Jimi Hendrix, Jim Morrison, the early Rolling Stones, the Beatles, James Brown and groups like the Marvelettes, whom she danced to until she dropped. And she worshipped Bob Dylan.

Patti soon fell in with the New York underground arts movement and with Robert Mapplethorpe

Early on she began toying with words, jotting down thoughts at random and scribbling rambling poems about love and death, epics that she has said were atrocious. She also loved to draw in a spidery hand with pencil. As a teenager she had a baby, who she gave up for adoption. She had no intention of being a single mother in New Jersey.

In 1969 Patti and her sister Linda took off for Paris. There Patti scraped by as a street performer and walked the streets Rimbaud had wandered a century earlier. She kept on painting and sketching, but was being drawn back to poetry — many of her drawings featured more words than images. It wasn't long before she gave herself entirely to the written word.

The next year she was back in the USA. Moving to New York, she immersed herself in alternate theatre, performing in independent productions including *Cowboy Mouth*, a play she co-wrote with Sam Shepard.

New York's Greenwich Village was teeming with artists. Patti fell in with the underground arts movement and with Robert Mapplethorpe, who later become a renowned photographer. Mapplethorpe, reportedly her lover for a time, was homosexual and in 1989 died of AIDS. The pair lived in the famously decadent Chelsea Hotel. At the time Patti was there the hotel was home to William Burroughs, Shepard and Janis Joplin when she was in town. Patti frequented Max's Kansas City, which had become the 'in' spot for the 'in' crowd. She became friends with Beat poets Allen Ginsberg and Burroughs.

She was in her element.

By 1971 she had teamed up with guitarist Lenny Kaye. They performed their first poetry-to-music reading at St Mark's Church on the Lower East Side. Their originality got a positive response and the two continued to explore the form over the next couple of years.

Patti began appearing at the Mercer Arts Center with various bands, including the New York Dolls. The Center, a warren of performance spaces, was a creative breeding ground for the new wave. She performed without accompaniment. Often the audience was less than receptive to the intense young woman. Patti was yet to start singing, although her poems were always written like song lyrics and lent themselves to rhythmic accompaniment.

She published three volumes of poetry — *Seventh Heaven*, *Kodak* and *Witt* — and contributed lyrics to several Blue Oyster Cult songs. In 1973 she and Kaye performed *Rock'n'Rimbaud* at Le Jardin near Times Square. Shortly after Patti began to experiment with singing. Her transition into performance-poetry-come-rock'n'roll was a natural progression.

As her confidence grew, she and Kaye decided they needed to round out their sound. They auditioned for a piano player, grilling tens of young hopefuls, and found the missing link in Richard 'DNV' Sohl (DNV is supposedly an acronym for Death in Venice). There was no doubt he could play — at the audition he swept from classical to jazz and everything in between — but for Patti the real clincher was that Sohl had been brought up a Jehovah's Witness and had rejected it. They were on the same cosmic plane. Patti recalled all three were stoned during the audition — she liked to smoke dope and eat hash, but the drugs were a brief interlude and never took over her life.

In 1974 Mapplethorpe, Kaye and Patti's manager Jane Friedman (who had worked on Woodstock) funded production of the single, 'Hey Joe' backed by 'Piss Factory'. The latter song was about Patti's experiences working in a toy factory in the late 1960s, when her fellow female workers had persecuted her by sticking her head in a urine-filled toilet bowl. 'Hey Joe' began with a monologue

critics were wowed by her audacity and her manipulation of voice, words and music — all without the slick embellishment of her contemporaries

about kidnapped heiress Patty Hearst toting a machine gun with her abductors. The songs were recorded at Electric Ladyland, the studio Jimi Hendrix built but never recorded in, located in the Village. Tom Verlaine, guitarist with Television and one of Patti's lovers, also played on the record, which was issued on the Mer label.

That year the Patti Smith Group, as the trio was named, performed a couple of gigs in California. Another band member was added — guitarist Ivan Kral — and the quartet launched into performances at Max's Kansas City in New York.

A two-month residency with Television at CBGB followed early in 1975.

The grimy, claustrophobic, dimly lit club appealed to Patti, who was in her element on the tiny cramped stage. She drew her energy from the sea of bodies heaving and rolling with her voice. Dressed in black, she seemed lacking in any female definition. Many assumed she was lesbian — had they read *Seventh Heaven* they would have been convinced. Patti laughed off the suggestion that her sexuality was that easily defined. She very clearly loved men, but as an artist she was amorphous.

The CBGB residency gave the band an opportunity to hone their skills. It also got them a record deal. Clive Davis signed them to his Arista label in 1975. Within weeks they were putting down tracks for *Horses*. Drummer Jay Dee Daugherty had been added to the line-up, and Verlaine and Allen Lanier from Blue Oyster Cult performed and contributed songs. John Cale from the Velvet Underground was brought in to produce, but he and Patti clashed, sometimes spectacularly. She was determined not to compromise her vision.

Horses captured the Patti Smith Group's live essence, which was what Patti was after — she loathed the over-produced 'manufactured' rock current. The group was about three-chord rock delivered without frills. It was a raw, bare, honest sound that would carry Patti's music directly to that

place in the brain where random thoughts tumble across emotional landscapes.

The album contained an eclectic mix of covers, original songs and the spoken word. Patti tackled Van Morrison's 'Gloria' and 'Land (of a Thousand Dances)' written by New Orleans songwriter/performer Chris Kenner. Both songs were features of Patti's live performances. *Horses* also captured the brilliance of her improvisational skills — the track 'Birdland' was recorded as a stream-of-unconscious poetry that went on for nine minutes and which Patti attributes to the angst she felt about working with Cale, who at times drove her insane.

Making it into the top fifty on the US charts, *Horses* opened the door for alternate musicians and took the provocative New York underground art to a wider audience. To support its release, Patti and the boys toured the USA and Britain, where her anarchistic, outrageous on-stage antics were likened to those of the Sex Pistols.

Patti confused many. She dressed like a man and tackled subjects that were verboten for women. When asked by *Penthouse* magazine in 1976 if she masturbated, the reply was a definitive yes. 'To me fucking and masturbation and art is all the same because all it is is total concentration ... a good artist's always got his hand in his zipper.'

she was no longer the angry volatile artist. Her happiness left her unable to produce the gut-wrenching emotion of earlier work

The next year Patti and her band were back in the studio to record *Radio Ethiopia*. Produced by John Douglas, Patti's friend Lou Reed and the New York Dolls, it featured nine original tracks all co-written by Patti. *Radio Ethiopia* failed to re-capture the creative freedom of *Horses*. Critics suggested the band had lost its innocence. Unmoved, Patti stated she was proud of the record.

The next Patti Smith Group album was *Easter*, released in 1978. It featured the single 'Because the Night', which became her greatest commercial success. The lyrics were written by Patti for her new lover Fred 'Sonic' Smith, the leader of Sonic Rendezvous Band and ex-MC5 guitarist, and the music by another New Jersey singer, Bruce Springsteen. Jimmy Iovine, producing his first solo album, would go on to make a name for himself working with Tom Petty and the Heartbreakers and Stevie Nicks.

'Because The Night' shot to number thirteen and the album settled at twenty on the Billboard pop charts. The songs on the album reflected Patti's continued fascination with sex and religion.

she channelled her grief into work. By 1995 she felt strong enough to start performing again

Her version of 'Privilege (Set Me Free)' included a recitation of the Twenty-third Psalm and 'Easter' evoked images of Christ's resurrection.

After touring extensively, the Patti Smith Group recorded their final album *Wave*, which was released in 1979. It was produced by Todd Rundgren, whose pop treatment left Patti's diehard fans wanting. Despite the album becoming her highest charting release, the creative forces that had defined the group and put Patti on the world stage were waning.

She was no longer the angry, volatile artist who had blown everyone away with *Horses*. Her obvious personal happiness — she and Fred Smith were deeply in love — shifted her focus and left her unable to produce the gut-wrenching emotion that had fuelled her earlier work. She performed to more than 70,000 fans at a farewell concert in Florence, Italy, before dropping out of sight for nearly a decade. She traded her rock'n'roll life for one of wedded bliss.

Patti married Fred Smith in 1980 and they set up house in Detroit. In 1982 Jackson, their first child, was born, followed five years later by daughter Jesse. She threw herself into the role of mother. Both Patti and Fred continued to compose material together, but they were content to lay low and live quietly.

In 1988 she released *Dream of Life*, which featured songs written with Fred, including 'People Have the Power' and 'Paths That Cross'. Co-produced by Fred Smith and Jimmy Iovine, the album was another step away from her previous work, reflecting a more mature and content Patti. She published more poetry and gave intermittent readings, but in the main was happy to stay at home.

Fred and Patti worked on a collection of songs they intended to record in 1995. But Fred died from heart failure in November 1994. Patti's heart was broken. As she struggled to cope, her brother Todd, who she was very close to, died unexpectedly from a heart attack.

She channelled her grief into work. By 1995 she felt strong enough to start performing music again. Lenny Kaye and Jay Dee Daugherty rejoined her, and along with bassist Tony Shanahan formed the nucleus of the Patti Smith Group. They embarked on a tour of the West Coast of the USA.

performing for more than three hours, Patti was as compelling at fifty-nine as she had been in her twenties

Returning to Electric Ladyland, where she'd made her first single, she laid down tracks for her next album. Tom Verlaine, John Cale and Jeff Buckley as well as Patti's youngest sister Kimberley on mandolin played on the album.

Patti went back to Michigan with her kids to start the school year. But the need to submerge herself in work continued. *Peace and Noise*, her seventh album which she dedicated to William Burroughs, was released in 1997. The album featured a number of songs written with a new collaborator, guitarist Oliver Ray, who first appeared on 1996's *Gone Again*.

It was three years to the next album, *Gung Ho*, on which her son Jackson played guitar along with Tom Verlaine, Oliver Ray and Lenny Kaye. Michael Stipe from REM added vocals. *Gung Ho* heralded a new era — less attention to personal meanderings and more focus on social and political statements.

In 2002 she had an exhibition at the Warhol Museum in Pittsburgh. The eighty-five drawings spanned four decades and included various self-portraits, images of Christ, a sketch of Rimbaud and a portrait of Robert Mapplethorpe.

Continuing her preoccupation with politics and social justice, *Trampin'* included plenty of material about 9/11 and the war on Iraq, against which she has protested loudly. The album was released in 2004 with Lenny Kaye, Jay Dee Daugherty, Tony Shanahan and Oliver Ray on board again. It sounded closer to her earlier work than anything she had done in the previous two decades.

The following year she curated the Meltdown Festival in Britain, putting together a program that featured works by Bertold Brecht and performances by Yoko Ono, Television and Sinead O'Connor. One of the festival highlights was a full performance of the *Horses* album — something never done before.

Since then she has appeared as a support act for U2 at Madison Square Gardens and for the Red Hot Chili Peppers. She was the last performer to take the stage at CBGB before the club closed its doors in 2006. Performing for more than three hours, Patti was as compelling at fifty-nine as she had been in her twenties.

Patti was inducted into the Rock and Roll Hall of Fame in 2007. The closing song of the award's ceremony featured Patti and Fred's 'People Have the Power'. On stage she was joined by her son Jackson, Keith Richards, Eddie Vedder, Stephen Stills, Sammy Hagar, the Ronettes and the evening's other inductees, who included close friend Michael Stipe, the man who said *Horses* defined his musical destiny.

Twelve, her first album of covers, was released the same year. In it she pays tribute to real rock'n'rollers, including Hendrix, the Rolling Stones, Jefferson Airplane and Kurt Cobain. Patti Smith has no intention of fading away into the ether: 'I want to be a thorn in the side of everything as long as possible.'

Of her body of work she has said, 'we never compromised any record for a company, we never compromised for money or career ... I feel good about all of them.'

In a career spanning four decades,

Stevie Nicks has been called everything from the

Queen of Rock

to a 'transgendered arena-rock god in all his/her grand self-regard' and

Queen of the Stoned Age.

Almost as much has been written about her addiction to cocaine as her stellar career, her love life and her unbridled fascination for the supernatural.

Stephanie Lynn Nicks was born in 1948 in Phoenix, Arizona. From the age of five, the little girl with gorgeous blonde locks and the face of an angel was singing and dancing with her grandfather Aaron Jess Nicks, a country singer, at a bar owned by her parents. Even at that age she was confident and bubbly, aware of the audience and their appreciative responses.

Much of her childhood was spent on the move in Texas, Utah and New Mexico, as her father Jess rose up the management ladder of major corporations. The constant moves made it difficult to develop friendships and Stevie and her brother Christopher relied on each other, and their imaginations, to entertain themselves.

On her sixteenth birthday she was given a guitar and promptly sat down to write her first song. From that moment Stevie became a compulsive songwriter, locking herself away in her room for hours at a time as she created imaginary tales of loves lost, pouring her heart out in her lyrics.

Her parents encouraged her musical aspirations. Both loved gospel music and Stevie learned from listening to its harmonies. She also had a solid diet of country music via her grandfather. In her teens her tastes shifted to the Beach Boys, the Ronettes and the Spinners. When Janis Joplin and Grace Slick hit the airwaves, Stevie switched allegiance to rock.

By the mid 1960s the Nicks were living in Los Angeles and Stevie was singing in Changing Times, a group modelled on the Mamas and the Papas. Before she finished high school, the family moved to San Francisco, where Stevie met Lindsay Buckingham at a church social. There were no romantic sparks at first. But Stevie made quite an impression with her beautiful singing voice.

San Francisco — then at the height of its flower-power hippy fame — would be the last move she made with her family. When they left for Chicago in 1967 Stevie stayed behind. In the same year she joined Fritz, a band of high school seniors — Brian Kane (lead guitar), Bob Aguirre (drums), Javier Pacheco (keyboards) and Lindsay Buckingham (bass and vocals). Fritz played mostly local gigs around Santa Clara County and soon they were on the bill at local festivals with Jimi Hendrix and Janis Joplin. Joplin made a huge impact on the impressionable Stevie, who was mesmerised by the woman's magnetism and the way she controlled the crowd.

Fritz moved to LA, having been promised a record contract that never eventuated. By 1971 they had folded. Buckingham and Stevie, who by now were romantically involved, wanted to move in a different musical direction. They stayed in LA.

Buoyed by the interest shown by sound engineer Keith Olsen, who worked at Sound City Studios, Stevie and Buckingham worked tirelessly, putting down demo tracks at night. They recorded in the coffee factory owned by Buckingham's father. Olsen, who was keen to turn his hand to producing, worked with the duo — now performing as Buckingham Nicks — on their self-titled album and brokered a deal with Polydor in 1972. Sales of the album, a mix of country/rock/folk songs written by the pair, were hampered by a lack of promotional support and Polydor dropped the duo shortly after its release.

They were back to square one. Moving into a share house, Stevie went out to work as a waitress while Buckingham worked on his music.

He dominated the relationship. 'He was the artist: he didn't know how to do anything except music. What was he going to do, sell shoes?' Stevie said. She paid for the rent, the food, the car. It was 'going to take my strength' to 'make it in the music business'.

By 1974 they were no closer to signing a new record deal. The constant struggle to make ends meet was taking its toll on the relationship and on Stevie, the breadwinner. She made a deal with her father to give it another six months and then to go back to study — her fallback position was to become a teacher. Her parents were not only concerned about her financial struggles. They were worried by the constant fighting between Stevie and Buckingham.

Stevie was mesmerised by Joplin's magnetism and the way she captured the crowd and held them in her grasp

One month before her deadline their fortunes changed. Mick Fleetwood was in LA looking for a new guitarist to replace Bob Welch, who was tired of all the emotional dramas rocking their band. Olsen had been enlisted to produce the next Fleetwood Mac album and played Mick Fleetwood a track on which Buckingham played. On New Year's Eve 1974, when Mick Fleetwood put in a call to Olsen saying he wanted Buckingham to join the band, he was told Stevie was part of the package.

Within weeks the duo was in the studio with Fleetwood Mac, recording the self-titled album that became known as *The White Album*. Stevie contributed material, including 'Landslide' and 'Rhiannon'. The latter song cemented her ethereal, mystical on-stage power. Performing 'Rhiannon' was like an out-of-body experience that left her exhausted. As Mick Fleetwood said, ' "Rhiannon" was like an exorcism' for Stevie.'

Plucked from obscurity to driving in limousines and travelling first class, Stevie began living the fantasy life that is rock'n'roll. 'It was one big outrageous morning til night party everyday for years,' she marvelled.

'it was 'going to take my strength' to 'make it in the music business'

Fleetwood Mac, originally from London, had been around since 1967 and had a reputation as one of the best British blues bands. In 1970, Peter Green, Mick Fleetwood and John McVie were joined by Christine Perfect (who would marry McVie — she had been singing with popular blues band Chicken Shack and had been voted female vocalist of the year by *Melody Maker*.

From the outset Fleetwood Mac was plagued by internal strife. Peter Green left in 1970 with a serious psychotic disorder after downing too much LSD. Guitarist Jeremy Spencer departed to join the Children of God cult and was replaced by Bob Welch. At that point the band left behind the blues and began playing soft rock. Then guitarist Bob Weston left after having an affair with Fleetwood's wife. By 1973 Fleetwood, the McVies and Welch had moved to LA and set their sights on cracking America. They had achieved critical acclaim, but nothing like they would experience with the addition of Stevie and Buckingham.

Stevie's voice, mellifluous and at times quavering with emotion, brought a distinctive resonance to Fleetwood Mac. Her ability to harmonise was now in full flight. The combination of vocals from Stevie, Christine McVie and Buckingham created the sound for which Fleetwood Mac became renowned.

The White Album reached number one and its three singles — 'Over My Head' and 'Say You Love Me', both written by Christine McVie, and Stevie's 'Rhiannon' — made it into the top twenty, with 'Rhiannon' charting at number eleven.

Stevie added a sexual spark and quickly became the pin-up girl. Everyone wanted Stevie, which created tensions with the other band members.

But she was the star. Ninety per cent of the people who went to Fleetwood Mac concerts wanted to see Stevie. Decked out in ethereal garb —platform boots, long flowing dresses and scarves she twirled across the stage — she spun a web of sex,

sorcery and mystique, with her soul-reaching vocals and mesmerising tiny twirling body. Watching her was like taking LSD — a real head trip that took the audience soaring as she emptied her heart on stage in front of thousands of strangers.

Women related to her. Men desired her. But not everyone appreciated her style. Early critics dismissed her as an airhead and a 'California girl prone to writing songs about witches, mysticism and all the other shit one would conjure up sautéing in a Jacuzzi.'

Stevie's on-stage persona, her stage costumes, were an extension of her personal style. She still wears the long dresses, velvet, lace, leather and chiffon. 'I love the same eye make-up. I'm not a fad person.' she explained.

She spoke openly about her belief in reincarnation and of the influence of the supernatural on her life. For a time rumours abounded that Stevie was a white witch and groups formed around the world to worship the new queen of the occult. She did little to quash the misperception. She loved

'Halloween and fairy tales', including the one she was living.

As the adoration of her fans and her sexy, confident on-stage persona grew, her relationship with Buckingham began to erode. The band's popularity was skyrocketing and its two warring couples, Buckingham and Stevie and the McVies, were pulling each other apart. At the same time Fleetwood Mac was recording its second album, *Rumours*. Buckingham admitted later to deliberately sabotaging the work he did during the recording of *Rumours* because he was angry with Stevie for ending their relationship.

The split was incredibly acrimonious, but that had been the tone of their relationship right from the outset. Buckingham had a vile temper and Stevie retaliated with equal venom. 'He's scary when he gets mad,' Stevie said.

Rumours was a torturous exercise that took a year to complete. The songs on the album document the heartbreak, anger and frustration in their relationships. Angst makes for great creativity and the album includes some of Fleetwood Mac's most brilliant material. The result was twenty-five million sales and a smash hit that charted for thirty-one weeks

there were rumours that Stevie was a white witch and groups formed around the world to worship the new queen of the occult

upon its debut. In comparison, *The White Album* had sold five million.

Rumours spawned numerous top ten hits, including Stevie's 'Dreams', which became the band's only number one hit in the USA and was voted best single in *Rolling Stone*'s US readers' poll in 1977. The album's release was supported by a world tour that took in the USA, Australia and Europe. During the tour Stevie embarked on a clandestine love affair with the then married Mick Fleetwood.

The success of *Rumours* meant instant wealth. Stevie went on a spending spree, buying cars and houses in LA and Phoenix. She decorated her mansions with rich fabrics, hundreds of cushions, candles, lamps, dolls and antique furniture. Indulging her passion for all things English, her home in Encino, California, was a mock Tudor sprawl. She believed Anne Boleyn had lived there.

She evoked the image of a slightly unhinged woman writing songs, painting pictures at all hours of the night — her painting of Rhiannon was sold for a princely sum at a charity auction — and crocheting many-coloured garments surrounded by dolls, dogs and cats. 'To say that Stevie Nicks is flaky is a mild understatement,' one journalist said. But her fans loved it.

While Stevie's fans found solace in her music, she began to lean heavily on cocaine. Her addiction grew to the point where she was reaching for a line the minute she woke up. Stevie wasn't the only band member in the clutches of the white powder. It would be the undoing of Mick Fleetwood financially, sending him bankrupt at one point.

Coke wasn't the only excess on tour. Stevie insisted her hotel rooms were decorated with her own things. Cushions, shawls, fabrics, netting hung from the ceiling, incense, candles, lamps and her typewriter all had to be set up for her arrival. 'If Stevie wanted a hotel suite painted pink with a white piano in it, what are you going to do, say no?' Mick Fleetwood commented.

A prolific and compulsive songwriter, Stevie carried her journal and typewriter around the world with her, ready to jot down thoughts or poems, many of which she turned into songs. Few of Stevie's songs were recorded by Fleetwood Mac. With two other songwriters — Buckingham and Christine McVie — she was lucky if three of her songs appeared on an album. So she recorded a solo album, *Bella Donna*, which was released in 1981 under her own label, Modern Records. Her less-than-thrilled band mates were worried it would be the death knell for Fleetwood Mac, particularly given the bad reception of 1979's experimental *Tusk*, which had sold less than *The White Album*.

Paul Fishkin, a record executive who became Stevie's partner in Modern Records, brought in producer Jimmy Iovine on *Bella Donna*. He enlisted some seasoned musicians, including Waddy Wachtel on guitar and keyboard genius Roy Bittan from Bruce Springsteen's E Street Band, and two back-up singers Sharon Celani and Lori Perry, who became Stevies's close friends (Perry later married Christopher Nicks). Iovine was a hard taskmaster, telling Stevie there was no place for a rock'n'roll diva in his studio. She took up the challenge and in 1981 *Rolling Stone* magazine crowned her queen of rock'n'roll.

Bella Donna reached number one on the Billboard charts and spawned three major singles — 'Edge of Seventeen', 'Leather and Lace' with Don Henley of the Eagles and 'Stop Dragging My Heart Around' with Tom Petty. But the day the album got to number one, Stevie found out that Robin Snyder, her closest friend who was married to Warner's promotions man Kim Anderson, had been diagnosed with terminal leukemia. 'I really didn't get to enjoy *Bella Donna*. ... It was a very sad, yet balancing, thing for me.'

despite the success of *Bella Donna*, it was not mentioned by her fellow band members. It was as if it had never happened

With her album riding high, Stevie went back into the studio to record Fleetwood Mac's *Mirage*. Despite the success of *Bella Donna*, it was not mentioned by her fellow band members. It were as if it had never happened.

She was on tour with the Mac in 1982 when she got the news Robin had died. ' I went crazy. I just went insane,' she said. In her grief Stevie became involved with her dead friend's husband, marrying Anderson in January of 1983. Three months later they parted. She has never re-married.

The constant speculation about her love life drove Stevie to distraction. Lovers were numerous, if short lived. She has been 'connected' to Don Henley, Warren Zevon, Jim Iovine, Joe Walsh and others. She is reported to have had a love affair with Tom Petty — twice. Petty wrote her smash hit

'Stop Dragging My Heart Around' and has been credited with snapping her out of the blues engulfing her after she left Fleetwood Mac in 1993. Stevie has described Petty as a valued and true friend, a sentiment that doesn't apply to all her ex-lovers. 'I especially don't like men rock'n'roll stars, mainly because of the size of their egos.' Henley was a renowned womaniser. During their affair, Stevie was spirited away in his Lear jet, making her think that 'being a rock star really is wild'. She became pregnant to Henley and had an abortion, one of four she endured.

Stevie's relationship with Mick Fleetwood is one of extremes — she either loves him or she hates him. The first time she saw Mick, 'I was awestruck. ... I still am ... The whole air around him is power.' But when his autobiography was published in 1990 her awe turned to fury as he revealed details of their affair. Later, when she had calmed down, she said she thought Mick had dealt with

'I especially don't like men rock'n'roll stars, mainly because of the size of their egos'

their relationship 'pretty well'. In a matter of months she was vilifying him when he refused to give up rights to her song 'Silver Springs', which was to have been on *Rumours* but was axed. Fleetwood Mac held the rights and Stevie was refused permission to include it on her solo album *Timespace*.

Addicted to work as much as to drugs, in the space of three years Stevie had recorded *Mirage*, her fourth album with the Mac, and put down two solo albums, *Bella Donna* and 1983's *The Wild Heart*, which reached number five on the charts. *The Wild Heart* featured a similar line-up of artists as *Bella Donna* with the addition of Mick Fleetwood and Toto's Steve Lukather. Prince played on 'Stand Back', which stayed in the charts for nineteen weeks and peaked at number five.

In 1985, when she began recording her third solo effort, *Rock a Little*, her manic pace and escalating cocaine use were taking their toll. Iovine began producing, but Stevie's drug habit was interfering and he walked out of the production and their relationship.

Musically, *Rock a Little* was a departure. It was blacker in content than Stevie's previous works and her voice was harsher and more raspy. Critics said that Stevie was a relic of the 1970s and no match for the likes of Cyndi Lauper and Madonna, whose upbeat pop tunes were dominating the charts.

Stevie's demons finally caught up with her in 1986. She had

a hole inside her nose large enough to stick a pencil through. There were rumours she paid someone to blow coke up her arse because she couldn't snort anymore. What scared her into action was a doctor telling her she could have a brain hemorrhage the next time she did cocaine. She checked into the Betty Ford Clinic.

Now free from her addiction, Stevie was encouraged to see a psychiatrist to help her cope with her re-entry into the cocaine-fuelled world of rock'n'roll. The psychiatrist prescribed Klonopin, an anti-depressant, and so began an eight-year battle with a drug she has labelled 'horrendous'.

Stevie's demons caught up with her in 1986

Stevie continued to work at a relentless pace. She went straight into the studio in 1987 to record the Mac's *Tango in the Night*, an album that clearly showed her voice was in bad shape. By the time the band hit the road for the obligatory promotional tour, they were minus Lindsay Buckingham who had left in a hail of acrimony.

The tour was a disaster for Stevie. Suffering from Epstein-Barr, a chronic fatigue illness linked to breast implants, and hammered by the Klonopin, she stumbled through. After four months she hit the wall. The last shows were

cancelled and Stevie retreated to Phoenix where she stayed for the next eighteen months, a virtual recluse, spending her time resting and writing songs.

the anti-depressant wrapped her brain in fog

Sufficiently recovered, but still hooked on Klonopin, Stevie went back into the studio in 1989 to record *The Other Side of the Mirror*. But the Stevie everyone had come to know and love was in the main missing. The album reached ten on the Billboard charts, clocking up platinum sales, largely due to Stevie's massive existing fan base.

The adverse effects of Klonopin on Stevie were significant. The anti-depressant wrapped her brain in fog, crushed her creativity and pushed her into an apathy that numbed her physically and emotionally. The drug became her worst nightmare — at least when she'd been snorting cocaine she had still been functioning creatively, but now the well had dried up.

In January 1993 Stevie, who was by that time operating on automatic pilot, performed with the Mac at Bill Clinton's inauguration, singing their hit 'Don't Stop', which the new US president had used as his campaign song. A month later she officially left Fleetwood Mac and headed back to her sanctuary in Phoenix.

It wasn't until Stevie fell and smashed her head that year — and didn't feel a thing — that she realised she was in deep trouble. She took herself off to rehab, checking into hospital for forty-seven days to go cold turkey. Then she retreated to Phoenix to work on songs for *Street Angel*, released in 1994 and the worst of her albums to date.

The album's chart performance wasn't her only concern. Stevie's weight had been creeping up, after years of drug abuse, prescription medications and an erratic lifestyle. On her 1994 *Street Angel* tour, she was fourteen kilos heavier than she had ever been. The media had a field day and endless jokes about her weight added to her distress.

U pset by the lacklustre performance of *Street Angel* and the constant media bashing, Stevie took herself out of the spotlight, resolving not to perform in public again until she had lost weight.

In 1997 she went back into the studio with Fleetwood Mac to record *The Dance* album, which saw Buckingham return to the fold. By the time *The Dance* tour hit the road she had regained her figure and the band had reclaimed its position at the top of the charts.

The following year Stevie, along with the original Fleetwood Mac line-up, was inducted into the Rock and Roll Hall of Fame. When the three-CD box set *Enchanted* was released, *Rolling Stone* magazine commented that 'you can hear how faithfully Nicks has followed her vision'.

For her next solo album, 2001's *Trouble in Shangri-La*, she teamed up with Sheryl Crow, who produced five of the album's tracks and challenged Stevie to play with her voice and expand her range. Crow and Stevie clicked musically and personally. The album also featured the talents of Macy Gray, Sarah McLachlan, Natalie Maine from the Dixie Chicks, some of the Heartbreakers and old flame Lindsay Buckingham. The album reached number five on the Billboard charts. Stevie Nicks was back.

In 2007 *Crystal Visions: The Very Best of Stevie Nicks* reached number 21 on the Billboard Top 200, her highest position since 1989. In 2009 she performed across the USA, Europe, Australia and New Zealand with Fleetwood Mac. At the Grammy Awards in 2010 she sang 'Rhiannon' with Taylor Swift.

The lyrics to her songs are like a map of Stevie Nicks's life. 'Rhiannon', 'Gold Dust Woman', 'Stand Back', 'Edge of Seventeen', 'Landslide', 'Dreams' describe what life has been like for this extraordinary performer who has sacrificed much for her art.

A petite woman with model features and dyed blonde hair stormed the stages of New York's underground clubs in the 1970s and became one of the

great rock'n'roll women

— a place she's held for more than three decades.

On the way to stardom, she stopped off to visit the land of the junkie for a few years, working at any dead-end job to get enough money to score. When the party became old hat, Debbie moved on, dropping bad habits and acquaintances as quickly as she procured them.

The Debbie Harry story begins in 1945 in Miami, Florida, where a three-month-old baby girl was adopted by Catherine and Richard Harry and christened Deborah Ann.

The Harry family lived in Hawthorne, New Jersey, a typical suburban enclave where Debbie's parents owned a gift shop. By the age of eight Debbie was singing in the Hawthorne Church Choir, which kept her amused until she hit her early teens. At this point she left behind the gawky kid who didn't think she was pretty and evolved into a head turner. She learned the power of sex appeal early and used it to her advantage.

Entertainment in the 1950s came largely through films and via the radio, Debbie's lifeline to the world of music. The airwaves heralded a new era, in which Elvis Presley, Bobby Darin, Bill Haley and the Comets and the Platters were changing the face of popular music.

Debbie and her younger sister Martha grew up in an extremely conservative environment where girls were expected to get married and have babies. It was a scenario Debbie rejected, and she felt this made her weird. But what she was experiencing was happening in homes around the Western world, as teenage girls of the 1950s began questioning their place in society.

she was sent to an all-girls finishing school in New Jersey. There she studied art but was more creative with the colours she dyed her hair

School held little interest for Debbie, who lacked any real ambition — although she was a reasonable student and stayed out of trouble. She had a vague idea she'd like to be an artist, maybe a painter. Her parents had other ideas and after high school she was sent to an all-girls finishing school in Hackettstown, New Jersey. There she studied art but was more creative with the colours she dyed her hair.

As the 1950s morphed into the 1960s, Debbie was grooving to the New York City girl group the Ronettes, along with the Crystals, the Shangri-las, the Supremes and R&B artists like

Smokey Robinson. She was itching to cross the Hudson River to Manhattan. She would sneak over on the weekends and walk around the city, fantasising about the future when she could live in New York.

She got her chance in 1965 when she was twenty. Setting up camp in Greenwich Village, the centre of cool, Debbie was in her element. But the reality was not quite what she'd imagined. She battled just to pay the rent. Poverty was an integral part of an artist's struggle for greatness and there was much struggling going on in

Debbie lived in dingy walk-ups, with urine-soaked stairwells, leaky plumbing, no heating and rats the size of cats

the Village in the mid 1960s. The city was a writhing mass of pent-up desires, full of young people from the suburbs looking for a new way to live. Like her contemporaries, Debbie lived in dingy walk-ups, with urine-soaked stairwells, leaky plumbing, no heating and rats the size of cats. Wanting to explore everything that life had to offer, she experimented with drugs and bisexuality and in the process shed the remnants of her suburban upbringing.

Debbie landed a secretarial job at BBC Radio, which gave her an entrée into the music scene. One of the musicians she met was Paul Klein, who was singing and playing guitar in a seven-piece folk ensemble, Wind in the Willows. The band needed another female singer. Debbie joined in 1967.

Wind in the Willows released one record, produced by Artie Kornfeld who worked for Capitol Records and later went on to co-create Woodstock. The self-titled album was a mix of psychedelic pop and folk tunes. A dark-haired Debbie can be seen on the classic hippy cover among a swirl of multi-coloured paisley patterns. The band hit the road, playing support to acts like Melanie. By the end of 1968 they had disbanded.

Debbie and the band's drummer Gil Fields became lovers. The pair moved in to a typical cheap, slummy East Village apartment. Fields was into heroin and it didn't take long before Debbie got involved. She was waitressing at Max's Kansas City, a restaurant and nightclub that had opened in 1965 and quickly became a hang-out of artists and writers. Andy Warhol could often be found there holding court, along with Lou Reed, Allen Ginsberg and Larry Rivers.

Hedonism ruled at Max's. Customers snorted cocaine on the tables and blew joints while quaffing $200 bottles of French champagne. It wasn't unusual to find couples copulating in the restrooms and even the phone booths. Debbie waited on Hendrix and Joplin, Jane Fonda and her then husband, avant-garde French film director Roger Vadim. 'What an education I got!' she told *Penthouse*. She lasted at Max's for less than a year before taking off to Los Angeles on the spur of the moment. But within a month she was back in New York.

she waitressed at Max's Kansas City, a restaurant and nightclub that was a hang-out of artists and writers. Hedonism ruled at Max's

To make ends meet she took a job at the Playboy club, strapping on a fluffy bunny tail to serve drinks. Tips were generous and you could earn good money without having to put out, money that Debbie used to feed her habit. She was stoned most of the time now.

Living in an almost derelict apartment on the Upper West Side near 107th Street and Manhattan Avenue, a decaying neighbourhood frequented by drug dealers and addicts, Debbie was engulfed in drug culture. Being an addict impacted on everything in her life. Any ambitions she may have held were sucked up into the needle along with the harsh brown liquid. The rush of the hit extinguished the desire to do anything else.

Then Fields overdosed and died. Debbie dropped heroin like a hot potato, replacing it with vitamin shots laced with speed, which she got from a neighbourhood doctor. But she knew she was just transferring dependencies. It was time to get out.

Around 1971 she moved up to Woodstock in upstate New York — she'd been to the festival two years earlier — to hang with a group of artists for a couple of months. Then she headed home to Mom and Dad in New Jersey. She knew she needed to stay away from the city and all its temptations until she felt strong enough to cope without drugs. She got a job as a beautician and tried to knuckle down to life in the suburbs. But Manhattan was magnetic, calling her back.

In the early 1970s the New York music scene was exploding. Bands like the New York Dolls, fronted by smack freak Johnny Thunders, were leaving the hippies behind in the wake of a new sound. Free from dope, Debbie started hanging out at Max's again. In 1972 she met singer Elda Gentile. They formed the Stilettos with Rosie Ross. The Stilettos, wearing evening gowns and backed by a four-piece band, modelled their music on the girl groups of the 1950s and added rock attitude. They played sporadically at clubs around the city for a couple of years before musical differences, and egos, split them apart.

The guitarist with the Stilettos was Chris Stein, who became Debbie's lover, soul-mate and Svengali. He reignited her passion for music and gave her a real sense of purpose and direction. In 1974 Stein, along with the Stiletto's bass player Fred Smith and drummer Billy O'Connor, formed a new band with Debbie. This line-up played under various names but didn't last long. O'Connor dropped out and Smith bailed to play bass for Television.

the name Blondie came from the constant cat-calls the platinium blonde got when out and about

Stein and Debbie ran an ad in the *Village Voice*, which brought in drummer Clem Burke, then bass player Gary Valentine and keyboard player Jimi Destri. The five clicked. Blondie was born, the name coming from the constant cat-calls the platinum-blonde Debbie received from passers-by when she was out and about the streets of New York.

Debbie brought an overtly sexual charisma to a time when butch females ruled. Patti Smith, her antithesis, reportedly told Debbie to 'get the fuck out of rock'n'roll' — although that may have been out of jealousy because Debbie was getting too close to Smith's lover Tom Verlaine, frontman of Television. But Debbie certainly wasn't interested in following Smith's tomboyish lead. She knew that sex sells and she wanted to explore how far she could take it. She was challenging the female singer stereotype as much as Janis Joplin had.

By 1975 Blondie was performing as the house band at underground club CBGB in the Bowery, along with the Ramones, Talking Heads, New York Dolls and Television. Blondie also took the stage at Max's Kansas City — the irony of being the celebrity was not lost on Debbie, who often found herself sitting with Warhol and his posse.

her natural shyness evaporated as she lost herself in her performance

The club environment suited the seductive, sexy, punk-glam rock chick Debbie conjured on stage each night, her natural shyness evaporating as she lost herself in the performance. A petite 160 centimetres, Debbie was a Marilyn Monroe replica, in clinging, low-cut dresses and make-up that accentuated her enormous eyes, pert lips and high cheekbones framed by bleached blonde hair. She projected a butter-wouldn't-melt-in-her-mouth persona, who sang about the dark side of human nature — lustful violence and psychotic tendencies — and seduced her audience with promises of intimacy. Her sexy manner playfully mocked the darkness that lay beneath the lyrics — death, violence and rape were delivered with an almost cruel ambivalence.

In 1976 the band was signed to Private Stock Records, an independent label. Their first recorded song, written by Debbie with bass player Valentine, was produced by Craig Leon at Plaza Studios in New York. Originally titled 'Sex Offender', and changed because of concerns it wouldn't get any airplay, 'X-Offender' was the first single from the band's debut album *Blondie,* produced by Richard Gottherer, who at that time was known for his work with the Angels. When Private Stock was bought out by Chrysalis, the album was re-released at the end of 1977.

With the Chrysalis muscle behind them, Blondie hit the road, performing with Television in Britain and supporting the Iggy

Pop/David Bowie tour in the USA. Bowie and Pop both hit on Debbie backstage one night. It was 'mind-blowing' to be touring with them, Debbie said, and having flirtations was 'just the icing on the cake'.

The re-released *Blondie* album launched other singles, including 'In the Flesh' and 'Rip Her to Shreds'. Always prepared to shock, one night Debbie appeared on stage at CBGB in a wedding dress, which she proceeded to tear from her body while singing 'Rip Her to Shreds'. 'This is the only dress my mother ever wanted me to wear,' she told the audience. Wearing the dress on stage would be the closest she got to being a bride.

Blondie successfully melded pop and new wave punk with the musical tones of the 1950s girl groups. Debbie's voice, which at times was almost lethargic in its little-girl delivery, could handle the gutsier, punk-rock moments of songs like 'Rip Her to Shreds'. It separated Blondie from the other new wave bands.

By the time the band went back into the studio in 1977 to record their second album *Plastic Letters*, guitarist Frank Infante was standing in on bass, replacing Valentine who had moved to LA. *Plastic Letters* spawned two singles: 'Denis', a reinterpretation of 'Denise' by Randy and the Rainbows, and 'I'm Always Touched by Your Presence Dear', which had been written by Valentine. Both singles made it into the British top ten, giving the band the exposure it needed on the other side of the Atlantic.

Blondie successfully melded pop and new wave punk with the musical tones of the 1950s girl groups

Towards the end of 1977 Blondie toured Australia, where 'In the Flesh' and 'Rip Her to Shreds' had reached the top five. In Brisbane there was a near riot when a concert was cancelled because Debbie had an upset stomach, supposedly as a result of eating too many cherries. Blondie came back to Brisbane at the end of their tour to honour the cancelled date.

As soon as they came off the road, they were hustled back into the studio to make the next album. Recorded in Britain with producer/songwriter Mike Chapman at the helm, *Parallel Lines* launched Blondie into the big time. It reached number six on the American Billboard charts and included four major singles. 'Heart of Glass', by Debbie and Stein, reached number one in the USA and Britain.

perceiving
herself as a late
starter — she
was now thirty-
six — Debbie
was working at
a relentless pace
trying to make up
lost time

'Picture This', written by keyboardist Destri, made the British top twenty, Stein's 'Sunday Girl' went to number one in Britain and Australia, and 'Hanging on the Telephone', a cover of the Nerves song, reached the British top five. Another single, 'One Way or Another', written by new bass player Nigel Harrison and Debbie, hit the US top thirty. Harrison had been brought in to replace Infante, who could then go back to what he did best, play lead guitar.

Parallel Lines secured Blondie's place in rock'n'roll history, selling more than twenty million copies worldwide and making Debbie a mega-star. Photographers clamoured to snap the sexy songstress and her face began to appear not only on music rag covers but also in fashion and men's magazines.

As the media attention increased, Debbie became cagey. Because she conducted few interviews without Stein, some journalists suggested she was Stein's puppet. That was far from the truth. Debbie was very much her own person. The press assumed

she projected a butter-wouldn't-melt-in-her-mouth persona, who sang about the dark side of human nature and seduced her audience with promises of intimacy

the woman and the onstage extrovert were one and the same. But the offstage Debbie was shy and didn't care to share her personal life with the world.

In 1979 it was back into the studio for the fourth album, *Eat to the Beat*, produced by Chapman again. The album failed to recapture the brilliance of its predecessor and its performance in the US was disappointing, although the single 'Atomic' reached number one. *Eat to the Beat* was also released as a video album, the first of its kind. Chrysalis was getting maximum bang for its buck.

Around this time Debbie tried her hand at acting in a full-length film, starring in the indie *Union City*, with Stein writing the score and Pat Benatar in the cast. As Debbie's star continued to rise, her fellow band members began to feel like they were a backing band. As far as the record company was concerned Debbie Harry was Blondie and she was the only one who was irreplaceable. Understandably, the rest of the band were less than thrilled with this position. In a bid to counter this perception, and plump up deflated egos, the band launched the 'Blondie is a Group' publicity campaign in 1979, but it fell on deaf ears.

Before the release of their next album Debbie worked with producer Giorgio Moroder to write 'Call Me', which featured in *American Gigolo*, starring Richard Gere. The song became a smash hit, topping the American and British charts.

On the band's 1980 album Blondie continued to break new ground. *Autoamerican* featured the first mainstream pop song to incorporate rap. Written by Debbie and Stein, 'Rapture' is exactly what the song sent DJs and the listening public into and its video was played on the day MTV first went to air in 1981. 'Rapture' hit number one in the USA, as did the album's other notable single 'The Tide is High',

Blondie had deteriorated into a cesspool of infighting fuelled by alcohol and drug abuse. It was nasty

a cover of a song by Jamaican group the Paragons. Producer Mike Chapman used a host of session musicians to give *Autoamerican* its fuller, more opulent sound.

That same year Debbie played a down-and-out fairy godmother in *Downtown 81*, a film that followed a day in the life of graffiti artist and Warhol protégé Jean-Michel Basquiat (who appeared in the 'Rapture' video).

Whether it was intentional or just bad planning, the release of *Autoamerican* coincided with the launch of Debbie's first solo album *Koo Koo*, which was not well received by the music press. *Koo Koo*'s first single 'Backfired' didn't even make it into the top thirty. The most startling thing about the album was its cover of Debbie's face and neck seemingly pierced by giant nails. *Koo Koo* marked the beginning of a downward spiral, professionally and personally.

Perceiving herself as a late starter — she was now thirty-six — Debbie was working at a relentless pace trying to make up lost time. In addition to her Blondie commitments and recording her solo album, she sported a mop of dark red hair in the film *Videodrome* with James Woods. The film, about a pirate TV channel that broadcasts snuff movies, became an 1980s cult classic.

Blondie's last album was released in 1982. *The Hunter* was clearly by a band under duress. Made to fulfill their contract with Chrysalis, the material reflected the crumbling relationships within the band. The album didn't rate on the charts and its one single, 'Island of Lost Souls', barely made it into the US top forty. Blondie had deteriorated into a cesspool of infighting fuelled by alcohol and drug abuse. They hardly talked to each other. It was nasty.

Debbie busied herself with other projects. In 1983 she recorded 'Rush Rush' with Giorgio Moroder for the soundtrack of the Al Pacino movie *Scarface* and also took to the Broadway stage with comedian Andy Kauffman in the play *Teaneck Tanzi: The Venus Flytrap*. The New York production was based on a successful London play, but whatever magic had existed in the original production seemed to have been lost in translation. It was canned by critics and canned by the theatre owner — closing after its first night.

Then Stein became gravely ill. He had a genetic skin disease that flared due to chronic stress. He lost weight to the point of emaciation, prompting suggestions that he had succumbed to heroin. Debbie didn't think twice about looking after him. That's what you do when you are in a relationship, she said.

There were many dark days ahead for the pair, their misery compounded by the fact that they went bust. Blondie ended up with 'no record contract, no manager and we all had tax problems,' she said.

Debbie was facing forty and a bleak future. But she is nothing if not a survivor. She stood up to face the music with the same New Jersey bluntness she'd always displayed. 'I do have to take responsibility for my stupidity and for things that happened to me.'

The experience of going broke made Debbie smarter fiscally. She and Stein hadn't bothered to look too closely at figures or contracts. Artistic abandonment had equalled financial ruin. She wasn't taking that path again.

When she signed to Geffen Records and reignited her career with the album *Rockbird* in 1986, she knew she had to cooperate with the record company if she were to have a future as a solo artist. *Rockbird* evolved over the years when she was nursing Stein, who had recovered sufficiently to perform on the album along with dozens of session musicians. Debbie co-wrote most of the songs, a number with Seth Justman, the former keyboardist for J Geils Band. The album's only hit, 'French Kissin' was written by Chuck Lorre, a TV sitcom producer.

Debbie was continuing her interest in film, appearing in *Hairspray*, an off-beat comedy centred around a TV dance show, with Ricky Lake, Sonny Bono, Divine, Ric Ocasek from the band the Cars and Pia Zadora.

In 1987, after fifteen years together, Stein and Debbie parted ways. They remain friends, Stein marrying and Harry being the godmother of his children. She has successfully remained under the gossip columnists' radar and the media has been unable to link her to anyone, male or female.

Signed to Sire Records, the same label as Madonna, Debbie released *Def Dumb & Blonde* in 1989, the first album to bear the name 'Deborah Harry'. This was closer to Blondie than her previous solo efforts and it spawned the dance hit 'I Want That Man', which went to two on the modern rock chart.

The release of *Def Dumb & Blonde* coincided with Madonna's Blonde Ambition tour. Debbie was on Sire Records' 'B list' and it hurt.

Debbie admitted it was hard going from being the 'it' girl to a less celebrated star — something all beautiful women in the entertainment world face at some point.

But Debbie Harry was not going to be relegated to the bargain bin. In 1990 she recorded a duet with Iggy Pop, 'Well Did You Evah!' for an album of Cole Porter classics, performed in front of 72,000 people at the Summer XS concert headlined by INXS at London's Wembley Stadium, and appeared in *Tales From the Darkside: The Movie* playing a suburban housewife who kidnaps a small child with the intention of having him for supper. Two years later she was on screen again in *Intimate Stranger*, playing a struggling musician who makes ends meet as a phone sex girl.

Stein worked on Debbie's 1993 rock-oriented album *Debravation* as co-producer, songwriter and musician. Members of R.E.M. also made an appearance and the album's highest charting single, 'I Can See Clearly', made it into the top five in the British and American dance charts.

Debbie left rock behind in 1994 to take up with New York band the Jazz Passengers. She enjoyed exploring a new musical dimension and was a guest vocalist on the band's 1994 album *In Love*, along with Jeff Buckley and

the offstage Debbie was shy and didn't care to share her personal life with the world

Mavis Staple, then spent four years as a permanent member of the band. One of the high points of the Jazz Passengers 1996 album, *Individually Twisted*, was Debbie's duet with Elvis Costello, 'Doncha Go Way Mad'. She stayed with the group until the reformation of Blondie in 1999. During this period she also recorded with Argentinean ska/jazz/rock band Los Fabulosos Cadillacs, on a cover of the Lennon/McCartney song 'Strawberry Fields Forever'.

No Exit was the first Blondie album to be released in seventeen years. But two of the original Blondie band members were left out of proceedings. Frank Infante and Nigel Harrison were replaced by Leigh Foxx on bass and guitarist Paul Carbonara. Infante and Harrison launched law suits against the rest of the band. But Blondie fans responded positively and *No Exit*'s first single 'Maria', written by original keyboardist Jimi Destri, became a surprise hit, topping the charts in fourteen countries. In the United States 'Maria' reached number fourteen on the Billboard top forty. *No Exit* also delivered Debbie an honour she would probably prefer to forget — the 2000 Guinness World Book of Records named her as the oldest female vocalist to reach number one in Britain.

In 2000 Debbie appeared on the Andy Summers tribute to jazz legend Charles Mingus, *Peggy's Blue Skylight*, singing 'Weird Nightmare'. On stage again, she was in the emotionally dark play *Crave* by English playwright Sarah Kane, who hanged herself at the age of twenty-eight. *Crave* — and Debbie — received rave reviews, with Ben Brantley in the *New York Times* stating that she gave a 'subtle, pitch-perfect performance'. She also appeared in a number of indie films: *The Fluffer* (2001), *Spun* (2002) and *Deuces Wild* (2002).

Another Blondie album, *The Curse of Blondie*, was released in 2003. Giorgio Moroder produced the single 'Good Boys', which became a hit on the dance club scene and was the album's only real chart success. *Curse* was more aligned to the Blondie of old, but it wasn't *Parallel Lines* by any stretch and many thought it was time they called it a day. The band followed up the album with a tour to Japan and Australia as well as more dates in Britain. Another tour — of South America and the USA — and another film, *Full Grown Men*, followed.

Now in her sixties, Debbie hasn't slowed down. In 2006 she was back on stage in *The Show (Achilles Heels)* at the Kitchen Theatre in New York, penned 'Dirty and Deep' as a song of support for embattled singer L'il Kim, which was available as a free download, and sang 'New York, New York' with Moby for his best-of album. Still considered one of the great beauties, Debbie was named as one of the stars of the MAC Viva Glam VI campaign.

In 2006 Blondie was inducted into the Rock and Roll Hall of Fame. Frank Infante and Nigel Harrison were part of the induction in name only. Debbie — reportedly still furious at their failed attempt to sue her — and Stein refused to allow them to perform. Infante's altercation with Debbie at the event, when he pleaded with her to let him play, generated more publicity than the band's actual performance.

The same year Stein and Debbie dropped keyboardist Jimi Destri when Blondie toured the USA with the New Cars fronted by Todd Rundgren. Citing drugs as the reason for his sudden departure, Debbie despaired that Destri was still battling the same demons he had twenty years earlier.

she left rock behind in 1994 to take up with New York band the Jazz Passengers. She enjoyed exploring a new musical dimension

Although Debbie has broken down many doors during her career, she believes women have regressed, that the musical rebellion has lost some of its oomph. She says music doesn't have an edge anymore. 'When Blondie were starting out ... we were fighting the idea that the only decent music was the Eagles or Chicago.'

In 2007 she joined the True Colours tour along with Erasure, the Dresden Dolls, Margaret Cho and the event's creator Cyndi Lauper. The national tour across America was in support of gay, lesbian, bisexual and transgender equality.

The same year Debbie went on tour to promote her latest solo effort *Necessary Evil*. Then in 2008 she teamed with Fergie for a rendition of the Blondie hit 'Call Me' for Fashion Rocks at Radio City Music Hall in New York City. And she picked up a Billboard Icon award. She was touring with Blondie again in 2009 and critics claimed her in fine voice. The tour continued with dates scheduled for London in June 2010.

Now in her sixties Debbie values her independence more than a relationship with a man, living alone in a swanky apartment with her dogs in her beloved New York. Her only real complaint, she doesn't like getting old. It sucks she says.

1980s

When Dance & Pop ruled

In December 1980 John Lennon was shot outside his home near Central Park in New York. The murder shook the music world and brought home the vulnerability of the famous in an age of celebrity-mania.

'Call Me', the Blondie hit, was on top of the charts in 1981 and Pat Benatar was picking up the first of four consecutive Grammys for best female rock singer. The Pretenders' 'Brass in Pocket' was named one of the top singles for the year. Although disco was still alive, it was in its twilight days. Punk had morphed into new wave, or vice versa. In Britain the new romantics — Duran Duran, Depeche Mode and Spandau Ballet — were winning the hearts of teenage girls. At the other end of the musical spectrum, Kim Gordon's Sonic Youth was pushing the sound barrier in New York.

On 1 August 1981 MTV went to air. It revolutionised the way music is marketed. Pat Benatar's 'You Better Run' video was the second played on the new music network. Video became the primary vehicle for promotion and artists were expected to pay for the production of their videos out of royalties earned from their albums.

In the space of two short years video clips went from simple footage of live performances to mini-cinematic productions. When Michael Jackson enlisted the help of film director John Landis to produce the fourteen-minute 'Thriller' video in 1983, he set the benchmark much higher than most artists could afford. *Thriller* went on to be a multi-platinum album, clocking up more than twenty million record sales worldwide and crowning Jackson king of pop.

'Bette Davis Eyes' was a monster hit for Kim Carnes in 1982 and Sheena Easton and Juice Newton made their debuts on the charts. But the year was dominated by pop music bands — Daryl Hall and John Oates, REO Speedwagon and Australian success story Air Supply — with love the central theme. Benatar was there with 'Hit Me with Your Best Shot' and so was Blondie with 'Rapture'. But the rocking vibe of the 1970s was waning.

The world became conscious of a new threat. AIDS stopped the promiscuity of the last few decades in its tracks. Safe sex became the words on everyone's lips as artists, actors, musicians and other public figures succumbed to the disease. Rock Hudson was the first big star known to die of AIDS. Others lost their fight with drugs, including comedian John Belushi, who died of a cocaine heroin cocktail known as a speedball in his room at Chateau Marmont in LA.

In Boston musician and songwriter Kim Deal answered an ad for a bass player in a band that would become the indie super group the Pixies.

Olivia Newton-John was back on top of the charts in 1983 with her *Physical* album and a new sporty look that tapped into the aerobics craze that was sweeping America. Multi-coloured lycra tights, floppy tops and headbands became part of everyday wear, complementing the big shoulders, big hair look of the TV soaps *Dallas* and *Dynasty*.

Newton-John's success seemed to spark a flurry of activity from Australian musicians, and Men At Work and INXS made it in the USA that year. These bands laid the groundwork and Paul Hogan threw a few more shrimps on the barbie, making Australians very popular in America. The Divinyls rode in on the Aussie wave, Chrissy Amphlett with her hard rocking arrogance giving American audiences more than they bargained for. Chrissy's feral cries and slamming stage performance paved the way for the riot grrrls of the future.

The musical movies *Flashdance* and *Footloose* were released a year apart. The themes — young dancers struggling for personal freedom — struck a chord and dance music became the rage again. It was the first time since disco that dance moved into the mainstream, mainly due to Madonna, who was clearly the leader of the *zeitgeist*.

By the mid 1980s Madonna held the minds and hearts of teenagers around the world firmly in her hand. Cyndi Lauper also had an impact with her crazy-coloured hair, penchant for ripped and layered clothing and her lyrics claiming all a girl wanted was to have fun. Whitney Houston was charting as were Bonnie Raitt and Janet Jackson. Heart's self-titled album started a renaissance in the rock anthem that had dominated the late 1970s. But overall the rock chick wasn't as prevalent in this decade as the one before.

From the mid-decade on everyone had a Walkman. But tapes and vinyl were being superseded by CD technology. Video games became the latest craze with Pac Man and Space Invaders the most popular. Plastic money, in the form of credit cards, was new —for the first time you could get what you wanted right now instead of having to lay away products or save. The 'shop till you drop' mantra became firmly entrenched and the protagonist in Oliver Stone's movie *Wall Street*, Gordon Gekko, proclaimed that 'greed is good'.

But in 1985 the music industry showed the power of the collective coming together, raising awareness and funds for famine victims in Africa. Bob Geldof, who had gained cult status as the lead singer of Irish band the Boomtown Rats, spearheaded the Live Aid concerts. That year Apple Mac released its first personal computer, and the first radio station dedicated to rap music was launched in LA.

In London Vivienne Westwood was dressing Adam and the Ants with ruffles, tailored pants and boots with buckles. Designer names became important for the first time across socio-economic divisions and brands like Calvin Klein and Ralph Lauren became household names. Everyone had a pair of CK knickers.

Strutting her new stuff, Tina Turner made the comeback of the century. Her multi-platinum album *Private Dancer* positioned her firmly in the mainstream rock category. Prince had a number one hit with 'When Doves Cry'. The Rock and Roll Hall of Fame was launched.

The world's worst nuclear power disaster, at Chernobyl in the Soviet Union in 1986, was out of the scale of known disasters, foreshadowed a few months earlier by the spaceshuttle *Challenger* exploding on lift-off, killing all on board. Terrorism was rearing its head too, with Libya held responsible for the bombing of a Berlin nightclub frequented by US soldiers, and the first bombing in one of Australia's cities, of the police headquarters in Melbourne.

The Bangles reached number one with 'Walk Like an Egyptian' the following year. Heart was still releasing hit singles, but most women on the charts — Whitney Houston, Tiffany, Debbie Gibson — were soft-sell, reflecting the conservative wind that was blowing. Pushed along by the largest fall on Wall Street, Ronald Reagan's America bunkered down and lost its humour.

In New York, censorship reached ridiculous levels with the banning of classic novels such as *Catcher in the Rye*. In response to the oppressive overtones, rap music emerged from the streets and ghettoes. A revolution had begun. Blondie were one of the first all-white rock bands to incorporate rap into their music with the song 'Rapture'.

Schmaltzy love songs pervaded late in the decade. George Michael's 'Faith' topped the singles chart for the year, while the pop girls dominated. Kylie Minogue, Samantha Fox, Taylor Dayne and Belinda Carlisle put in appearances. Rock made a comeback of sorts with glam rock band Cheap Trick and camp Def Leopard charting along with hard rockers like Aerosmith, INXS, Bon Jovi and Guns'n'Roses. But rock chicks were thin on the ground.

In 1988 CDs outsold records for the first time. Women continued to enter the charts, including comeback queens Sheena Easton and Cher, Martika, Neneh Cherry, dance music empress Madonna and Paula Abdul. But the only woman who came close to rocking was the pop queen from Swedish band Roxette, Marie Fredriksson.

At the close of the decade, Gorbachev's Soviet Union — and most of the Western world — was under the glasnost spell and the Berlin Wall came down after twenty-eight years. East and West met with trepidation, the separation between them not only physical. The reunification of Germany brought hardships for those who had lived under communist rule.

155

Milli Vanilli's hit 'Girl You Know It's True' propelled the German duo into the media spotlight in 1989. Turning quickly from celebration to ridicule early in the new decade, Milli Vanilli were exposed as frauds — neither of them had sung on their records. The scandal demonstrated how easily the music industry could be duped.

Countering the cacophony of manufactured sounds were musicians who were going back to their roots. PJ Harvey was scratching out songs for her first album, Nick Cave and the Bad Seeds were as black and brooding as ever, and Nirvana began to make music that would create a new genre — grunge.

ANNIE LENNOX

An Authentic Life

Scottish-born

Annie Lennox

is one of those artists who would have been happy to make her music and remain invisible to the media. But it's impossible to have the kind of success that she's had — Eurythmics alone has sold upwards of seventy-five million records — and

escape the spotlight.

The culture of celebrity has never sat well with the intensely private Scot whose continual internal battle with self-worth is at odds with the role of rock star. After nearly thirty years Annie still finds it hard to reconcile her rock'n'roll status.

An only child, Ann Lennox was born on Christmas Day 1954 in Aberdeen, Scotland. Her father worked the shipyards and the family lived in a two-room tenement flat. Life was hard, something her parents continually reinforced, urging Ann to be sensible and choose a career that would give her stability and a safe income. Wanting more for their daughter than they'd been afforded themselves, her parents sent her to an all-girls school where she took up the piano and flute. Her musical talents led to winning a place at the prestigious Royal Academy of Music in London, where she enrolled at the age of seventeen.

her musical knowledge had been confined to the classical — she was largely ignorant of the trends in contemporary music

In London Annie, as she was known, worked as a waitress to support herself while she studied, visions of playing in an orchestra or chamber ensemble driving her on. Before moving to London, her musical knowledge had essentially been confined to the classical genre — she hadn't had a record player and was largely ignorant of the trends in contemporary music. Radio had given her sound bites, but she'd never had the opportunity to really submerge herself in the new sounds.

Her first real exposure to popular music came via one of her flat mates. She worked her way through his music collection. Coming across Stevie Wonder's *Talking Book* was a pivotal moment. Joni Mitchell was another who inspired her.

Annie stuck it out at the Royal Academy for two years. But, disenchanted with the whole competitive and narcissistic scene, she dropped out before taking her final exams. What she had left behind was nothing compared with the manipulative environs of the rock music industry.

She continued to waitress while she contemplated her future. She didn't know what she was going to do, but was determined it would involve music in some fashion. One night while waiting tables she was introduced to a young musician, Dave Stewart. The pair became lovers as well as musical partners and began toying with the idea of forming a band with a mutual pal Peet Coombs. It was 1977.

Annie, Stewart and Coombs landed themselves a contract, initially as songwriters, with Logo Records. On a trip to Germany they met producer Conny Plank of Kraftwerk and Devo fame. When they returned to London they put together what became the Tourists, adding drummer Jim Toomey and bassist Eddie Chinn to the line up.

After extricating themselves from their songwriting contract — be wary of the pieces of paper you sign at the outset of your career — and re-signing as a band, the Tourists were off and running. The band was given three weeks to record their first album, which was produced in Germany with Plank at his studio in

Annie ingested the critical attacks as if pellets of poison. Her natural tendency towards pessimism began weighing her down

Cologne. It was a less than satisfactory process, but it was a matter of taking the time slot available. The priority was to get a record out.

With their self-titled album in the bag the Tourists hit the road as support act on Roxy Music's comeback tour in 1979. They also performed at the Reading Festival. But things were not going the way they had hoped. When the influential DJ John Peel declared his disinterest in the band, they became fair game in the press. Annie ingested the critical attacks as if pellets of poison. Her natural tendency towards pessimism began weighing her down. Rather than ignoring the press, Annie couldn't help herself devouring every nasty jibe.

What the band saw as exploring creative options, the media pronounced as lack of direction. Despite the fact that audiences seemed to enjoy their shows, Annie felt they couldn't win. That year they recorded another album, *Reality Effect*, which included their most successful single, a cover of Dusty Springfield's 'I Only Want to Be with You'. Annie had chosen the song because she thought it was fun, but the publicity outtake labeled her a 'nice, popsy, happy-go-lucky' airhead.

Their tour of Britain and Australia was marred by her increasing anxiety, which sapped at her self-confidence. 'We had quite a lot of success with the Tourists but when we were slammed … my God we were slaughtered … it drove me mad, seriously,' she told *The Face* later.

Stewart was nearly killed in a car accident, Annie rushed to his side … they decided their creative bond was too strong to ignore

They managed to put out a third album, *Luminous Basement*, in 1980, but the bad press wasn't the only thing hampering the band's ability to enjoy what they were doing. Artistic dissent was rife, with Annie and Stewart wanting to go in a different direction to Coombs. By the end of the year the Tourists had folded.

The band's demise coincided with the ending of Annie and Stewart's four-year relationship. Annie fell into depression and for months she laboured over the simplest activities, often in floods of tears. Not only was she feeling the emotional strain, but there were also serious financial pressures — she and the rest of the Tourists owed RCA, to whom they were signed at the time of the split, thousands of pounds. It seemed the walls were caving in on her.

Then Stewart was nearly killed in a car accident. Annie rushed to his side. During his convalescence they decided their creative bond was too strong to ignore. They began writing songs together again — Annie the lyrics and Stewart the music.

In Germany for New Year's Eve in 1980 the pair hooked up with Plank, the producer of their first album, and the seeds for Eurythmics were sown. More a project than a band, the concept was to stay fluid in terms of band members, the permanent core being Annie and Stewart.

On the strength of the demos they had recorded with Plank, Eurythmics were signed to RCA. Their first album *In the Garden* was released in 1981 in Britain, but not in the USA. Clearly a transition album between the Tourists and the new entity, it didn't set the charts on fire. But it did make a statement about the innovative musical style that was at the heart of Annie and Stewart's collaborative work.

It wasn't until 1983's release of *Sweet Dreams* that Eurythmics were propelled into the rock stratosphere, much to Annie's horror. She loathed the obsequious and superficial nature of the music industry. The two years between *In the Garden* and *Sweet Dreams* had been draining as commercial success eluded them. Then suddenly they were thrown into the international music spotlight. The media pursued the pair,

Annie's face appeared on music magazine covers around the world. For the intensely private Scot it was sheer torture

Annie in particular, and her face appeared on music magazine covers around the world. For the intensely private Scot it was sheer torture.

'Sweet Dreams', the single, reached number one on the Billboard pop charts with the album coming in at number fifteen. The song crossed pop, R&B and club playlists as did the album's other single, 'Love is a Stranger', which was a re-released track from *In the Garden*. The Eurythmics sound was described as synth-pop, but Stewart's experimentation ranged much wider, evoking pop rock, R&B and opera, and made full use of the versatility of Annie's voice.

MTV, which had gone to air in 1981, was becoming a force in the promotion of music. It was made for Eurythmics — their videos were visually and conceptually startling. In the 'Sweet Dreams' video, which was influenced by Luis Buñuel's 1930 surrealist film *L'Age d'Or*, Annie was dressed in a man's suit, her wide, red mouth and short cropped orange hair an effective contrast to her slender frame.

Her androgynous appearance was confusing, particularly to the Americans. Before MTV agreed to air the video it made an astonishing request of the record company — to sight Annie's birth certificate to confirm her gender. 'The moral majority in America was very concerned about anything that seemed to be pushing the

before MTV agreed to air the video it made an astonishing request of the record company — to sight Annie's birth certificate to confirm her gender

boundaries,' Annie said. They read her androgyny as a statement about her sexuality rather than a feminist proclamation about gender equality, which was her intention. She had thought it 'a very interesting statement to make through the media … [but] they missed my message.'

Satisfied that Annie was female and unlikely to morally corrupt young Americans, MTV put 'Sweet Dreams' on high rotation. The video won the award for best new artist at the inaugural MTV Awards in 1984 and began a dream run for the pair — Eurythmics videos were regularly nominated in future awards.

A third album was released in November 1983, *Touch*. Annie was really coming into her own as a songwriter as was Stewart as a composer and producer. Annie also played flute and keyboards on the album, which reached number seven on the pop charts and thirty-five on the R&B. *Touch*'s hit single, 'Here Comes the Rain Again', apparently written after a volatile clash between Annie and Stewart, made it to number four. 'In a musical field awash with deep-pocketed clotheshorses and hoary soul revivalists, Eurythmics are creating something unmistakably new,' *Rolling Stone* commented.

Eurythmics gave Annie the opportunity to explore her vocal range. Her voice moved easily among pop, rock, R&B and soul. However, the overuse of her voice, not only in performance but also in fulfilling her publicity commitments, resulted in a nodule on her vocal chords — a creeping huskiness told the singer something was amiss. Fretting that she might require surgery, she quickly learned how to look after her voice by undertaking extensive warm-up exercises and avoiding cigarettes — she is one of the few rock chicks who hasn't flirted with drugs.

Much of Annie's material is autobiographical. She has said she writes her best material when she is at her most miserable. She is not bi-polar, but admits she comes close — she's either on a searing high or an agonising low, there isn't much in between. In her younger years she had contemplated suicide. Annie's confident even bold on-stage persona masked a woman consumed with self-doubt, anxiety and pessimism. Every day she had to make a conscious effort to be positive. Her natural tendency was towards the bleaker side of life.

In 1984 Annie married Radha Raman, a Hare Krishna and a vegetarian cook who was part of the band's tour entourage. Her decision to marry shocked everyone around her. Her father advised her not to do it and Stewart had a meltdown. They needn't have worried. The union was short-lived and by the following year they were divorced. The divorce signaled the end of her interest in the Hare Krishna faith.

Annie has often said that the more unhappy she is, the more creative. The 1985 album *Be Yourself Tonight*, which contained material written after her divorce, was a massive commercial and artistic success, charting in the top ten and spawning a number of hit singles on both sides of the Atlantic.

Be Yourself Tonight was a departure from Eurythmics' previous work, which had been squarely centred on Annie's voice and Stewart's mastery in the studio. This album featured a number of guest performers. Elvis

she is not
bi-polar,
but admits
she comes
close —
she's either
on a searing
high or an
agonising
low, there
isn't much in
between

Costello joined Annie on the song 'Adrian', Stevie Wonder played harmonica on 'There Must be an Angel' and Aretha Franklin sang the duet 'Sisters are Doing it for Themselves' with Annie. 'Would I Lie to You?', another hit from the album, was nominated for no less than five awards in the 1985 MTV awards.

Aretha, who had been living a semi-reclusive life in Detroit, jumped at the chance to work with Annie and Stewart. When the pair met, Annie

> **when she gave birth to a stillborn son, Annie had to endure the reporting of her private ordeal in newspaper headlines**

was shocked Aretha was a heavy smoker: with her own paranoia about her voice, she thought it inconceivable that a voice like Aretha's was possible in a smoker.

The shift from pop-synth towards the pop-rock of *Be Yourself Tonight* was even more pronounced on 1986's *Revenge*, which again called on the talents of other musicians, including Blondie's drummer Clem Burke. The single 'Missionary Man' went to number one on the mainstream rock charts and won the duo their first Grammy. The album also featured 'Thorn in My Side, which was a hit in Britain, and 'The Miracle of Love'. Eurythmics embarked on a worldwide tour to promote the album — something Annie had wanted to avoid at the outset of her career, but the commercial reality of the music industry was impossible to avoid.

Savage, released in 1987, heralded a new direction in Annie's songwriting, revealing a darker, more psychologically intense side and prompting *Rolling Stone* to state that 'these are the dreams of the everyday housewife ... the everyday schizophrenic housewife.' Stewart's synth-dance compositions left behind the pop-rock sounds of the two previous albums. Sales of *Savage* were slow, particularly in the USA, but the duo's top forty run continued, with the single 'I Need a Man' entering the top ten on the Billboard dance charts, and reaching thirty-two on the mainstream rock charts. *Savage* was also released as a video album.

In 1988 Annie married film-maker Uri Fruchtmann, who is credited with producing *Spice World: The Movie*. In December that year she gave birth to a stillborn son. Annie had to endure the reporting of her private ordeal in newspaper headlines. She and Uri retreated to their home in Paris to work through their grief.

Part of her coping mechanism was to go back to work, encouraged by her husband and Stewart, who was by now married to singer Siobhan Fahey

(Bananarama and Shakespeare Sister). Eurythmics went on another international tour in 1989, the year *We Too are One* was released. Produced by Jimmy Iovine and Stewart, it displayed Annie's superior lyric-writing skills, proving her theory that misery makes for great art. A hit in Britain, it was less enthusiastically received in the USA. Annie also had a hit with Al Green in 1989 with the duet 'Put a Little Love in Your Heart'.

By the time the Eurythmics tour concluded in Rio de Janeiro, Annie was emotionally and physically spent. She and Stewart were also in desperate need of time out from each other. Eurythmics was shelved and the pair didn't speak for close on four years.

Annie delivered a healthy baby girl, Lola, at the end of 1990. Now living back in London, she recorded her first solo album at Mayfair Studios. Produced by Stephen Lipson (Pet Shop Boys) and released in 1992, *Diva* introduced a more mature Annie, who had successfully overcome her fear that she was incapable of making music without Stewart. Awarded best British album in the Brit Awards in 1993, *Diva* was also nominated for a Grammy. The album demonstrated Annie's incredible vocal range, moving from the haunting single 'Why' to the more pop-oriented 'Walking on Broken Glass', both of which were top forty hits. The single, 'Little Bird', was also a hit on the dance charts.

By the time she came to record 1995's *Medusa* she was the mother of two girls. *Medusa* was Annie's first covers album — reportedly she was too happy to write anything worthwhile. The album's biggest hit was 'No More I Love You's', a song earlier recorded by little known British band, the Lover Speaks. Annie tackled a variety of material, including songs by Neil Young, Al Green, Bob Marley and the Clash. Critics weren't fans of the album, but 'No More I Love You's' and 'A Whiter Shade of Pale' both reached number two on the Billboard hot dance charts and Annie picked up the Grammy the following year for best female pop performance.

During the 1990s, outside of her two multi-platinum selling solo albums, Annie focused on raising her daughters away from the prying eyes of the press. In 1997 the death of Peet Coombs of the Tourists brought Annie and Stewart back together. In 1999 the duo released another album, the critically acclaimed *Peace*, the first album from Eurythmics in a decade. *Peace* gave the duo another worldwide hit with the single '17 Again' reaching number two on the dance charts. 'I Saved the World Today' was another stand-out track.

In 2000 Annie and her husband of twelve years called it a day. Her pain and grief over the ending of her marriage provided ample material for her next solo album, 2003's *Bare*. On the cover Annie states, 'I am a mature woman facing up to the failed expectations of life and facing up to core issues,' which are exquisitely dealt with in the eleven songs on *Bare*. It included three number one hits on the Billboard hot dance chart. The album reached number four.

In 2005 she was one of the artists to perform at Live8 in London and at G8 at Glen Eagles in Scotland. The same year she sang on the 46664 tour to raise

> 'I despair of the women I see in music [today] ... the values are ignorant, materialistic., ... I think we've gone backwards'

funds for Nelson Mandela's AIDS campaign, performing in remote places, including Tromsø in the far north of Norway. A staunch supporter of Mandela's work in South Africa for victims of AIDS, in 2005 Annie took her daughters with her to visit an HIV/AIDS orphanage and hospice in one of the shantytowns.

In 2007 there was another solo release, *Songs of Mass Destruction*. One of the songs, 'Sing', named for her SING campaign for Africa and HIV/AIDS, features a stellar choir of superstars including Madonna, Celine Dion, Fergie, Melissa Etheridge and Gladys Knight. Currently she divides her time between making music, working on AIDS projects and raising her two daughters alone in west London.

After surviving more than thirty years in music, Annie laments what she sees as the regression of women in the industry and the videos which she believes equate to 'soft porn ... I despair of the women I see in music [today] ... the values are ignorant, materialistic. I don't think we've gone forward ... I think we've gone backwards.'

PAT BENATAR

The
Pixie
Who
Roared

When Pat Benatar was approached by VH1 to appear in the hit rock series *Behind the Scenes* she responded in her usual direct New York way: 'I know how these things end up, "they lost everything, and the shit hit the fan." I don't have any of this. And you can dig too baby cause …

you ain't gonna find shit.

My life is very boring.'

Boring is hardly the word for a rock chick like Pat. But her life is extraordinarily normal for someone who has lived in the public eye for the best part of thirty years. Pat has been married to Neil Giraldo, lead guitarist in her band, for over two decades. She's a superstar who does her own cooking and grocery shopping and hangs with the other moms at her kids' sports events.

Pat was initially another success story from the Chapman Chinn stable, who had written hits for Suzi Quatro and produced Blondie's *Parallel Lines*. Mike Chapman, producer of Pat's first album, was the man with the Midas touch. Just as he had launched others into the superstar stratosphere, so he worked his magic on Pat. Since that first album, *In the Heat of the Night*, she has sold over thirty-five million records.

Patricia Mae Andrzejewski, born in 1953 of Polish-Irish heritage, lived on the wrong side of the tracks in Lindenhurst on Long Island, New York. Her father was a metal worker, her mother a former opera singer. Money was tight and Pat and her brother Andrew grew up with few material possessions. Lindenhurst was divided by railroad tracks. The middle-class kids lived on one side, the don't haves on the other. 'I think I always worried about … our being so poor,' Pat said.

Her mother's love of music was passed on to daughter. Pat trained as an opera singer, encouraged by her mother to use her natural gift — a three-and-a-half octave range. As she grew into her teens she discovered rock and was a big fan of bands like Led Zeppelin. She found it hard to listen to popular music on the radio and then have to switch to classical tones, and even harder still to stick

it was a good way of gaining a broad musical education — she sang everything from cabaret and R&B to contemporary songs

to rigid practise sessions. Gradually her interest in opera waned. Pat turned her attention to Motown, R&B, the girl groups, the Beatles, the Stones. She performed in every school musical. She wasn't planning a career in music though. She wanted to be a school teacher.

At nineteen she married her high school sweetheart Denis Benatar, who was drafted into the army shortly after. The young newlyweds were shunted off to Richmond, Virginia, and Pat shelved any ideas of going to college. To alleviate the boredom she took a job as a bank teller, but it drove her to distraction. 'I was there with all these proper little Southern girls, which is such a whole other thing when you're from New York,' she said.

Pat took any job with a musical element, including a stint as a singing waitress in a roaring twenties restaurant where, dressed as a flapper, she would hit the stage to sing a few songs before going back to the tables to take orders. It was a good way of gaining a broad musical education — she sang everything from cabaret and R&B to contemporary songs in hotel lounges and smoky clubs.

By 1975 the pair were back in New York, but the marriage was on the rocks. Before long Pat filed for divorce. She took whatever singing work she could. There were months of performing at cabaret venues on Long Island and a role in the short-lived production of the sci-fi musical *Zinger*, composed by Harry Chapin.

She got her big break one evening at Catch a Rising Star, a Manhattan club that held open-mic nights. It was 1977. By the time Pat got her turn to take the stage it was around 3 am. The waning crowd was paying little attention to the wannabees on stage until Pat let rip. Singing the Judy Garland song 'Rock-a-Bye Your Baby with a Dixie Melody', she blew them away. 'Everybody just went crazy. I didn't do anything spectacular. It was just one of those magical things.' Afterwards club owner Rick Newman approached Pat about performing regularly. Shortly after he became her first manager.

Pat sang at the Star for the next year. One night she turned up in a Hallowe'en outfit she'd been wearing at a party and performed her usual routine. The costume — a black catsuit with heavy black eye make-up — gave her an added edge. The crowd was electrified.

The buzz around Pat was palpable. Jeff Aldrich from Chrysalis Records heard the rumours. He made the trip to the Star and liked what he saw, signing her on the spot. In no time Pat was in LA recording with one of the hottest record producers in the world. Mike Chapman.

Chapman had not intended to take on any new acts. But when he heard Pat's voice he couldn't resist. This woman had a vocal reach strong enough to shake the foundations and high enough to break glass. Sound engineer Peter Coleman also produced several tracks and formed a strong musical bond with Pat.

Chapman suggested she work with Neil Giraldo, the guitarist from Derringer who was known for his musical arranging skills. When Giraldo, with his dark wavy hair, tattooed arms and rock'n'roll vibe, walked into the studio it was love at first sight. 'I called up my girlfriend and I go, "I met the father of my children." She … says … "What is wrong with you? … It's 1979, you don't have to marry him to sleep with him." But I knew. I was in love … instantly.'

Her first studio effort was released in 1979. *In the Heat of the Night* eventually went multi-platinum, reaching number twelve on the Billboard pop charts. But early on it was a struggle to get airplay. After all, Pat was a woman and you could only have one female in the top ten at one time. Her debut single, 'If You Think You Know How to Love Me', written by Chapman and songwriting partner Nicky Chinn, was a slow mover. But 'Heartbreaker' delivered Pat's first top forty hit. It was emulated by 'We Live for Love', written by Giraldo. At Chrysalis everyone began to realise that Pat Benatar was on her way to being a rock star.

Despite her amazing vocal range she was on a steep learning curve when it came to making music. Before she'd recorded *In the Heat of the Night* she'd had little experience with real musicians. And she had found it difficult to articulate what she'd like to sing other than to say she wanted to rock. Giraldo took charge of the musical direction, but Pat the perfectionist wanted to learn as much as she could.

A touring band was formed with Giraldo on lead guitar and keyboards, Scott St Clair Sheets on rhythm guitar, bass player Roger Capps and ex-Derringer drummer Myron Grombacher. The live Pat Benatar shows rocked. She appealed to both sexes. Pat revelled in the attention, but also could see the humour in it. 'The guys get silly,' she said. 'They take their shirts off like they are guy groupies or something.'

early on it was a struggle to get airplay. After all, Pat was a woman and you could only have one female in the top ten at one time

Pat's opera training meant her voice had the stamina to tackle the big rock numbers she loved. But adapting to rock was no easy matter and, she said, took a good two years, finding out 'how I could scratch up my voice, rough it up, and still not rip my throat out.' Her range was a powerful tool. The transition from opera to rock came as a shock to Pat's mother: 'she was a little freaked out'. Her father was supportive, but not of the decibels. At his daughter's concerts, he resorted to wearing earplugs.

On stage she was a powerhouse. She clad her tiny, athletic body in spandex tights worn with a leotard or a top cinched in with a wide belt. She wore high heels and kicked, punched and stomped her way through sets. Pat's onstage persona drove the audience wild. As soon as the house lights went down, she was transformed into a 'vampish, sensual bitch everyone wants to love and to make love to,' one critic wrote. She 'struts and purrs, prowls and growls, and shakes and screams.'

Pat loathed the sex kitten image Chrysalis came up with to promote *In the Heat of the Night*. A poster depicting Pat in tights and leotard was the stuff of male fantasies, the publicity blurb painting her as a tough-talking man-eater: 'A lot of women singers today seem to be saying, "If you love me and then hurt me I'll die". I say, "If you love me then hurt me, I'll kick your ass".' But the sexy, hard-ass act proved its worth in platinum sales. Pat's records dominated the charts in the early 1980s and Chrysalis took every opportunity to prove that sex does sell.

As her first album climbed the charts she rebelled, discarding the tights, throwing on a jacket and lopping off her hair, much to the chagrin of her publicists. She also had a clause written into her contract that stipulated no photos would be issued without her approval. But it didn't matter how much she railed against the image. Pat was viewed as a sex symbol.

Less than a year after her first album was released, *Crimes of Passion* produced by Keith Olsen hit the charts. The public went nuts. *Crimes of Passion* went gold in less than two weeks, clocked up more than four million sales, reached number two on the charts and delivered Pat the first of four consecutive Grammys for best female rock

adapting to rock took a good two years, finding out 'how I could scratch up my voice, rough it up, and still not rip my throat out'

vocal performance — an unprecedented run. One of Pat's best known songs, 'Hit Me with Your Best Shot', was the first single and her first top ten hit.

Crimes of Passion positioned Pat firmly on the female rock'n'roll throne from where she would rule unchallenged for four years. The songs on the album were hard-hitting in their messages. Pat was keen to use her music to make statements: 'to sing a worthless lyric is like jerking the public off and jerking myself off.'

Managing the balance in her relationship with Giraldo — she was his employer as well as his lover — was difficult at times. By the time they were in the studio recording the next album both were feeling the strain. *Precious Time* was Pat's first album to reach number one. Its single 'Fire & Ice', written by Pat, guitarist Sheets and Tom Kelly, hit the number two spot on the Billboard chart. The album launched four top forty hits — 'Fire & Ice', 'Just Like Me', 'Promises in the Dark' and 'Take It Anyway You Want' — and delivered Pat her second Grammy.

In 1981 Pat and Giraldo decided to end their relationship but continue to work together. Pat put on a brave face, telling journalists, 'it came down to having a career or being Mrs Giraldo. We both love our careers too much to give them up. We could either be lovers or work together.'

In August, when MTV went to air for the first time, Pat's 'You Better Run' video was the second to be aired. Music videos became just another thing an artist had to do, and pay for, to support their records. Chrysalis wanted their star property to be a video star too. She became one of the stars of MTV, although she wasn't convinced the audience needed such literal translations of songs. She preferred they used their own imaginations.

The Benatar–Giraldo separation didn't last long. By the time her fourth album, *Get Nervous*, was released in 1982 they were married. Giraldo had popped the question while he was producing John Waite's solo album in New York. They were married in Hawaii on the beach, without any paparazzi, family or friends — just two strangers who acted as witnesses. Determined to work at their relationship and not let the music suffer, the pair made a series of compromises, such as making sure each had a room on tour, so they weren't in each other's pockets. Whatever they did worked because they're still married.

Get Nervous was another triumph, delivering four top forty hits, two of which made the top five — 'Shadows of the Night' and 'Looking for a Stranger'. *Get Nervous* rocked hard, but it also included more pop-oriented tunes. Pat wasn't happy with the album, feeling the record company had interfered too much, which had resulted in a manufactured feel. And they were still controlling her image.

The first line-up changes to the Pat Benatar band happened around this time with Scott St Clair Sheets leaving and Charlie Giordano coming in on keyboards, but the nucleus remained and the on-stage dynamics were clearly part of her success.

In 1982 Pat and Giraldo moved to LA with their animals, to suburban Tarzana in the San Fernando Valley. Pat was determined she could be a rock star and be married, and make both work. 'I don't want to be fried and I don't want to be dead.'

Money and fame didn't bring her any closer to the respect she wanted, respect she felt was automatic for her male counterparts. 'The attitudes never really changed. We'd be at board meetings with the president and vice president of the label and we're generating billions of dollars. But when I'd leave the meeting somebody would go, "hey, nice pants!" '

P at's contract demanded she deliver an album every nine months, as well as perform and do promotional tours. And it seemed the more money she made Chrysalis, the tighter their grip on creativity. They didn't want to alter a winning

she became one of the stars of MTV, although she wasn't convinced the audience needed such literal translations of songs

formula, but Pat was feeling stifled. She wanted a change, even if that meant risking her chart domination.

The next album was recorded during the 1982–83 world tour when Pat and the band performed across Europe and the USA to massive audiences. *Live from Earth* captured Pat's energy and vibrancy on stage and gave her one of her biggest hits and one of her most enduring songs. 'Love is a Battlefield' made it to the top ten and delivered her a fourth Grammy.

On her next record *Tropico*, Pat began to soften her sound and there were less hard rocking tracks. The album reached fourteen on the Billboard chart and delivered a top five hit with 'We Belong'.

Pat gave birth to her first daughter Haley in 1985. Twelve months later she was back on tour with hubby and baby in tow promoting her seventh album, *Seven the Hard Way*. The Benatar entourage travelled in luxury on a private plane. Pat approached motherhood in her usual pragmatic fashion and got on with the job.

Seven the Hard Way was Giraldo's first solo stint as producer for his wife. The album reached twenty-six on the Billboard chart and launched two singles, 'Invincible' and 'Sex as a Weapon'. It is her least favourite album. During its recording the record execs showed their true colours. 'I'd just had a baby … they didn't care … They wanted the record immediately … we had the contract from hell.' Her relationship with Chrysalis went into a downward spiral. Caught up in a contract that allowed the company to put an artist on suspension — which 'meant no royalties, no money' — she ended up in court, but couldn't break free from the label until 1993.

Her wry sense of humour and her ability to be self-deprecating were Pat's weapons against the overwhelming status of rock star. When they were not on stage or in the studio, Pat and Giraldo were at home in LA watching movies and playing board games or working out.

One thing she isn't fanatical about is

songwriting. Self-conscious about her ability as a writer, Pat would often give Giraldo one of her songs with the caveat that he read it when she wasn't around. She may have reached mega-star status, but her ego certainly hasn't.

It was nearly three years before the next Pat Benatar album was released, in 1988. Pat had insisted on some downtime. *Wide Awake in Dreamland* benefited from the

> we'd be at the record company and we're generating billions of dollars. But when I'd leave somebody would go, "hey, nice pants!"

hiatus. 'All Fired Up', the first single released, promptly went to number two on the mainstream rock tracks chart, and nineteen on the top 100. Giraldo and Grombacher, the only two of the original band line-up, were joined by Kevin Savigar on keyboards and bassist Fernando Saunders.

In 1991 Pat took a new musical direction, singing the blues on the album *True Love*. From a vocal perspective the material gave her no trouble. But she got considerable grief from those around her who said she was going to kill her career. Pat and Giraldo, both huge blues fans, pressed on regardless. *True Love* got a mixed reception. Some thought her segue into blues was a perfect fit, others labelled the effort atrocious. One rock reviewer even described her as a 'whitebread fluff peddler'. Pat shrugged off the bad press. It wasn't like she hadn't heard it before.

True Love featured a number of BB King songs, including 'Payin' the Cost to be the Boss', which made it into the top twenty. Giraldo called in Roomful of Blues, a band that had been around since 1967, to add the horns to his guitar work.

Pat and Giraldo took *True Love* on the road, performing in intimate theatres around the USA. Gone were the 1980s trademark tights, short wraps and clinging tops. On this tour she wore a dress, stockings and pumps and there wasn't a 'You Better Run' or 'Love is a Battlefield' in sight.

Getting back to her rock'n'roll roots, *Gravity's Rainbow*, released in 1993, was classic guitar rock with anthems, ballads and hard-hitting rock songs along with a touch of quieter moments that were almost R&B. The album was universally praised. *Rolling Stone* welcomed back 'Benatar the rock diva … Benatar sounds genuine once again.' The album's best performing single was the Benatar/Giraldo penned 'Everybody Lay Down'.

Gravity's Rainbow — named after Thomas Pynchon's novel, which Pat described as 'the most bizarre book … about man's inevitable race to destroy himself' — was the last album she did under the Chrysalis label. Released in the year she turned forty, the album allowed Pat and Giraldo to focus on social issues that were close to their

Gravity's Rainbow was classic guitar rock with anthems, ballads and hard-hitting rock songs along with quieter moments that were almost R&B

hearts. It wasn't the first time they had tackled tough subjects. Way back in 1981 'Hell is for Children', a song written by Pat after reading a newspaper article, had powerful lyrics that dealt with child abuse.

Pat's second daughter Hana was born in 1994. The next year she embarked on a major US arena tour, Can't Stop Rockin', along with Fleetwood Mac and REO Speedwagon. It were as if time had stood still and she was back rocking her heart out like she was still in her twenties. The onstage garb had changed though — there were no zebra jumpsuits or lurex tights.

In between ferrying her kids to sports matches and keeping house, Pat has continued to tour and record. She released an acoustic oriented album, *Innamorata* in 1997, her first independent release: 'there was no way … I was going to stand there and let a twenty-five year old tell me what do to.' Any notion that not being signed to a major label was a hindrance was quashed as quickly as it was raised. The album may not have reached the lofty heights that she enjoyed in the 1980s, but it did get positive reviews and, most importantly, Pat and Giraldo were happy with the work.

Pat Benatar still sells lots of records and she still pulls a good crowd after nearly thirty years of hard rocking. 'I don't know what the hell I thought I would be doing but I didn't think it would be this … I feel grateful as shit that I still get to do it.'

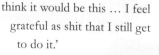

'I don't
want to be
fried and I
don't want to
be dead'

CHRISSIE HYNDE

Not
A
Pretender

Chrissie Hynde
of the Pretenders has the image of a woman
with copious amounts of
self-confidence
who isn't afraid to speak her mind
and stick her finger up at the
injustices of society, regardless
of the fallout. She is driven by an
undercurrent of self-belief fuelled by
a steely determination and
oodles
of talent.

A wandering soul in search of the next adventure, Chrissie, an American, opted for England. She landed there in the early 1970s and immediately immersed herself in the music scene. Being in her own band was her primary motive for getting off her ass every day, shrugging off the booze hangover and peddling her dream, but it took her nearly six years to form the Pretenders.

Born in 1951, Chrissie grew up in the Cleveland district of Akron, Ohio, the supposed tyre capital of America, a culturally barren landscape in the Mid West. The only daughter of a working-class family, Chrissie spent much of her time on her own, wandering in the woodlands, reading and listening to the birds sing. She enjoyed her own company and the quiet gave her time to think.

When she was fourteen she began to teach herself guitar. 'I was more like a guy, locked away in a room, practising obsessively,' she said. She also began to read Jack Kerouac and other Beat Generation writers.

After graduating from Firestone High School, she took an arts major at Kent State University where she spent most of the time 'doing a lot of drugs and having a good time', like the rest of her peer group. It was a time for freedom of expression, for self-exploration and for protest.

Chrissie was on campus the day of the Kent State massacre in 1970 when four students were shot by Ohio national guardsmen during a protest against US involvement in Cambodia. Chrissie was eighteen. It was one of her country's lowest moments. It didn't fill her with any great desire to stay in her homeland.

From childhood, Chrissie had been enamoured with England. She loved the accents, the strange British coolness that seemed far more attractive than brash, uncultured America. And the awesome music of the Beatles and the Rolling Stones captured the rocker within. When she heard Iggy Pop and the Stooges, Iggy became her idol. Jimi Hendrix was another musician who inspired her. Chrissie's musical education wasn't just confined to rock. She

Chrissie was on campus the day of the Kent State massacre when four students were shot during a protest against US involvement in Cambodia

watched her older brother Terry play saxophone in jazz bands and she got into R&B, particularly Candi Staton. But deep down, she knew her destiny lay in rock music.

While at university, Chrissie sang briefly in garage band Sat. Sun. Mat., (Saturday, Sunday, Matinee) with Mark

Mothersbaugh, later in Devo. Chrissie was terminally shy in those days and when the band rehearsed she would sit around the corner on her own to sing.

In 1973 Chrissie bought a one-way ticket to London. She had no plans, nowhere to live and no friends there, but it didn't stop the loud Yank, as she has described herself, from taking a gamble.

Chrissie had no problem fronting up to clubs and gigs on her own or heading down to the pub for a drink. Booze was her drug of choice. She got drunk a lot in those days.

she bought a one-way ticket to London. She had no plans, nowhere to live and no friends there

She worked at whatever gigs she could get — live modelling for art classes, cocktail waitressing and a stint as a handbag seller. She moved from one opportunity to another, sucking up as much of the atmosphere around her as was possible.

Much of her time she was penniless, living off the charity of strangers, many of whom became friends, in damp, decrepit squats, or cheap, vermin-infested hotels. But Chrissie had her bed roll, guitar and a few possessions — an Iggy Pop record was one of her most precious items although she didn't have a means of playing it.

The punk movement was in its infancy, Ian Dury and Elvis Costello were making music, Suzi Quatro was rocking up the charts and the glam-rock bands were dominating popular music. Musical experimentation was de rigueur.

Chrissie met Nick Kent, a journalist with rock bible *New Musical Express* (*NME*) at a party. He was her entrée into the London music scene, giving her the opportunity to live out her fantasy — to be part of the world of rock'n'roll.

Chrissie's relationship with Kent — their affair lasted about a year — led her to write for the paper too. But she soon grew weary of having to meet deadlines. It was an unwelcome contrast to the organic creation involved in songwriting. She had begun writing lyrics at the age of sixteen, jotting down thoughts as they came to her, often awakening in the middle of the night inspired by dreams.

One of the benefits of writing for *NME*, aside from the free entry to gigs and the opportunity to interview some of the legendary rockers of the 1970s, including Brian Eno, were the review copies of records she received. They were currency. She sold them — she didn't have a stereo so there wasn't much point keeping them and the money was useful.

During this time Chrissie became friends with Malcolm McLaren and

Vivienne Westwood whose shop SEX was a mecca for the new wave of punks littering the King's Road in Chelsea. Chrissie was drawn to the buzz around the pair and was briefly employed at SEX. But she didn't want to work in a fashion store anymore than she wanted to be a journalist.

McLaren was putting the Sex Pistols together. Chrissie began to teach Johnny Rotten how to play guitar while she attempted to find the right mix of musicians to form a band with. It was harder than she imagined.

'I went into SEX, and she just told me to fuck off.' Chrissie suspected that Westwood felt she'd gotten too close to the boys in the Sex Pistols

Then in early 1975 a Frenchman she'd met at SEX invited her to Paris to sing in a new band. Modelled on the New York Dolls, the Frenchies just didn't work for Chrissie. Unable to speak the language and on a tour that was hopelessly organised — the band opened as the support act for Flamin' Groovies — she quickly became disenchanted and on the spur of the moment headed back to Cleveland.

She mooched around her old stomping ground for a few weeks and played in an R&B outfit, Jack Rabbit. But Cleveland didn't have what she was looking for. She took off to Paris. Before long she had moved back to London, and was living in a squat in Clapham.

The musicians she hung around with were getting their acts together — Mick Jones with whom she'd shared rehearsal space was in the Clash, and the boys from Malcolm McLaren's Masters of the Backside, who she'd sung with briefly, had formed the Damned. Chrissie was getting frustrated.

Tony Secunda, then manager of Steeleye Span, agreed to listen to some of her songs. Chrissie played a few tunes from her songbook for him with just her guitar and amp, her earlier shyness long forgotten. He liked what he heard and for a time she went on his payroll while she tried to get a band together. But Secunda was busy with his own deals and after a few months Chrissie was back to square one.

And she was cast out of the Westwood–McLaren circle, Westwood moving on to her next new best friend. 'I went into SEX and she just told me to fuck off.' Chrissie suspected that Westwood felt she'd gotten too close to the boys in the Sex Pistols — a social experiment that McLaren and Westwood wanted to keep under close control. In retrospect, Chrissie was the least of the Pistols problems.

Despite her inability to find musicians she clicked with, she continually seemed to connect with the right people. A chance meeting with Anchor Records A&R man Dave Hill led her to bassist Pete Farndon. At last she had found a musician she felt she could play with.

seven years after arriving in London, Chrissie was living her dream. But 'Anything we get we deserve,' she said

Farndon was from Hereford on the border of England and Wales, where there was a thriving local music scene. He enlisted the talents of two other Hereford men — guitarist Jim Honeyman-Scott and drummer Gerry Mackleduff.

Hill became the band's manager and negotiated a deal with one of Warner's labels, Real through Sire Records. Once they had signed, the music machine went into full gear pushing the band at a pace Chrissie wasn't prepared for. She had hoped for rehearsal time and the opportunity to hone their live performance skills. But the record company had different ideas and they were in the studio before they even had found a name for the band.

'Stop Your Sobbing', a cover of the Kinks hit and a song that Chrissie had loved as a teenager, became the Pretenders' first single. It was produced by Nick

Lowe, who had started Stiff Records in 1976 and had worked on Elvis Costello's *My Aim is True* album. He was one of the hottest producers around.

Released in 1978, the single made a respectable debut on the charts and paved the way for the band's first album. The Pretenders' version of the song obviously impressed the Kinks, who re-recorded it after its newfound chart success. Chrissie, a huge fan, said 'they used part of our arrangement! Which was just the thrill of my life … orgasm after orgasm.'

By the time the Pretenders hit the touring circuit to promote the single, Mackleduff had been replaced on drums by Martin Chambers. They

performed in pubs and clubs and were well received despite the fact that Chrissie had never played guitar and sung live at the same time before.

the band discovered if you interrupted La Hynde when she wanted a quiet moment, all hell broke loose

The follow-up, 'Brass in Pocket', was released in 1980 and shot the Pretenders to number one on the British charts and four on the US Billboard top 100. Seven years after arriving in London, Chrissie was living her dream. But 'Anything we get we deserve,' she said emphatically.

The band's debut album *The Pretenders* was recorded at Wessex Studios in London where their producer, Chris Thomas, had worked with the Sex Pistols on *Anarchy in the UK*. *The Pretenders* featured what would become classic Hynde songs, including 'Precious' and 'Kid', which was also released as a single. Chrissie's lyrics were fresh and uninhibited. The band's sound was a mix of 1960s British rock and the newer punk influences set to Chrissie's individualistic beat, which even Honeyman-Scott admitted he found hard to follow at times. It gave the Pretenders a sound all their own.

The press praised the first album, many grappling to define Chrissie's vocal delivery, which at times was more like talking than singing. Her voice was distinctive and deceptive. At one turn she was a rough, tough rock'n'roll chick, and then she was a vulnerable young woman with a broken heart.

Her American frankness took many an unsuspecting journalist by surprise. 'I'm drunk a lot of the time and I'm out of order a lot of the time' she said of herself, a description that others readily accepted. She was loud, and some thought temperamental and aggressive. She made journalists nervous and didn't cut them any slack. There was something fascinating about a woman who lived so brazenly on the edge of society. She was like a man in her fearlessness and her lack of desire for the comforts of life.

For a woman who enjoyed her own company, often more than that of others, she found the confines of touring with a band suffocating. She insisted on her own room — she had shared too many times and it drove her insane — where she could be quiet, where there was no radio, no television and no one talking. It didn't take her fellow band members long to discover that if you interrupted La Hynde when she wanted a quiet moment, all hell broke loose.

The trappings of her newfound success did have some benefits, she conceded, including the luxury of having her own bath. After all those years of living in rundown hotels and on the move, Chrissie had become fanatical about bathing, often taking a soak two or three times a day.

Six months after the album

topped the British charts, the Pretenders made their assault on America, undertaking a forty-city tour. Part of their rapid rise in the USA was due to the pick up on both FM and AM radio of 'Brass in Pocket'. The DJs loved Chrissie and the boys. Chrissie was always referred to in the press as the lead singer and leader of the band. Despite her protests, there was no denying that she was the Pretenders, just as Debbie Harry was Blondie.

On stage Chrissie, clad in tight black pants, a high-necked ruffled shirt, and waistcoat, sized up the audience through kohl-rimmed eyes shaded by a fringe of dark hair — a look she has kept throughout her career. She gave the impression of being tough yet vulnerable, an enticing cocktail that prompted love letters from fans.

In San Francisco they supported the Irish band the Boomtown Rats, who hadn't enjoyed the kind of chart success the Pretenders had, prompting one journalist to assert 'man smart, woman smarter.'

Their debut album sold over two million copies and charted around the world from Australia to Japan, the USA and throughout Europe. Not a bad effort for

a woman who didn't give a toss about anything other than writing songs and

she was over the moon at the thought of meeting her idol. She thought Davies was a brilliant songwriter and musician

playing — all the other trappings of success were irritants except the money which, Chrissie conceded, gave you the freedom to do whatever the hell you liked.

During the US tour Chrissie took the opportunity to take her political views on the environment out for an airing. In an interview in Detroit she spoke about the need to find an alternative form of transport. The environment wasn't her only cause. A vegetarian since the age of seventeen, Chrissie told anyone who would listen about the evils of eating meat. At concerts she thanked the vegos for coming and told the meat-eaters to 'fuck off'.

Chrissie met Ray Davies of the Kinks while on the US tour. She was over the moon at the thought of meeting her idol. She thought he was a brilliant songwriter and musician — in one of her *NME* articles she had called Davies the only songwriter who could invest intense emotion into his songs, despite the brevity of the lyrics. They quickly became lovers despite Davies being married.

Shuffled back into the studio by the record company a week after ending the gruelling six month tour, the band struggled to come up with material. Chrissie was less than thrilled that the label had assumed she'd been penning songs for the next album in her spare time on the tour. In between playing, doing publicity and partying there was little time left for sleeping let alone writing.

The band headed to Paris to put down tracks for *Pretenders II*, which was recorded at Pathe Marconi Studios and at Wessex Studios. The vibe in the studio was anything but conducive to creativity and it was a chore to get tracks down.

The tour excesses — the booze, drugs, late nights and general raucous behaviour, including an overnight stay in jail for Chrissie for being drunk and disorderly — had taken their toll. Everyone was running on empty. Tempers were frayed and the band members couldn't stand the sight of each other.

Released in 1981, the album wasn't a patch on their debut offering, despite the singles — 'I Go to Sleep', another Ray Davies cover, and 'Talk of the Town' — making it into the British top ten. One of the band's staunchest supporters, Van Gosse from the *Village Voice* slammed it. '*Pretenders II* sucks every which way it possibly can … If the Pretenders can make a record as rotten as this, it raises the question of whether they were ever as good as they once seemed.'

Whatever impact the critics may have had on the band's reputation, it was nothing compared with what was going on inside the Pretenders. During their extensive world tour in 1982, Pete Farndon's drug abuse and whisky drinking had escalated to the point where it was impacting on his ability to perform. As the tour drew to a close the band were at breaking point.

The band determined to fire Farndon, a hard decision, but one Honeyman-Scott and Chambers insisted on. At a meeting they voted against Chrissie, who didn't want to make the call even though she knew that Farndon had become a liability. It tore Chrissie apart to see her friend and former lover shooting his life down the toilet.

In June 1982, two days after Farndon left the band, Honeyman-Scott was found dead. The official verdict was that he died from a cocaine-induced heart attack. Chrissie, pregnant at the time to Ray Davies with whom she was now living, was rocked by the death. 'No one saw that coming,' she said.

Always the pragmatist, and believing it would have been what Honeyman-Scott wanted, she and drummer Chambers soldiered on. They recruited guitarist Robbie McIntosh, bassist Tony Butler and guitarist Billy Bremner and recorded 'Back on the Chain Gang', which Chrissie wrote shortly after Honeyman-Scott's death. The single was released to critical acclaim and chart success in both the USA and Britain.

The heartache continued for Chrissie. Not long after the birth of Natalie, her daughter with Davies, Farndon was found dead from a cocktail of cocaine and heroin. The last time she'd seen him or spoken to him was at Honeyman-Scott's funeral. No doubt Chrissie's new bundle of joy saved her from being consumed

they had intended to marry, but the London registrar refused to grant a licence because the pair wouldn't stop arguing

by the blackest moments of this period. She also drew strength from channelling her pain and sorrow into song.

The next album from the Pretenders — now Chrissie and Chambers with Robbie McIntosh and Malcolm Foster on bass — was *Learning to Crawl*, which was released in January 1984. Chrissie's maturity as a songwriter was evident on this album, which dealt with the gamut of life experiences — birth, death, love, faith.

During the crisis in the band Chrissie was also warring with Davies. They had intended to marry, but the story goes that the London registrar refused to grant a licence because the pair wouldn't stop arguing. Chrissie has said that 'nobody ... can get angrier faster than I can. I'm like a phenomenon.'

Davies and Chrissie split shortly after the birth of Natalie, which must have niggled at Chrissie's belief that families should stick together. Years earlier she had lamented the fact that there were so many women who had children to different fathers. It wouldn't be long before she joined their ranks.

Learning to Crawl was supported by a massive world tour in 1984, with major dates in New York at Radio City Music Hall, Nashville, Los Angeles, Dallas and her native Cleveland.

Within twelve months of splitting with Davies, Chrissie was married to Jim Kerr, lead singer of Simple Minds, who she had met in Australia during the *Learning to Crawl* tour. In 1985 their daughter, Yasmin Paris, was born. Over the next two years Chrissie slowed down, devoting time to her daughters and her relationship with Kerr, although she did perform at the Live Aid concert.

By the time 1986's *Get Close* was released, Chrissie was the only original Pretender left standing. Rumours abounded that she and Chambers had fallen out, but the truth was they just needed a creative break from each other. Chambers played on one track, a cover of Jimi Hendrix's 'Room Full of Mirrors'. *Get Close* featured the singles 'Don't Get Me Wrong', which reached the top ten in the USA, and the folksy rock ballad 'Hymn to Her'. The album was almost too slick to be a Pretenders record.

The Pretenders toured the US in 1987, but it was fraught with internal fighting. Keyboardist Bernie Worrell and TM Stevens, who had played bass on the album, were fired mid-tour. There were more personnel changes to come before the tour reached South America. For all intents and purposes the Pretenders didn't exist anymore.

The disintegration of her marriage to Kerr collided with the 1990 release of *Packed!* When the album was recorded, Chrissie said, she was not functioning as a musician — she needed a band. It were as if the hands of time had turned back to pre-1978 and she was searching once again for the right group of musicians.

Chrissie began devoting more time to causes close to her heart — animal rights and vegetarianism in particular. Words can be powerful as Chrissie found out when she glibly suggested that she'd firebomb a McDonald's restaurant in the animal liberation cause. She copped some flack when a fan took her up on the suggestion.

Despite being most famous for her work with the Pretenders, she believes that saving animals is what she's here to do. 'This animal rights thing is my life's work … that gives me more satisfaction than anything I've done in the music business.' She has left instructions that when she dies a full-page ad is to be placed in newspapers with the words: 'Dead meat should be buried not eaten. Take it from Chrissie Hynde.'

Four years elapsed before Chrissie was ready to go into the studio again. *Last of the Independents*, released in 1994, was received with open arms by most music critics.

when she dies a full-page ad is to be placed in newspapers with the words: 'Dead meat should be buried not eaten. Take it from Chrissie Hynde'

The band returned to the British top ten with the ballad 'I'll Stand by You'. Recorded in Bath and London, the album was produced by Ian Stanley and featured a number of session musicians, as well as Martin Chambers who played drums on several tracks.

Another album followed the next year. *The Ilse of View* was recorded as a live performance with the Duke String Quartet and Damon Albarn from Blur on piano in front of a small studio audience. The album included previously unrecorded

tracks and some of the band's greatest hits, including 'Brass in Pocket' and 'Back on the Chain Gang'. Although not strictly unplugged, it did have acoustic elements that gave it an unusual feel, especially for a Pretenders offering. *Rolling Stone* was prompted to compare Chrissie to Joni Mitchell.

Viva El Amor! would have been titled *Biker* if Chrissie had had her way. But the record company didn't think it conveyed the right message

In 1997, aged forty-six, Chrissie married Colombian sculptor Lucho Brieva, fourteen years her junior, at a London registry office. The bride and groom wore jeans and later adjourned to a local pizza parlour to celebrate with close friends.

The Pretenders' 1999 album, *Viva El Amor!* would have been titled *Biker* if Chrissie had had her way. But the record company didn't think it conveyed the right message. Here the band was back to its truest form, with many likening guitarist Adam Seymour to Honeyman-Scott. Jeff Beck guest-starred on guitar on the track 'Legalise Me' and the Duke String Quartet made another appearance on the song 'Biker'. *Vive El Amor!* showed Chrissie in fine form as a songwriter and musician.

By the time she was on the road promoting 2002's *Loose Screw*, her marriage to Brieva was over. Alone again and hitting the big five-oh didn't daunt her. 'I've got pretty good at being on my own. It's better than feeling lonely with other people.' In 2005, along with U2 and Percy Sledge, the Pretenders were inducted into the Rock and Roll Hall of Fame at the Waldorf Astoria in New York.

Physically, the Chrissie Hynde of today isn't that different to when she first hit the stage. She may show some signs of wear and tear but she still has the same fringe, kohl-rimmed eyes and slim physique.

But 'Being in a rock and roll band is not my life. It's my hobby. I've got a life thanks.'

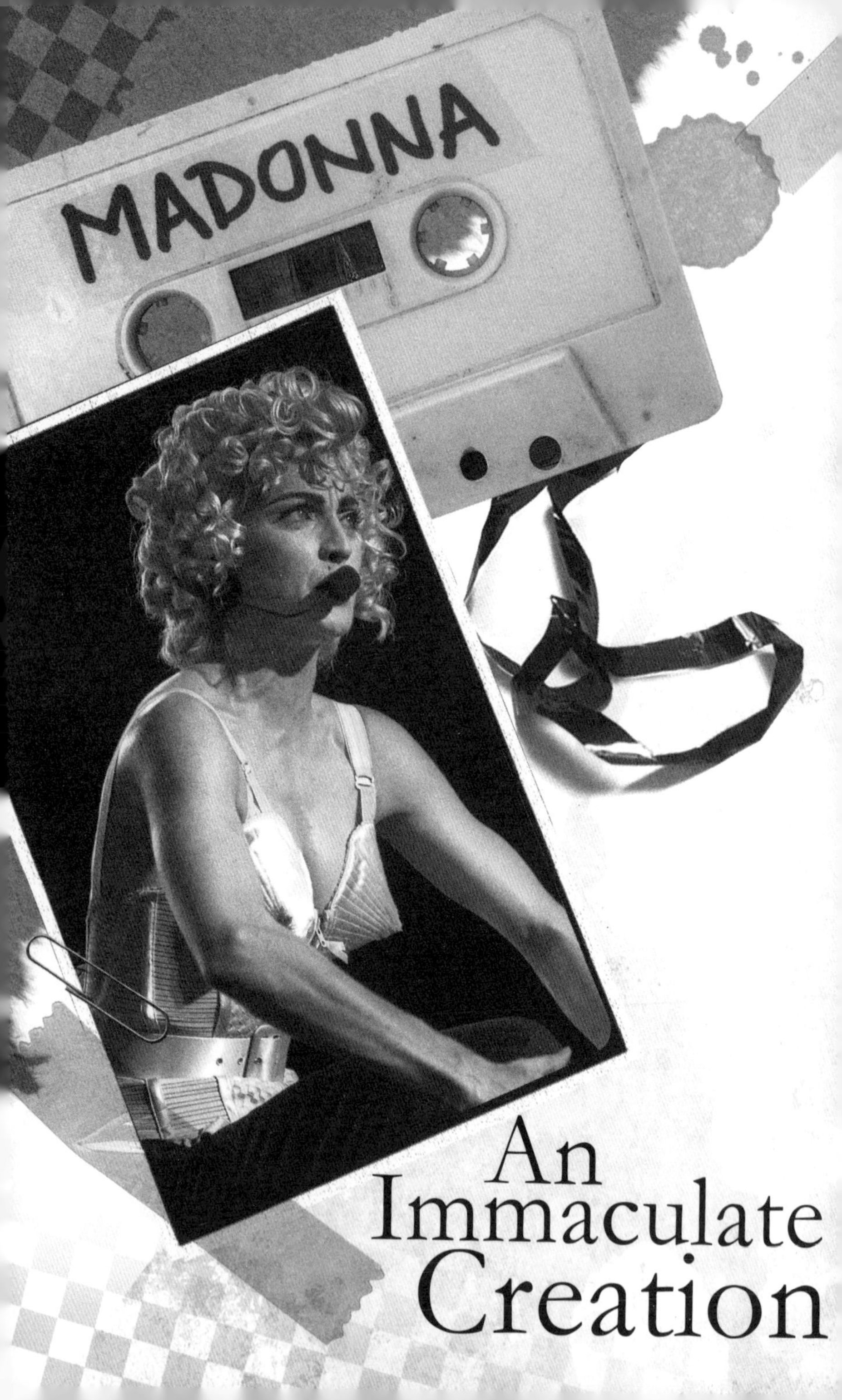

An Immaculate Creation

She is an
ever-changing
enigma.
When Madonna burst on to the scene in 1983 her street-smart, boppy dance tunes and theatrical stage get-up set her apart. She was a breath of fresh air, like Debbie Harry had been nearly a decade earlier. The media drew obvious comparisons. Madonna and Harry may look similar — sexy, blonde, knowing — but Madonna was driven by a ruthless determination. She didn't want to get into the groove.

She wanted to be it.

Born in 1958, Madonna Louise was the third child and first daughter of the Ciccones. Tony was a first-generation Italian-American, his model wife Madonna of French-Canadian descent. The Catholic family lived comfortably in a middle-class suburb in Detroit where Tony worked as an automotive engineer.

Three more children followed, two girls and a boy, then Madonna senior died of breast cancer.

Five-year-old Madonna reacted with anger and defiance, refusing, along with her siblings, to co-operate with the numerous nannies her bewildered father employed. But one nanny was different. She didn't take their cheek or rudeness. Tony Ciccone married Joan Gustafson six months after she started working for him.

Madonna was devastated. Despite her young age she had assumed the role of woman of the house, She saw the marriage as a betrayal on many levels. It took a long time for her to accept that her stepmother was there to stay.

A precocious child, always wanting to be the centre of attention, Madonna was prone to dancing on table tops. She was an outrageous flirt from a very young age. She excelled at school, a straight A student with a grizzly determination to succeed no matter the cost. She had few friends and seemingly no interest in trying to fit in, although she was a cheerleader — they always drew a crowd.

Former classmates claimed Madonna was promiscuous. The reality was she had one steady boyfriend at Rochester Adams High. Perhaps her reputation for putting out came from the fact that she liked to kiss boys and girls indiscriminately — and did so at every opportunity. 'I did a lot of bad things because I knew I could go to confession at the end of the week and all would be forgiven,' she said.

'I did a lot of bad things because I knew I could go to confession at the end of the week and all would be forgiven,' Madonna said

After haranguing her father, the fourteen-year-old Madonna replaced her piano lessons with dance. She was transformed. Suddenly she was doing what she felt she'd been born to do. Her teacher Christopher Flynn saw something in the young girl — she screamed 'star'. He gave her consistent praise and support over the next few years.

Madonna was impatient. She wanted to get her life started. At twenty she dropped out of university, where she was studying dance, and took off to New York. It was 1978. Landing at La Guardia airport with a few bucks and a trunk load of self-conviction, Madonna didn't have a concrete plan. She just knew she had to dance.

Control was core to her being. She loathed drugs and excess alcohol — and hated not being in charge of her body. She was known to have a drag on a joint occasionally, but no substances were going up that pert nose or into those steely blue veins. Madonna had enough adrenaline coursing through her body to satiate any addiction.

For a time she studied with Pearl Lang, the renowned dancer and choreographer. According to Lang, Madonna was undeniably talented and committed, but also young and reckless. She didn't like being told what to do.

In those early New York days Madonna eeked out a living working in fast-food outlets and passing out cloakroom tickets. Sometimes she posed as a nude model for artists and photographers. She had moved seamlessly from her safe middle-class suburban home to the seedy streets of the East Village, living in rundown tenements without utilities or furniture. She loved being deep in Bohemia.

But New York could be scary. Not long after arriving, she was sexually assaulted in a back alley. The incident frightened and at the same time galvanised the young dancer. She would not be beaten — by anyone. Madonna didn't know how to play victim.

She did know how to play though. Madonna always found a way to stand out. And where to find the party. In between her exhausting dance classes and odd jobs, she managed to frequent cool underground clubs and bars around the city where men, and women, would buy her drinks. With her striking figure, dark hair (the blonde came later) and revealing outfits, Madonna tantalised with promises of wild,

she moved seamlessly from her safe middle-class suburban home to the seedy streets of the East Village

uninhibited passionate nights ahead. She has said condoms saved her life. It was at the end of what was a promiscuous era, just before knowledge of AIDS, and nothing was going to rain on her sexual parade.

Her partying life was frenetic. But her dance career had stalled. In 1979 she tried out as a back-up dancer for Patrick Hernandez, who had a mega-hit in the dance clubs with 'Born to be Alive'. At the audition Madonna met the first of her financial benefactors.

Her exuberant singing and dancing sparked the interest of Hernandez's French producers. They flew her to Paris, put her up in an apartment and allowed her to run amok in clubs while they tried to figure out how to harness her obvious talents. There was a loose idea that she could be a singer, but Madonna consistently rejected the disco material suggested. Finally, she grew bored and three months later returned to New York.

Madonna picked up with an ex-boyfriend from Detroit, musician Steve Bray, moving into the run-down Music Building used by small entertainment businesses, musicians and squatters. It was almost derelict. Madonna was all bones and muscles, her thin body given definition by her rigorous dancing. She and Bray turned orange crates into furniture, slept on a rug and used public washrooms.

Going back to living in virtual poverty didn't dampen Madonna's spirit. She was still determined to make it to the top, but now she wanted to be a singer. Her flirtation with the life of a rock star — the limousines, shopping, endless partying — had appealed. She was destined for stardom. It was only a question of when.

Madonna was calculated in everything she did — the clubs she danced at, the people she attached herself to. She was always looking for the next leg up.

Camille Barbone became Madonna's next stepping stone. A partner in Gotham Productions, an entertainment agency in the Music Building, Barbone would see the waif in the hallways and the elevator. They began to talk and Madonna revealed her ambitions.

Barbone has said she had an almost maternal love for Madonna and treated her like a wayward child. Over the next two years Barbone introduced Madonna to important contacts in the music industry, believing she was leading the ingénue along a path that had room for them both. She was sorely mistaken.

Barbone invested heavily in her new charge. Madonna was moved into clean accommodation with a real bed and bathroom and given an allowance of $100 a week, a princely sum to the girl who could get by on air alone. Barbone planned to mould Madonna into another Pat Benatar. Madonna refused. She wasn't going to be another anyone. She was going to be herself.

The high priestess was fast growing weary of her minions.

The only tangible result from the partnership was a four-track demo tape that Barbone funded, sharing copyright with

Madonna and the studio where it was recorded. Madonna took the tape and moved on, looking for the next opportunity. The tape — the only way Barbone would see a cent from her investment — has never been released. Madonna has refused to give permission. Despite being her first manager, Barbone's brush with the gifted one left the coffers at Gotham Productions empty.

It was on to the next scene in which hot New York DJ Mark Kamins plays a central role. As ballsy as ever, Madonna approached Kamins at Danceteria, one of the city's coolest clubs. Before long they were lovers. Once she had him in her grasp she lent him the demo tape. Kamins played her track 'Everybody' at Danceteria one night. The crowd loved it.

Kamins wanted to be a record producer. He saw Madonna as an artist who could go places. Taking the initiative, he gave the demo tape to a mate at Sire Records, part of Warner's. Sire's president was in hospital recovering from heart surgery, but he liked what he heard. Madonna was summoned to his bedside and the deal struck. She was on her way. It was 1983.

Madonna always found a way to stand out. And where to find the party

But those who had thought they could climb on board for the ride, like her pal Steve Bray, were left out in the cold. Even Kamins was passed over for album producer — in favour of Reggie Lucas. Madonna rationalised that she needed the most experienced people on her first record to give her the best shot.

'Everybody' was released first to test the waters. Madonna promoted the single tirelessly, going to clubs and radio stations to pump up interest. When the song jumped from the dance charts to the US Billboard top 100 a murmur ran through Sire Records. They were on the cusp of something big. Madonna went into the studio to record her first album.

With offers coming left, right and centre she needed a manager. Enter Freddy DeMann, the man who had taken Michael Jackson to mega-stardom. Madonna was delighted when she heard that DeMann was no longer with Jackson. It meant he could focus on her. Her first album sold nine million copies. DeMann knew he'd gotten lucky and he remained her manager until 1997.

Madonna was unleashed in July 1983. The singer and her band did the New York club circuit, driving audiences wild as she pumped up her volume. The first single 'Holiday' took some time to gather momentum, but eventually it reached number one on the Billboard club playlist along with 'Lucky Star', which was written by Madonna. Two more singles, her 'Burning Up' and 'Physical Attraction', co-written with Lucas, reached the top five of the club playlist. 'Borderline', another Lucas/Madonna collaboration, broke through into the mainstream hot 100, reaching number ten. Not a bad performance for a debut album.

A vision of movement and colour, Madonna was made for TV. 'Borderline' was the first Madonna video that MTV gave serious airplay, but it was 'Lucky Star' that introduced the world to her gyrations and reignited mass interest in popular dance music. Her routines were sexually charged and playful, and her costume — with its ripped fishnet stockings, lace, dangling crucifix earrings, chains, calf-length boots, rags in her dyed hair and an exposed midriff — was something to covet. Young girls around the country began to emulate their new idol.

One of the standout features of Madonna's wardrobe was her Boy Toy belt, named after a moniker from her early New York days when she used to hang out with graffiti artists. She needed a street name and Boy Toy was it. This one badge sparked a merchandising empire that brought in millions of dollars as young girls everywhere mimicked the Madonna look. They wore crucifixes dangling from their ears and Boy Toy belts strapped low across their hips so as not to obscure their belly buttons. Showing the belly was critical to getting 'the look' right.

The launch of her first album coincided with the filming of *Desperately Seeking Susan*. Madonna had a supporting role. In the off-beat comedy her character Susan is a mirror of Madonna herself. She 'washes in a public bathroom, latches on to total strangers, bums food and money, lives out of a suitcase'.

During filming, her record was climbing the charts and sparking a flurry of Madonna-mania. It was like there was a hypnotic message

no one
had exposed
themselves
so graphically
and so
intimately on
camera

in her music that converted the listener to the new religion. Her influence was unprecedented, especially in the time it took her to take hold of the American, and later world, public.

On the movie set, the star Rosanna Arquette despaired at the growing interest in this amateur. Playing the lead in a quirky Susan Seidelman film was meant to deliver Arquette a giant step up the showbiz ladder. Instead, there were security guards on set keeping Madonna's fans away. *Desperately Seeking Susan* became Madonna's film.

Her triumphant debut album was followed in 1984 with *Like a Virgin*. The success of the title track written by the little-known Billy Steinberg and Tom Kelly began a run for the songwriting pair that would lead to more number one hits, including Cyndi Lauper's 'True Colours'. On this album Steve Bray got his break as a producer, but in the driver's seat, along with Madonna, was Nile Rodgers of Chic fame.

Like a Virgin, the single and album, firmly positioned Madonna's star at the top of the tree. Both reached number one on the Billboard hot 100 and the single topped the club playlist chart as well. 'Material Girl', written by disco dynamos Peter Brown and Robert Rans, further cemented her position as the queen of dance. She was unstoppable.

they were a strange couple, almost unattractive, more often seen arguing than in a loving embrace

At the inaugural MTV awards in 1984 Madonna took the stage to perform the opening song, 'Like a Virgin'. Wearing a white wedding gown, she writhed with an energy that blew the minds of her audience, all those years of dance paying off in a spectacular routine. She was in her element.

Hollywood brat packer Sean Penn invited himself on to the 'Material Girl' video set for a closer look. It wasn't long before the pair became an item.

It was an unlikely union, this publicity-seeking newbie on the brink of unimagined fame and the moody, at times violent, actor. They were a strange couple, almost unattractive, more often seen arguing than in a loving embrace. In the early days of their relationship the press interest in Madonna was escalating. She enjoyed the media exposure but it drove Penn to drunken nights and ugly brawls. He tried to keep himself in check, but one intrusion after another wore away at his resolve.

Their relationship was fuelled by a strong sexual attraction. Madonna enjoyed Penn, but even he wasn't enough to quench her thirst. Throughout their courtship she continued her liaisons with other men — among them graffiti artist Jean-Michel Basquiat who she used to hang out with — despite Penn's increasingly violent jealous outbursts.

The two surprised everyone by announcing their engagement. At their 1985 wedding, on Madonna's twenty-seventh birthday, journalists went to extraordinary lengths to gain access — even dressing as waiters and climbing the patrolled boundaries of Penn's Malibu mansion. All were discovered and thrown out.

The incensed bridegroom scrawled FUCK OFF in the sand to the flock of helicopters that buzzed above. But the paparazzi were undeterred. Before the ceremony Penn could be seen raging around the garden firing shots indiscriminately at the helicopters. Madonna wasn't adverse to a burning helicopter — the more publicity the better. The drone of the choppers was so loud it was hard to hear the marriage vows. Madonna was in her element. Penn was desperate.

Off on the Virgin tour in 1985 Madonna had little opportunity to comfort the brooding Penn, who was pining for his wife. The two tried to keep the spark alive, she travelling to his film sets and he to her concerts. But their efforts were fraught.

The Virgin tour played the USA and Canada with sell-out shows at Radio City Music Hall and Madison Square Garden in New York. The critics who said she couldn't sing and wouldn't outlast Cyndi Lauper are still eating their words. Madonna eclipsed all comers.

fans loved 'Like a Prayer' but it was a red rag to the Catholic Church. Unholy desire and burning crucifixes left it bleating about blasphemy

Her third album, *True Blue*, was released in 1986. It had more number one hits — 'Live to Tell', 'Papa Don't Preach', 'Open Your Heart' and the album itself. As Stephen Thomas Erlewine said, *True Blue* is 'one of the great dance-pop albums, a record that demonstrates Madonna's true skills as a songwriter, record-maker, provocateur, and entertainer through its wide reach, accomplishment, and sheer sense of fun.'

She was enraging all sorts of groups with her songs, her scanty outfits and her smart mouth. The feminists were up in arms — her outrageous, overtly sexual stage performances and videos, almost soft porn at times, reportedly setting the women's movement back thirty years. 'Papa Don't Preach' made family groups believe she was anti-abortion and encouraging teen girls to have babies. She laughed off the criticisms. Madonna was more interested in selling records than advocating moral reforms.

In 1987 she embarked on her first world tour, Who's That Girl, to Japan, Britain, US and Europe. Many of the shows were massive stadium events with crowds of 70,000 or more. By the end of the tour she'd entertained around two million fans. Earning an estimated half million dollars per show, Madonna donated all the proceeds of her Madison Square Garden concert to the American Foundation for AIDS Research — she had lost close friends to the disease.

That year the film *Who's That Girl* was released. Directed by James Foley, Madonna played the lead role in the quirky comedy, which was canned.

Even though she'd only released her first album four years earlier, *You Can Dance*, a compilation of dance hits, was released in 1987. The album featured long-play singles and remixes of 'Holiday' and 'Into the Groove'.

Her marriage ended in 1989 with Penn screaming he would have preferred to have annulled his wife not the marriage. Madonna moved on as if nothing had happened. Penn has said 'he can't remember ever having a proper conversation with her ... It was a miserable marriage.' For her part she said it failed because 'I just wasn't ready to be married. I was completely obsessed with my career and not ready to be generous in any shape or form.'

At the time she was caught up in the controversy over the video of her number one hit single 'Like a Prayer'. Fans loved it but it was a red rag to the Catholic Church. Madonna couldn't have cared less. Unholy desire and burning crucifixes left churches bleating about blasphemy. Once again Madonna was in the press, just as she had intended — this time in battle with the Vatican.

Albums kept coming in rapid succession. *I'm Breathless* was released in 1990 to coincide with the launch of her next celluloid catastrophe, *Dick Tracy*, with the equally publicity fond Warren Beatty. The album's most notable hit 'Vogue' went to number one on the Billboard hot 100 chart. Slick and elegantly choreographed, the video for 'Vogue' introduced Madonna with cropped blonde hair and tailored suits — creating another fashion trend. The song paid tribute to women Madonna admired: Marlene Dietrich, Bette Davis, Marilyn Monroe, Grace Kelly and Greta Garbo.

Beatty and Madonna embarked on a brief affair, the intimate details of which were shared in her documentary *In Bed with Madonna* (known as *Truth or Dare* in the USA) filmed during her Blonde Ambition tour. It offered a ghastly close-up look at the Material Girl in all her ugly greediness.

No one had exposed themselves so graphically and so intimately on camera. Audiences loved it. The more outrageous she was the better. As the media wailed, the *New York Post* calling her a tramp — 'Vulgar Madonna is the Degenerate Queen of Sleeze' — the movie became a box-office smash.

The Blonde Ambition tour was an epic, drawing the 'ire of law enforcement officials' for its saucy, even naughty content and sexy costumes. It introduced conical breasts and bustiers, created by Jean Paul Gaultier. Suddenly wearing underwear on the outer was in vogue. The concert was a Hollywood spectacular with all the

her descent into the weird, dark, psycho-sexual world of her album *Erotica* and the book *Sex* genuinely shocked many with her depravity

production values of a blockbuster movie. Catholics were beseeched by the Pope not to attend. The Italian concerts were the only ones not to sell out.

As her fame grew, so did her ego. It didn't matter what she did, the public, her subjects, would continue to adore her.

Then, shock horror, she took a wrong turn. Her descent in 1992 into the weird, dark, psycho-sexual world of her album *Erotica* and the much publicised coffee table book *Sex* genuinely shocked many with her depravity. Had the woman lost her mind?

Sex was a strange compilation of simulated sexual situations — everything from Madonna masturbating in front of a mirror to lesbian sex and implied bestiality. 'Catholicism inspired the sadomasochistic photos in *Sex*. I think a lot of Catholicism is based on punishment. A punishment-equals-pleasure kind of a thing,' Madonna said. Whatever the reason for its existence, *Sex* produced by her new enterprise Maverick Recording Company, became a huge seller.

The album wasn't received with the same vigour. The video for its number one single 'Justify My Love' was yanked from airplay by MTV after only a week. Its S&M imagery was too much. Madonna wouldn't be intimidated. She retaliated by releasing the video into record stores — and she made a fortune.

The following year's *Bedtime Stories* went a long way to restoring the faith of her fans. It reached number three on the album charts and its singles, 'Secret', 'Take a Bow', 'Bedtime Story', co-written by Bjork, and 'Human Nature', made the top five of the hot dance charts. The queen of dance was back.

Madonna pushed the sanctimony further, taking on the role of Eva Peron in the movie version of *Evita* — and winning a Golden Globe. Buoyed by the success, Madonna appeared in Quentin Tarantino's episode in *Four Rooms*, the awful *Blue in the Face* and Spike Lee's *Girl 6*.

In 1996 she gave birth to a daughter, Lourdes. Carlos Leon, the willing sperm donor, was Madonna's personal trainer at the time. He soon faded into the background and Madonna took full charge of her daughter's life.

Her post-motherhood triumph was the emotionally and spiritually rich *Ray of Light*, a 1998 masterpiece that had the media hailing a more mature Madonna. Despite the heavy emphasis on god in various guises and the preachy, sometimes corny lyrics, Madonna had timed it beautifully, reinventing herself as a spiritual goddess. *Ray of Light* reeled off the hits — the album's title song, plus 'Frozen', 'Nothing Really Matters' and 'The Power of Goodbye'.

she had timed it beautifully, reinventing herself as spiritual goddess

Madonna always attracts as much publicity for her personal behaviour as for her music. Her adoption of ancient Kabbalah in the late 1990s became a source of speculation. She told CNN, 'studying Kabbalah is actually a very challenging thing to do.' Belief in Kabbalah also requires followers to shed their egos, something the Material Girl is unlikely to do. She once said 'she wouldn't be happy until she was bigger than God.'

Within a decade Madonna had taken herself from heretic to devout. No wonder she said she wouldn't change her life for anything. Money, wealth, fame, beauty, motherhood. The only thing missing was the love of a man.

In December 2000 she married British film director Guy Ritchie of *Lock Stock and Two Smoking Barrels* fame, with whom she'd had a son Rocco earlier that year. Ritchie is

ten years her junior. The two set up home in a house in Notting Hill, West London, with Lourdes, Rocco and the nannies, servants and personal assistants.

In 2001 she hit the road on the Drowned world tour, which featured songs from *Ray of Light* and *Music*. It was the first time audiences had seen her since 1993 and fans lined up in their thousands to get a glimpse. At forty-three, Madonna was incredibly agile. A relentless yoga and dietary regime had kept her in top shape.

The 2003 album *American Life* featured the techno influence of Mirwais. It was her worst sales performer, not even reaching a million copies in the USA. The touchy subject matter of the title song, and its overtly war-mongering video, clashed with the Iraqi War. Recognising she was out of synch with the public, Madonna recalled the video, claiming it was out of respect for soldiers and civilians caught up in the horror.

Desperate to regain the headlines, Madonna appeared on the MTV awards French-kissing Britney Spears and Christina Aguilera. This time the antic wasn't shocking, just boring — and a little sad.

Just when it looked like she had lost her grip, her Reinvention tour became the biggest grossing tour of 2004. With her 2005 album, *Confessions on a Dance Floor*, she was back on top, rocketing to number one around the globe. It was a triumphant return to her dance club roots and was firmly steeped in the musical genre Madonna had claimed as her own more than twenty years and 250 million records ago. *Hard Candy* of 2008 was Madonna's most sexual album, more graphic than *Erotica*. That didn't stop it topping the charts in the USA, Britain, Australia, Canada and countries throughout Asia and Europe. In 2009 Madonna said goodbye to husband Guy Ritchie. It didn't take long for photos of her with her latest love conquests to appear in the tabloids. Divorce gave her more column inches than marriage and she played that hand heavily.

Whether you're for or against her, Madonna has undeniably influenced popular culture, her insatiable appetite for power and fame, making her a true rock chick.

KIM GORDON

Noise
Queen

Kim
Gordon

Crowned the

Queen
Mother
of Punk

or the Godmother of Grunge, depending on your perspective, Sonic Youth's Kim Gordon has been led into the realm of music by her love of art — drawn in by a handsome young punk, Thurston Moore, her lover and musical collaborator for more than twenty-five years.

Their band Sonic Youth has its own flavour made of the 1980s no wave, noise, alternative and experimental music genres, but with its own signature sound. Their music is still relevant today to both diehard fans and newcomers.

Born on 23 April 1953 in Ferguson, Missouri, Kim Althea Gordon, is the younger of a pigeon pair. She has a brother named Keller. In 1958, when Kim was five, the Gordon's moved to Rochester, New York. Over the coming years Kim also spent time in Hawaii and Hong Kong. But the family's base was in Los Angeles where her father was a lecturer in sociology at UCLA. Her brother was into the hits of the day, quintessential 1960s music, including Bob Dylan and Kim shared his interest.

Both her parents held progressive outlooks. They sent Kim to University High School in LA where she could explore her artistic side. She took private dance lessons and art classes. After graduating high school in 1971, Kim studied art at Santa Monica College. But her father convinced her to study for a degree at York University in Toronto, Canada. Kim moved there in 1975 to study dance and the arts. She also performed in a band at the Ann Arbour Film Festival.

But soon she was back in LA studying at Otis Art Institute of LA County. Much of her work involved appropriation — finding objects to create art from. Kim favoured advertisements in magazines. Music, pop culture and painting were also interests. She graduated in early 1977 and at 24 made her way to New York.

Kim earned a living doing odd jobs while she tried her hand at everything from writing articles to playing the drums. She waitressed, painted upper-class apartments and pretended to be a secretary (she didn't type). One of the best day jobs was working in a copy shop frequented by the art crowd. Artists would come into the shop to make copies of their work, print off flyers for exhibitions or create fanzines. The graffiti-neoexpressionist artist, Jean-Michel Basquiat, was a customer.

Home was a typical rundown walk-up on the Lower East Side where junkies and prostitutes prowled day and night. Kim's mentor Dan Graham lived upstairs. Graham was a conceptual artist who Kim had met when he'd given a lecture at Otis in LA. He introduced her to the New York art world and to the secrets of the Lower East Side with its clubs and human curios.

In 1980 she made another live musical appearance, this time in one of Graham's performance art pieces at the Massachusetts College of Art in Boston, a gig that gave Kim the music virus.

Not long after, Kim first saw Moore performing with the Coachmen at Manhattan club Plugg on West 24th in Chelsea. Within months they were living together. Moore, a guitarist and singer, began to teach Kim bass. She was still learning when they took the stage at A's in SoHo in December 1980 to play an experimental musical set under the name Red

Milk. Performing with them were Dave Keay (drums) and Anne DeMarinis (keyboards), the first of many line-ups. The gig lasted fifteen minutes and was a cacophony of insanely loud and incoherent noise.

After Red Milk came the Arcadians, with whom Kim played her first gigs at CBGB in January 1981. Then came Sonic Youth, who debuted at Club 57 in May. The name is a combination of Sonic, from Patti Smith's husband Fred 'Sonic' Smith, and DJ Big Youth.

Sonic Youth's first real break came at the Noise Festival that year at White Columns, an art gallery in New York. The festival ran for nine days and was centred on experimental music. Glenn Branca, who

created symphonic scores for multiple electric guitars and percussion and who Moore would later play with, was on the bill as well as Rhys Chatham, Dog Eat Dog and Ad Hoc Rock.

By December 1981, when Sonic Youth recorded its first EP at Radio City Music Hall's recording studios, the line-up had changed again — Lee Ranaldo was on guitar with Moore. Glenn Branca was so taken with the band that he started Neutral Records to sign them. The eponymous EP featured five songs: Kim's 'I Dreamed I Dream', and 'The Good and the Bad', 'I Don't Want to Push It', 'She is Not Alone' and 'The Burning Spear'.

Kim wrote the lyrics to 'I Dreamed I Dream' from slogans and words she'd read in magazine advertisements — another example of using appropriation, as she had done in her art school days. Moore and Ranaldo played their guitars at full throttle and used power drills and metal pipes to create an exchange of noise that would define Sonic Youth's sound. The band hit the road on a six-date tour. They didn't sell many copies of the EP, but that didn't dampen spirits. Kim and the rest of Sonic Youth weren't looking for fame and fortune. They just wanted to make music. Getting paid for it was a bonus.

Their first LP *Confusion is Sex* was released in April 1983. Reviewers grappled to describe the assault on their senses. One compared listening to the album with major dental surgery. Another likened it to Hell. But there was consensus that Sonic Youth was pushing the boundaries in the way no other band had before.

Another two tours followed, but now they were playing to audiences in Europe and drawing the biggest crowds to date — up to a hundred hyped-up, aggressive and out-of-control indie music fans who were crazy for the band. They played in fields, industrial sites and discothèques in Italy, Germany and Switzerland. And slept wherever they could find a floor or a couch. It wasn't glamorous and often Kim and Moore, the only couple on tour, would find themselves sharing with another band member. But this lack of privacy didn't faze Kim and few outside the band would have known she and Moore were a couple, they were so understated.

Tired from touring and irritated by a perceived lack of support from their label, Sonic Youth split with Neutral Records. By 1984 they were without a contract. They continued to make music and everyone went back to their day jobs to make ends meet.

On 9 June Kim and Moore were married in Bethel, Connecticut. Sonic Youth went back to Europe where the band had its strongest following. Drummer Bob Bert was ditched during the tour, and Steven Shelley, ex-Crucifucks, signed up. Shelley has been at the musical heart of Sonic Youth ever since and the line-up has stayed stable since.

Around this time Kim teamed up with Lydia Lunch, an avant-garde performance artist who was part of the Greenwich Village crowd she hung with. They performed together only once as an all-female noise-rock duo on the LP *Naked in the Garden Hills*.

Leaving behind another label, Homestead, Sonic Youth signed to SST. Their first album for the label *EVOL* ('love' spelt backwards) was released in 1986. It was their highest selling album to date, clocking up forty thousand copies in the first year of release. But it wasn't all smooth sailing. Like other bands of that era, Sonic Youth had signed away publishing rights before they knew what they were doing. That experience caused Kim to call in a lawyer to go over the SST contract before they put pen to paper.

Sister followed in 1988 and gave the band their first *Rolling Stone* review. The magazine called it a 'howling broadside'. Sonic Youth also recorded a cover of Madonna's 'Into the Groove' called 'Into the Groovey', under the alias Ciccone Youth. The dance clubs in Britain lapped it up.

Sonic Youth's style of music was enjoying a level of success it hadn't seen before. The band was finally attracting attention from the major labels. They met with Atlantic and Sony, but settled for Geffen. Their contemporaries, such as R.E.M. and Hüsker Dü, had consistently delivered respectable sales figures. Now it was Sonic Youth's turn to enjoy commercial success with a major label behind them.

At the end of the 1980s, Sonic Youth played to their biggest audience ever at the Ritz in New York. And toured the Soviet Union. *Rolling Stone* declared their double LP *Daydream Nation*, 'the sound of the New Rock Nation rising'. *Record Mirror* claimed Sonic Youth the 'best band in the Universe'.

Kim's celebrity rose beyond the band's diehard fans. It was spurred on by the release of their music video for 'Kool Thing', from the album *Goo* (1990). The video was peppered with images of a sexy new-look Kim, who at one turn is wearing black vinyl, at another sparkling silver or all white. Boots, hotpants, halterneck tops. Faux fur. The words 'sex symbol' became to appear with her name.

In the early 1990s Sonic Youth played the Reading Festival in Britain where incredulously Kim made friends with Courtney Love, whom she deemed a real talent. She was so enamoured with Love and her band Hole that she produced their debut album *Pretty on the Inside* with Gumball frontman Don Fleming. Around the same time, Sonic Youth toured with Neil Young. At the other end of the musical spectrum was an upcoming band from Seattle, Nirvana. Sonic Youth and Nirvana were together on the Year Punk Broke tour. And Kim was instrumental in getting Nirvana signed to Geffen.

By the time 1995's *Washing Machine* was released, Sonic Youth had put down ten albums. They were being hailed as the most prolific of the indie bands.

In the year she turned forty Kim fell pregnant with daughter Coco. While Coco was a baby Kim recorded another two original albums, *A Thousand Leaves* and *SYR 4: Goodbye 20th Century*. As the year 2000 approached, Sonic Youth played to a sell-out crowd in Paris, at Mutualit'T theatre in the Latin Quarter.

Touring was what the band did. There hadn't been a year since their formation that Sonic Youth hadn't gone on the road. In the 2000s they crossed the Atlantic many times to satiate the hunger of their European fans. Sonic Youth is still creating new music. Loud music. *The Eternal*, released in 2009, was their highest ranking album on the Billboard Independent Charts and the Billboard 200.

Throughout her career, Kim has been somewhat of an enigma. As one journalist said, 'Attempting to pin a label on Kim Gordon is like trying to understand the lyrics of Sonic Youth's songs: it's beside the point.'

As well as her work with Sonic Youth, she's dabbled in side projects. Free Kitten, her collaboration with Julie Cafritz and Yoshimi P-We, released a debut album, *Sentimental Education*, in 1997 and eleven years later the second, *Inherit*. Kim once said, 'Music is really supposed to be about freedom'. She continues to spread her wings and soar.

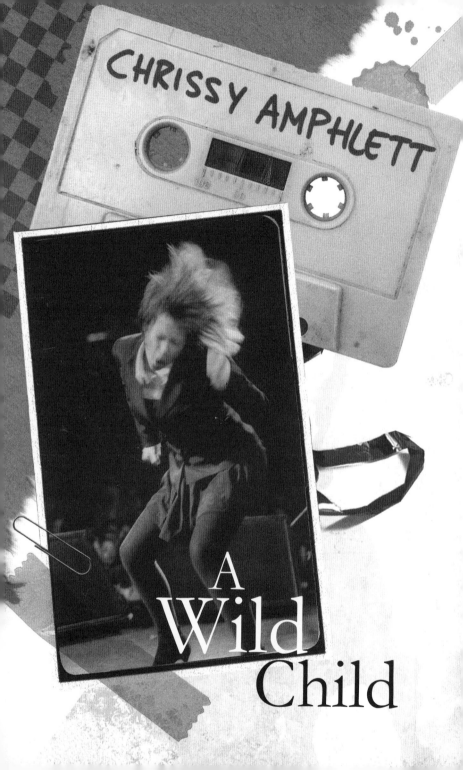

CHRISSY AMPHLETT

A
Wild
Child

Chrissie Amphlett spent almost two decades as
the lead singer of the
Divinyls,
but she is etched upon the
rock'n'roll
psyche
of Australia
forever.

She embodied everything that is rock'n'roll — her lyrics were guttural and the music was driven by rock guitar rifts, electronic keyboards and a thumping bass line and drums. Sex was Chrissy clad in an outrageous schoolgirl uniform with suspenders and high heels. Drugs were ever present as was booze. The Divinyls were a party band. The sneering, pouting quick-tempered retorts she dealt everyone who crossed her path, though, belonged to her alone.

Chrissy was quick to develop a scary reputation. Her eyes could spit venom at anyone who dared look at her. She had firmly planted the rock queen crown on her head and woe betide anyone who thought they were worthy of the royal attention. She was monstrously intimidating and incredibly fantastic. Everyone loved to hate her, but no one could deny the forcefulness of her personality. She oozed rock chick charisma and was magnificent in her reign.

Chrissy started life as Christina, born in the seaside town of Geelong on the Victorian coast in 1959. Geelong then was regional, not part of Melbourne's urban sprawl as it is today. She was the younger of two daughters. Like most kids who lived by the sea, she gravitated to the beach on weekends, smoking pot and watching the surfers while car radios blared the Rolling Stones, Dylan, the Beatles and Sly and the Family Stone.

She found her voice at a young age and would often break into song. Sitting around the fire with her mates after a day's surfing, Chrissy was the songbird. Singing ran in the family — she was the cousin of Little Patti, who had enjoyed success as a singer in the 1960s. Chrissy received more schtick about her famous relative than she did kudos for her strong vibrato voice. She sucked it in and kept on singing.

she had watched Debbie Harry climbing the charts and was inspired by the rock persona that Harry had created

Dropping out of school at fifteen, she wanted to be a rock singer. Heading for the big smoke of Melbourne, she hung around the live music scene, which was thriving in the early 1970s, and sang in a couple of bands. Daisy Clover took her to Sydney as the support act for Darryl Cotton and Zoot. One Ton Gypsy was an eight-piece ensemble playing Joe Cocker. But she was restless.

At seventeen she headed to London with a girlfriend on the *Fairstar Princess* ocean liner. For the next three years

Chrissy bummed around Europe, forming impromptu rock groups and busking wherever she happened to be. The crowd she picked up with always had acid, pot and vodka on hand. Chrissy indulged in whatever was on the go. She lived in squats in London and *pensiones* in Spain and Italy. A little trouble with the Spanish police meant two months in prison and an escort to the border.

Facing her twentieth birthday, Chrissy determined to get serious about music. She flew back to Melbourne ready to start her rock career. She had watched Debbie Harry and was inspired by the rock persona that Harry had created. Chrissy wanted a taste of that life, and she knew her voice could take her there.

She skirted around the edges of the music industry, performing in *Let My People Come*, a bizarre musical that had critics and the moral fraternity up in arms about its nudity and sexual dialogue. At one point, Chrissy's character, the porn queen Linda Lips, appeared wearing a corset and curlers in her pubic hair to sing 'Cum in My Mouth'. After the show closed in Melbourne, Chrissy headed with the production to Sydney. There she threw herself headlong into the rock'n'roll scene. She began smoking heroin, but shied away from mainlining — too many of the surf crowd of her youth had died shooting smack.

Working at whatever musical jobs came her way, Chrissy sang with radio station 2CH's choir and had a part in *Jesus Christ Superstar* as a back-up singer and understudy for Marcia Hines's Mary Magdalene. Singing in the musical and the choir paid the bills, but Chrissy wanted to be a rock singer. She formed a band, Baton Rouge, with Shayna Stewart, another singer in *Superstar*, and Jeremy Paul from the show's band. But Baton Rouge was a basic covers band and she quickly became bored.

In 1980 she made the first significant connection, the one that would put her on the path to becoming a rock star. From the moment she met guitarist Mark McEntee she knew he was her creative doppelganger. The pair threw themselves into songwriting with a passion, producing what became iconic Divinlys songs, including 'Science Fiction', 'Elsie' and Chrissy's ticket to rock stardom, 'Boys in Town'.

When Baton Rouge died a natural death, Chrissy and Jeremy Paul toyed with putting a new line-up together. Henk Johannes, a former castmate from *Let My People Come*, joined along with rhythm guitarist Bjarne Ohlin, McEntee and drummer Richard Harvey. It wasn't long before Johannes, who fancied himself as lead singer, was out of the picture. The band, named Divinyls, recorded their first demo.

While they waited for WEA to make a decision about the demo, they worked on their live act. Divinyls took up residency at the Piccadilly Hotel near Kings Cross, where they played to hardcore rock fans who threw beer cans and other projectiles on stage. Chrissy learned to give as good as she got, the verbal and physical assaults bouncing off as if she were encased in a forcefield of energy. At one of these gigs film director Ken Cameron saw Chrissy in action and cast her in his film *Monkey Grip* as a rock chick. Around the same time WEA signed the band. It was 1981.

she was the rock queen and woe betide anyone who thought they were worthy of the royal attention. She was monstrously intimidating and incredibly fantastic

The soundtrack of *Monkey Grip* lifted Divinyls from Sydney pub band to a national act. It featured a number of Divinyls songs, which were released as an EP. The single 'Boys in Town' became a hit on radio. Reviewers couldn't find enough adjectives to describe Chrissy's vocals. Her natural vibrato was twisted into something that sounded at times like Lena Lovich in its frantic rise and fall, laced with an aggressive, seething rock inflection. Prickly, feral, angry, volatile and demanding, her voice was an extension of her personality, leaving no doubt she was in control. She came across as a bossy bitch — and that was pretty much on the mark.

Chrissy's powerful personality caused rifts within the band. By the end of 1981 Jeremy Paul was

her trademark squat, which led to rumours she peed on stage, added to her image as the wild woman of rock

gone after trying to overthrow her. Rick Grossman, a mate of McEntee's, took his place. Chrissy had now won two internal coups. It was clear Divinyls wouldn't exist without her.

As the *Monkey Grip* EP took off, the music industry started to take notice. Divinyls became part of the Dirty Pool stable, which included all the major acts of the time. Divinyls was booked as support to Cold Chisel, the Angels and Icehouse. In 1982 they supported Simple Minds on a national tour and Chrissy was nominated for an Australian Film Institute (AFI) award for best supporting actress for *Monkey Grip*.

That first EP featured some of the best material Chrissy and McEntee wrote — 'Elsie', 'Only Lonely' and 'Boys in Town' are all classic Divinyls material. In a natural transition, their relationship evolved and McEntee, who was still married, left his wife for Chrissy.

She was fast gaining a reputation for being wild, uncontrollable and hardnosed, a persona she channelled into her on-stage routine and one that was fuelled by the band's escalating drug and alcohol consumption. She wore a gymfrock, suspenders and high heels, a costume invented by Chrissy and the band's manager, Vince Lovegrove. Often she brandished a blue neon tube from the 'Boys in Town' video clip like a sword, swiping she was playing diva 24/7. She was rude, crude and impatient, and revelled in her notoriety at the audience and band members as she raged around the stage. Frantically caught up in the music, at times she would leap on McEntee's back mid-song — like an animal in heat. Her trademark squat, which led to rumours she peed on stage, added to her growing image as the wild woman of rock.

Long before Courtney Love, Chrissy was stage-diving into the audience, the frenzied crowd obediently passing her around before returning her to the stage unharmed. She was scary. Divinyls' live gigs rocked like no other. Often there were brawls in the crowd and bottles and cans thrown on stage. Chrissy read them the riot act, abusing them and at the same time egging them on. She was addictive.

> they hard-toured for weeks on end ... it was rock'n'roll at its dirty best and Divinyls were one of the hottest live tickets

The live music culture in pubs was at its zenith. Divinyls were essentially a pub band and they hard-toured for weeks on end up and down the east coast of Australia. It was rock'n'roll at its dirty best and Divinyls were one of the hottest live tickets.

Chrissy's ego paralleled the band's growing success. There was no downtime between the on-stage and the at-home woman — she was playing diva 24/7. Her volatile relationship with McEntee, growing dependency on alcohol and the never-ending pills and powder on tour continued to feed her ego. She was rude, crude and impatient, and revelled in her notoriety.

In 1982 the band signed to Chrysalis and later that year they flew to New York to start work on their first album, *Desperate*. Bob Clearmountain was in the producer's seat along with Mark Optiz, who had worked with the band on their EP. The singles from the album included a raucous

cover version of the Easybeats' hit, 'I'll Make You Happy', which Chrissy made her own, 'Science Fiction' and a new recording of 'Elsie'. The album reached number three on the Australian charts. It received positive reviews in the USA and Divinyls set off on a North American tour.

That year Australian artists were taking the US by storm. Men at Work and INXS had songs in the charts and Olivia Newton-John opened Koala Blue in LA. Chrissy blew the American audience away with her wild on-stage antics.

The band played legendary venues like CBGB in New York, the stage Debbie Harry owned in 1975. It was a powerful moment. Later that year Divinyls joined the New Zealand leg of the Dire Straits world tour before touring the US with Psychedelic Furs. The highlight of the year was the massive US Festival where they played in front of 200,000 concertgoers, along with Bowie, the Pretenders, the Clash, U2, INXS and Men At Work.

Divinyls and Chrissy Amphlett had arrived.

The band finished off 1983 supporting the Ramones and U2 on two separate tours in the US. The pace Chrissy was moving at was taking its toll. Her short fuse further diminished as her dependency on liquor escalated. She was now drinking every day, as well as swallowing pills, smoking dope and snorting cocaine. Chrissy was rarely sober.

Despite the intense touring to promote *Desperate* and the positive reviews, the album didn't do great business in the States. Divinyls were gaining a cult status there, but that didn't translate into the volume of record sales Chrysalis had set as the album's target. The band had been given a substantial advance against royalties to pay for their relocation to the US, studio time, wages and travel, all of which had to be paid back in record sales. Falling well short of the target, Divinyls returned to Australia in debt to Chrysalis for tens of thousands of dollars.

Weighted down by the debt, they took to the road and toured Australia from coast to coast the next year. The only time they stopped was to go into the studio to put down tracks for their second album, *What A Life*.

Producer Gary Langan started working with the band in Sydney, but it soon became apparent that his overtly studio-mixed British DJ sound distorted Divinyl's vibe. Chrysalis called in its big guns to salvage the production. Mike Chapman, who had long admired Chrissy's voice, remixed Langan's work and recorded new songs They included a Chapman and Holly Knight song, 'Pleasure and Pain', which became the band's biggest hit to date.

The album was released almost eighteen months after they had begun. It had been an agonising process for the impatient Chrissy. Her arguments with McEntee had become vicious tirades which resulted in days, sometimes months, of frozen silence. But agony often produces great work. *What a Life* shot to number two in Australia and made it into the Billboard top 100, settling at seventy-five. The real success was with 'Pleasure and Pain' which hit the US top forty. The other singles, 'Heart Telegraph' and 'Sleeping Beauty', didn't make much noise.

falling well short of the sales target, Divinyls returned in debt to Chrysalis for tens of thousands of dollars

Now in even more debt despite the chart success of *What a Life*, Chrissy and the band returned to Australia and continued to tour in an attempt to pay their bills. In 1986 they headed back to the States to pick up the Aerosmith tour. As the support band, Divinyls were pelted with all manner of flying objects. But the next tour was worse. They joined the Cult with whom they feuded from the moment they met.

Chrissy was now consuming substances, but not shooting. The concoctions she downed would rival her idol Marianne Faithfull, but she still got up to perform. The drug and booze hangover made her more cantankerous than ever and her acid tongue was out to lash everyone, particularly McEntee.

When the wife and son of Vince Lovegrove, the band's manager, were diagnosed with AIDS, his priorities changed overnight. Despite her sympathy for his situation, Chrissy could see disaster written all over Divinyls' future. She was proven right.

At the end of 1987 bassist Rick Grossman checked himself into rehab to rid himself of a long-term addiction to heroin, something he had kept secret from the band for nearly seven years. With Grossman's departure, only Chrissy and McEntee were left of the original band.

When the album *Temperamental* was released around the middle of 1988 Chrissy had put the schoolgirl back in the closet and taken out a sexy vamp in a clinging black dress, feathers and fishnets. The smudged lipstick, fringe and black doe eyes were still there, but the neon pole had been replaced with seductive hand and body gyrations.

the smudged lipstick, fringe and black doe eyes were still in place, but the neon pole had been replaced with seductive hand and body gyrations

Temperamental's singles were pure Divinyls — 'Hey Little Boy', 'Back to the Wall' and Chrissy's 'Punxsie'. The album received positive reviews, but sales were once again too low for Chrysalis's liking.

Three strikes and you're out. After the sales failure of *Temperamental*, Divinyls and Chrysalis parted company. It coincided with management changes. In twelve months, they went through three managers, including Madonna's Freddy DeMann, who got them signed to Virgin.

The record company hustled their new charges into the studio to put down 1991's *Divinyls*. Virgin put their faith behind the band, calling on the services of seasoned musicians: Randy Jackson on bass, the Heartbreakers' Benmont Tench on keyboards and African-American drummer Charley Drayton.

The first single from the album, 'I Touch Myself', became the band's greatest hit, reaching three in the US and one in Australia. Written by Chrissy with Billy Steinberg, Tom Kelly and McEntee, it was blatantly pornographic in its depiction of masturbation. It raised interest and ire — and was Divinyls' only British hit.

The band continued to tour, one pub gig after another, in their bid to pay off the Chrysalis debt. In 1992, while she watched her album bomb, Chrissy sang the Rascals hit 'I Ain't Gonna Eat Out My Heart

Anymore' for the soundtrack of *Buffy Vampire Slayer*.

More trouble was headed their way. Freddy DeMann dropped them suddenly in 1993 in favour of running Madonna's new label Maverick. Chrissy was devastated, her depression exacerbated by Virgin dropping them too. She drank her sorrows over and over, often vomiting before she went on stage. She lived on uppers and downers washed down with liberal glasses of vodka, bourbon and gin, topped off with a generous sprinkling of ecstasy.

Chrissy sparked up when Charley Drayton agreed to join the band on tour. As her friendship with Drayton intensified, her relationship with McEntee faltered. When they did split, McEntee agreed to continue their professional relationship. Not long after, Chrissy and Drayton became a couple.

With no label behind them, in 1994 they went to Nashville and recorded 'I'm Jealous', written by Chrissy with Steinberg and Kelly. The single appeared on the band's next album — for their new label BMG. *Underworld* was recorded in early 1995.

Underworld was only released in Australia and the band hit the road to promote the record. With Joan Jett and the Blackhearts as their support act, the band — Chrissy and McEntee — financed their own tour. Ticket sales fell short and it threw the pair further into debt. It was a black time. Chrissy plunged into the bottle. The album was a dismal failure too. By the end of 1996, after sixteen years, Divinyls folded.

Chrissy went cold turkey and stopped drinking. Following the twelve-step program, she holed up on her farm in New South Wales. Once she felt strong enough she joined Drayton in New York. In 1998 she took on the role of Judy Garland in the Australian production of the Peter Allen musical *The Boy from Oz*. Since her marriage she has been relatively quiet. Now living in New York, she has performed only a handful of times over the last decade. She played with Drayton at the September 11 benefit concert in New York in 2002. Four years later she was back on the stage in *The Boy from Oz*, with Hugh Jackman.

When Chrissy took the stage in February 2010 at the Palais Theatre in Melbourne, she moved with the gait of someone suffering from multiple sclerosis. She has spoken about the disease and how every day is different. On this night she came on stage with a walking stick, but the moment she opened her mouth she was the rock queen from the Divinyls standing defiant once again before her adoring subjects.

KIM DEAL

The
Real
Thing

Kim Deal

The bass player and vocalist of the über-successful indie band the Pixies and lead singer of the Breeders, Kim Deal is a quintessential rock chick, independent (head strong), opinionated (fuck you), rehabilitated (alcoholic) and abundantly creative. (songwriter, bass player, guitarist, singer, band leader)

Born in Dayton, Ohio, on 10 June 1961, Kim is the younger of identical twins. Her doppelgänger Kelley was born eleven minutes earlier. They lived with their parents and younger brother in the suburb of Huber Heights, known as America's largest community of brick homes. At thirteen Kim started playing guitar and writing songs. Inspired, she began recording in her basement and playing her tapes for friends. As her songwriting matured, the 'sweet, smarmy' lyrics became deeper and more insightful. Kim declared her songs would be from the heart and loaded with meaning.

Fanatical about making music, on birthdays and at Christmas Kim asked for equipment for her studio. She got her early musical education from her father, a physicist at the Wright Patterson Air Force Base who loved soul music and the blues. Kim recalled seeing Ray Charles with her father who was moved to tears.

While Kelley was getting stoned and being anti-social, Kim was making music in her makeshift studio. She was an honours student and cheerleader. By fifteen she too was getting stoned. And playing imported records with her friend Pat Rohr. Rohr introduced Kim to such bands as Blue Oyster Cult, Stray Cats, James Blood Ulmer and Captain Sensible. She also listened to rock — ACDC and Led Zeppelin were two favourites. By the time she was seventeen, in 1978, she had written 'hundreds' of songs.

They'd met at a Breeders gig in New York, Cobain a fan, Kim oblivious to who he was

Kelley started to show an interest in making music with Kim as their teens came to a close. A guitarist and also a singer, Kelley joined Kim in her studio and the pair began working on songs that would influence their first playlist. In Dayton the only roles for girls in bands were as Pat Benatar clones or tambourine players. There wasn't a man in town prepared to play with the twins. Kim and Kelley began their live performance careers as a folk-rock duo, the first incarnation of the Breeders, playing a hotel bar. And opening for Steppenwolf in a bikers' hangout, playing covers of Elvis Costello, Hank Williams and Kim's own compositions.

Kim attended university but never completed a degree. In 1983 she married pop-rock musician John Murphy of the Boston band Mente. When they met, Kim was performing as a country singer at the Ramada Inn in Dayton. Her sultry mid-western air and creative spirit captured Murphy's heart.

The newlyweds moved to Boston and Kim answered an ad for a bass player and vocalist for a band whose influences included folk trio Peter, Paul & Mary and punk band Hüsker Dü. The only applicant, Kim didn't really want to play bass — her dream had been to be a rock guitarist — but she was itching to do something musically and she took the gig as a member of the embryonic Pixies. As the line-up settled down, Charles Thompson (aka Black Francis aka Frank Black) was on lead vocals, Joey Santiago guitar, Kim bass and David Lovering drums.

While Mrs John Murphy, as she referred to herself, settled down in Boston, Kelley chose life in Los Angeles rather than filling the drummer slot in her sister's band. As Kim's star rose, Kelley worked an IT job in LA and sank further into substance abuse.

The band got an early break when they scored the supporting act on the Throwing Muses tour. The Pixies music was described by journalists as shrieking, primal, visceral, grinding guitar hell. *Melody Maker* went further in 1986 saying, 'the Pixies are the disfigurement and degradation of language'.

In 1987 the Pixies made a demo tape that was released by British indie label 4AD. The eight-track recording, put out as the album *Come On Pilgrim,* topped the British indie charts. This was followed by the landmark *Surfer Rosa,* which had the music press salivating and fans clamoring. It got rave reviews and was called a 'brilliant step sideways' from the Pixies' earlier madness. Later Kurt Cobain opined that Kim should have been allowed to write more material for the band because 'Gigantic', co-written by Kim and Thompson, he said, 'is the best Pixies song'.

Although others were ecstatic about the album, Kim was not. Making the record had been an ordeal because of producer Steve Albini's rudeness and overbearing manner. But Kim doesn't hold grudges and later Albini would be enlisted by the Breeders, Kim's other super indie rock band.

In three short years the Pixies had gone from performing at the Rat in Boston to being college-radio kings and drawing fifty thousand screaming fans at the 1990 Reading Festival in Britain. And Kim had gone from being Mrs John Murphy back to Kim Deal after her 1988 divorce.

In 1989 *Doolittle,* the band's

first album for major label Elektra, charted at number 98 on the Billboard 200 and gave the Pixies two top five singles. Gil Norton (Echo and the Bunnymen) came on board as producer and his pop-culture edge gave the album its commercial flavour.

Rolling Stone awarded the Pixies 'Best New American Band'. Being the next big thing didn't sit well with Kim, who shunned the accolade. The collective music media claimed the Pixies was the most successful indie band since the Smiths. But after an exhaustive tour Thompson declared the Pixies on hiatus. Kim used her time to get the Breeders together and put out an album, *Pod*, which was produced by Albini and hailed as a masterpiece. The line-up featured Lovering from the Pixies, Tanya Donelly and David Narcizo (Throwing Muses), and later Josephine Wiggs (Perfect Disaster).

The Pixies followed up *Doolittle* with *Bossanova*, produced by Norton, who was now known as the fifth Pixie. Another grueling tour took the band across the top of the world for eight months. In London they played Hammersmith Odeon and proved the critics correct — they *were* the biggest thing since the Smiths.

But 1991's *Trompe Le Monde* would be the last album from the Pixies. While supporting U2 on the USA leg of the Zoo TV behemoth, the friction among band members was palpable and the volatile relationship between Kim and Thompson brought the band to a halt in 1993.

She pushed her energies back into the Breeders. Kelley took over on lead guitar, and Jim MacPherson was on drums. Donnelly left to start her own band and other members had been lost along the way. The Breeders followed up the previous year's EP *Safari* with the platinum album *Last Splash* with Kim in the producer's chair along with Mark Freegard. The single 'Cannonball' gave the band a hit, taking out second spot on the Billboard Modern Rock Tracks.

The Breeders were on the bill for MTV's New Year's Eve show in Seattle, along with Nirvana, Cypress Hill and Pearl Jam but the latter didn't show. Kim was pissed. In an interview with *Melody Maker,* a very stoned Kim said she didn't like Pearl Jam's music or their attitude. The interview also involved Kurt Cobain, who said when he first met

Kim she was 'condescending' and 'generous' at the same time. They'd met at a Breeders gig in New York, Cobain a fan, Kim oblivious to who he was. Within months the world would know Cobain through Nirvana's *Nevermind*. Later the Breeders would support Nirvana on tour and even later Kim would mourn Cobain's death.

In 1994 the Breeders played on the main stage at Lollapalooza. Kim was dating Jim Greer, a music journalist and sometime bass player for Boston band Guided by Voices. Then Kelley was arrested for possession of heroin and entered rehab putting the Breeders on hold. According to Kim, watching her twin sister go through her heroin hell was the 'worst f——ing feeling in the world'.

K im put her restlessness into another side project, The Amps (formerly Tammy and the Amps) with MacPherson on drums. Towards the end of 1995, The Amps put out the album *Pacer*, making full use of Kim's vast library of songs. By 1997 The Amps was over and Kim went back to the Breeders. But this time it was just Kim and Kelley. The pair put together a demo tape, but there wouldn't be another Breeders album until 2002 with the acclaimed *Title TK*.

In 2002 it was time for Kim's turn in rehab — for alcoholism. The withdrawal symptoms were truly dreadful, she said, not 'cool junkie sick'. But Kim bounced back and in 2004 joined the Pixies on a hugely successful six-month reunion tour of the USA, Canada and Europe. It was twelve years since Kim had spoken to Thompson. 'Bam Thwok', which Kim wrote, was released as an iTunes single, one of the rare times one of her songs has been used on the Pixies' records.

Juxtaposed against the heady success of the Pixies resurrection was the personal heartache Kim was suffering. Her mother was diagnosed with Alzheimer's and Kim moved back home to help care for her.

Late in 2007 the Breeders released their first album for six years, *Mountain Battles*, which reached number 12 on the Billboard Top Independent Albums, but only managed 98 on the Billboard 200.

As her forties come to a close, there are no signs of the hyperactive state that inhabits Kim lessening its grip. This rock chick's race is only partly run.

1990s

Pop Princesses & Riot Grrrls

A new rock chick emerged in the dawn of the decade. When PJ Harvey hit the airwaves, her feral, raw, sexually charged songs sung in an angst-ridden voice to scathing guitar riffs was just the ticket to shake up the staid environment. The American music rags sang her praises, spiriting the notoriously shy and private musician into the bright lights of celebrity.

PJ despised the attention, shrinking like a violet. The other new rock chick on the scene, Hole's Courtney Love, couldn't get enough attention. But Madonna blitzed them both.

Her Blind Ambition tour in 1990 set a precedent for live rock concerts. Choreographed routines, professional dancers, acrobats and Jean Paul Gaultier bustiers turned the show into a theatrical performance. Blind Ambition rewrote the record books for live music performances and Madonna sold millions of albums. Her single 'Vogue' became the mantra on the dance floors. Her power dressing, close-cropped blonde hair and scarlet lipstick was the new fashion.

Roxette, Mariah Carey, Taylor Dayne and Janet Jackson were making the charts and Heart's anthem 'All I Wanna Do is Make Love to You' became another hit for the sisters from Seattle.

Kylie Minogue emerged out of her pop princess shell with hits like 'Locomotion' propelling the former *Neighbours* star into celebritydom. In 1990 Kylie hooked up with the bad boy of Aussie rock, Michael Hutchence, the troubled lead singer of INXS. Their relationship gave Kylie the cred she needed to move up to the next rank of pop royalty.

Music fans turned out in the hundreds of thousands to attend the Berlin Wall concert, masterminded by Pink Floyd's Roger Waters. Beamed into millions of homes around the globe, it was more like a theatrical play in which songs from Pink Floyd's *The Wall* album were transformed into a series of stage acts performed by singers, actors and musicians. Thomas Dolby, Albert Finney, the Band, the Scorpions,

236

Sinead O'Connor, Ute Lemper, Joni Mitchel, Bryan Adams, Jerry Hall, Van Morrison, Marianne Faithfull and Roger Waters were supported by Waters' Bleeding Heart Band, the East Berlin Rundfunk Symphony Orchestra, the East Berlin Radio Choir and the Marching Band of the Combined Soviet Forces in Germany.

For a short time the world was bathed in optimism. By 1991 the Gorbachev-led Soviet Union was dissolving in glasnost and the Cold War was officially over. Nelson Mandela was released from prison and two years later would be awarded the Nobel Peace Prize.

But the first Gulf War erupted in February 1991. In Africa war raged in Somalia. NATO was kept busy with peace-keeping troops in Bosnia and the USA participated in air strikes on Yugoslavia.

In 1992 the world wide web was launched, changing the way we ran our lives. By the end of the decade its negative impact on the music industry would be apparent, with the first online free music download site Napster. Music lovers could only see its benefits. But the music industry went ballistic at the thought of their revenue being eroded. Although the big record companies bemoaned the theft of copyright, it was the artists who ultimately suffered, missing out on royalty payments that were rightfully theirs.

Bill Clinton rode into the White House in 1992 with Fleetwood Mac's hit 'Don't Stop' as his campaign song. The president asked the Mac to perform at his inauguration and later again at the conclusion of his administration. He is the only president to have a sexual act named after him — doing a Clinton became the slang for fellatio.

In the early 1990s the Gallagher brothers of Oasis, Londonbeat and New Kids on the Block were infiltrating the British and US charts. The Spice Girls, created in 1994, had a hit around the world with their first single 'Wannabee' two years later. The band became the voice for 'girl power' and the five members — Posh, Sporty, Scary, Ginger and Baby Spice — icons for the tweens and teenagers who bought more than fifty million Spice Girls albums over the next four years.

Alternative rock bands were gaining popularity, largely thanks to the acceptance of grunge rockers Nirvana. The Seattle trio took the music world by storm in 1991, with the release of the landmark album *Nevermind* spurring on the likes of Pearl Jam and Soundgarden. Of course Nirvana wasn't only famous for its music. The marriage of lead singer Kurt Cobain to the fame-hungry Courtney Love, and his untimely death in 1994, kept the band's name in the media well into the new millennium.

Although slightly more alternate rock, Courtney Love was part of the riot grrrl movement, along with L7, Bikini Kill, Babes in Toyland and Bratmobile. The riot grrrls were a new wave of feminist, singing with attitude and their collective finger up at the world. Some were marked as man-haters and others tried too hard to rebel. But their music made listeners think. They sang about rape, incest, discrimination, racism and sexual abuse. The riot grrrls was part of a cult movement that published its own online magazines — zines — and communicated through chat rooms.

Sheryl Crowe and Melissa Etheridge brought a softer rock, almost folk, feel back to the airwaves. Meatloaf made a surprise comeback with the number one hit 'I'd Do Anything for Love (But I Won't Do That)', proving that the music-buying public still loved a good rock anthem. 10,000 Maniacs did a cover of Patti Smith's classic 'Because the Night', written by Smith and Bruce Springsteen, and Crash Test Dummies made it into the charts with 'MMM MMM MMM MMM'.

Sheryl Crowe's 1996 album was banned in Wal-Mart stores across the US because one of its songs referred to children being killed in mass shootings with guns bought at the superstores. The issue of gun control became a topic that musicians focused on as more of their peers — including rappers Tupac Shakur and the Notorious B.I.G. — lost their lives to street violence.

In the latter half of the decade the music charts began to get a little more interesting. New York band the Goo Goo Dolls made an assault on the mainstream charts after years playing the alternate scene. Their singles 'Name' and 'Iris' gave

them a level of success they hadn't experienced before or since. The Smashing Pumpkins and Collective Soul were charting with a new sound that previously would have been relegated to the alternate charts — mainstream music was beginning to change its face. What had been known as AOR — adult or album oriented rock suited to radio airplay — was morphing into a sound that was edgier and more connected to emotions other than love. Alanis Morissette gave us hope that a new rock chick was emerging. Her 'You Oughta Know' rocked and ranted with a seething anger and indignation that had been missing. But Alanis didn't follow through and her future work pushed her into the pop/folk genre.

As the 1990s came to a close Jennifer Lopez, or J Lo, Britney Spears, TLC, Christina Aguilera, Destiny's Child and Mariah Carey were all singing songs of love and dancing their butts off in highly choreographed videos. Cher made her mainstream chart comeback with 'Believe', but there wasn't a new rock chick in sight.

The racial and civic turmoil that had seen the world map redrawn would continue into the next decade as would our continued reliance on technology. By the end of the millennium more than 100 million people were using online technology. Email had become a way of life and so had mobile phones. There was a gadget for everyone. As we counted down the new year on 31 December 1999 everyone waited for the technology governing the world to be thrown into a spin, but the impending disaster didn't eventuate.

PJ

The
Reluctant
Rock Star

ARVEY

The natural talent of
Polly Jean Harvey
has led her
kicking
and **screaming**
into the spotlight, delivering
the kind of fame and wealth
that many covet.
Celebrity at times has
driven PJ almost
insane.

Her music, which is in a constant state of evolution, crashed on to the alternate music charts in 1991. It defined her as the messenger of intensely sexual, black and visceral songs that were anything but comfortable listening — even for the artist, who has said listening to some of her tracks makes her nauseous.

Born in 1969, PJ grew up in Dorset, in a small picturesque village on the south-west coast of England. A happy little kid, PJ frolicked around the family farm, collecting eggs and helping her father tend the animals. She was the one who twisted the balls off baby lambs and wrenched dead foetuses from sheep wombs. Her father was too squeamish to do it.

Her father, a stonemason, and her sculptor mother had escaped London to live off the land. Both were huge music fans and dabbled in music promotion, organising for various bands and R&B ensembles to play locally. The Harvey home was filled with musicians, including her father's best friend, Ian Stewart, one of the original Rolling Stones. It was a very stable environment. Her parents, whom she refers to fondly as old hippies, had Jimi Hendrix, Pink Floyd, Janis Joplin, John Lee Hooker, Ella Fitzgerald and Captain Beefheart pumping on the stereo — it was an eclectic mix and offered PJ a broad musical education.

She grew up a tomboy, hanging out with her brother Saul and his mates. Up until her mid teens she was often mistaken for a boy. Then she grew her

she broke the news to her parents that she wanted to be a musician. They were delighted

hair and wore dresses. It was only when she started having relationships with men that she began to feel that she had made the transition from tomboy to woman. PJ didn't start dating until she was twenty.

As a teenager she flirted with popular music, listening to Duran Duran, Spandau Ballet and U2, much to her parents' horror. But it wasn't long before the pull of rock and R&B drew her back to her roots and heroes such as Keith Richards, Tom Waits, Howlin' Wolf, Bob Dylan and Willie Dixon.

Up until the age of seventeen PJ's instrument of choice was the saxophone. When the songwriting bug hit, she picked up a guitar and taught herself with the help of the Police songbook.

She began to think of a future in music when she met John Parrish of Automatic Dlamini, which played experimental percussion. She joined the

she couldn't switch to carving stone, her mind was full of songs

band in 1988 and remained for three years. While singing backing vocals and playing guitar and saxophone, she worked relentlessly on her songwriting, refusing to present any of her material until she was certain of its worth.

Automatic Dlamini undertook a five-week tour to Europe in the summer of 1989. The following year they recorded *Here Catch, Shouted His Father*, but the record was never released. Today bootleg copies are prized. The band's 1992 independently produced *From a Diva to a Diver* featured PJ, but she'd already left to start her own band with ex-Automatic Dlamini members, drummer Rob Ellis and bass player Ian Olliver. Her musical connection with John Parrish would continue.

Before she gave herself to the world of rock, PJ had enrolled to study sculpture at St Martin School of Art in London. But she couldn't switch to carving stone, her mind was full of songs. Accepting her fate, she broke the news to her parents that she wanted to be a musician. They were delighted.

The original PJ Harvey line-up didn't make it past the first gig in a club in April 1991. The audience, thinking the band so awful, began to leave in droves. Olliver left and was replaced by Steve Vaughan, whose five-string fretless bass brought a new element to the PJ Harvey mix. Six months later, they were signed to independent label Too Pure and their first single, 'Dress', was released to rave reviews. PJ was being hailed as the first real rock chick of the 1990s.

Influential DJ John Peel fell in love with the single and played it ad nauseum. The band performed live in the studio for one of his famed *Peel Sessions* — the tracks were later released by Too Pure in 1992. Peel's advocacy for the wraithlike creature and her seat-squirming lyrics helped to propel her star into the stratosphere. But the speed of this would prove too much for the shy and deeply intense Polly Jean.

The band's second single, 'Sheela-na-gig', celebrated the Celtic stone carvings of the same name, believed to be fertility charms. The Sheela-na-gig, a hunched-over old woman, adorned churches, her hands clasped either side of her vagina pulling it apart, her mouth carved into the grin of madness. PJ liked the contradiction the image presented, and the song's lyrics gave flight to the artist's macabre sense of humour.

Less than twelve months after playing that disastrous first gig, PJ Harvey had an album on the indie charts — *Dry,* released in March 1992 — major labels sniffing around and more media attention than she wanted. Within weeks of *Dry*'s release, it was number one on the British indie charts. Even the Americans were paying attention, hailing PJ as the new Chrissie Hynde.

The change in her life was dramatic. Moving to London, PJ was living away from home for the first time at the age of twenty-one. She shared a flat with a girlfriend. The euphoria of being in the 'big smoke' shifted to angst as she tried to cope with the impersonal nature of the metropolis and juggle her new commitments. She began escaping back to Dorset whenever the opportunity presented itself.

Dry was a collection of songs focused on unsatisfying sexual encounters, menstrual cycles and fertility mysticism. The raw anger and visceral nature of the lyrics were delivered with a savage humour that few detected, much to PJ's chagrin. The eclectic arrangement of raw punk rock and blues riffs was almost intimidating. PJ's voice, described as a wailing banshee, was the most distinctive John Peel said

fans sent her bodily fluids through the mail and others shared their thoughts about suicide. The attention terrified her

he'd heard in some time. As *Melody Maker* noted, 'sex and bile and rock and roll. It's been a long while since it was done so well ... these songs punch holes in your life.'

In 1992 *Rolling Stone* named PJ songwriter and best female singer of the year, *Spin* ranked *Dry* at number eighteen of the best albums of the year, *NME* had it at seventy-first in its 1993 list of greatest albums of all time, *Melody Maker* lauded it at number six and it was four on the *Village Voice*'s best albums of 1992.

The *Dry* album cover set the tone for PJ's public face. She wasn't interested in doing pretty. It was a close-up of her large lips, a smudge of red lipstick wiped across one side of her face. The photograph, taken by Maria Mochnacz, was a strikingly unattractive representation reeking of insolence.

PJ's decision to pose topless, albeit with her back to the camera, for an *NME* cover, caused a commotion. To PJ there wasn't anything sexual about the photo — she didn't think of herself in those terms,. She didn't think she was attractive. Quite the opposite. She was consumed by how ugly she felt, commenting about the disproportionate size of her head, her large eyes and over-sized mouth.

Her lack of self-confidence also manifested itself in her on-stage persona. Incredibly shy, PJ was unable to talk to the audience between songs, which drew comments about her being arrogant and aloof. The motivation behind her stage garb was also misconstrued — hair pulled back tightly in a bun, black trousers and turtle necks, and perhaps a smear of lipstick. It was designed to obscure her sexuality,. Her fans had other ideas. She began to attract the kind of attention that belonged in Stephen King novels. Fans sent her bodily fluids through the mail and others shared their thoughts about suicide with her. The attention terrified her. The bone thin star lost more weight and began to fall apart.

In the beginning it had been fun to do press interviews and read reviews. But the inexperienced PJ had much to learn about dealing with the media. Behaviour that she presumed normal — like peeing in a kettle she kept in the bedroom of her London flat in front of a *Melody Maker* journalist, or not washing her hair for two years because she believed it was self-cleaning — gave the media the hook they were after. PJ's eccentricities became a talking point, as did her anxieties.

Stress is very much a part of PJ's makeup and she often suffered from the pressures she put upon herself in her pursuit of perfection. Being in control was central to her ability to function.

As the career demands mounted, PJ began to unravel. By the time her first real romance ended in mid 1992 she was no longer coping. The crunch came at the Reading Festival in August when her stress level reached a crescendo. PJ fell in a heap. It took her months to recuperate.

It was reported that she had suffered a nervous breakdown. Some intimated that perhaps her woes were the result of anorexia, or drug abuse — after all, her stick-like appearance was not dissimilar to that of a heroin addict, although it was a rumour that couldn't have been further from the truth.

PJ may have flirted with marijuana, but drugs made her feel nauseous and had no part in her life. More often she'd have a cigarette and glass of wine in hand, but even her drinking was largely measured.

Her mother came to the rescue. She retreated to her parents' farm before taking up digs in a seaside flat in Dorset, where she began to regain

the crunch came at the Reading Festival when her stress level reached a crescendo. PJ fell in a heap

her grip on her strange reality. For the next two months she lived as a virtual recluse and started to pen songs, many of them about her feelings on the ending of her love affair with an un-named musician.

During those quiet days she breathed in the calm of the country as she readied herself to re-enter the world of rock, this time with therapist in tow. As others may take a stylist or hairdresser, PJ takes her stress management counsellor on tour.

Back on her feet, and now signed to Island Records, PJ went back into the studio to record *Rid of Me*. Determined to do things her way, and with no perception of the supposed barriers that women in music faced, she shunned

the list of producers the record company put forward and instead chose Steve Albini, formerly of 1980s US cult band Big Black, after hearing his work with Jesus Lizard and the Breeders. Albini had a reputation for deafeningly heavy and distorted guitar sounds which appealed to PJ.

Rid of Me wasn't for the faint-hearted. Its scarified delivery of visceral sexual encounters was anything but easy on the psyche, but the album captured the ferocious energy of the band live. PJ's vocals raged from gutsy punk rock howls to high-pitch squeals and quietly ferocious hisses, prompting one reviewer to describe her as 'a demonic fusion of Siouxsie and Patti Smith with a bit of Sinead and Kate Bush'.

The album spawned the single '50ft Queenie', inspired by the movie *Attack of the 50ft Woman*. The songs included 'Man Size', 'Rub 'Til It Bleeds' and 'Me Jane', and all focused on a favourite PJ theme — sex. The only one not written by PJ was a torturous cover of Dylan's 'Highway 61 Revisited'. Although the songs were lyrically mature, many reviewers felt Albini's harsh treatment didn't do them justice. PJ disagreed. It was exactly what she was looking for.

Released early in 1993, *Rid of Me* was unlike anything at the time, a scathing collection of vitriolic songs of betrayal, lust and control with guitar riffs that flayed you alive. Her diehard fans and the music media took to the new offering as if it were the holy sacrament. Her songs fired overtly aggressive missives at men. Was she a feminist? Or a riot grrrl? PJ shrugged off the attempts to pigeonhole her, saying it was patronising to be labeled.

the music was stripped back and raw, PJ's vocals raged from gutsy punk rock howls to high-pitch squeals and quietly ferocious hisses

The album's cover was as contentious as its content. Again photographed by Mochnacz, on the front PJ is whipping back a long trail of dreadlocks. On the back sleeve is a close-up of her face with what looked like rope burns — in fact marks made by rubber bands — making her look like a victim of violence.

Late in 1993 the band played their first major stadium gigs supporting U2. The mega-band's manager Paul McGuinness would bring PJ into his star-studded management stable the following year.

On her continual quest to extend her creative boundaries, PJ threw out the tight turtle necks and black clothing of *Dry* and introduced the PJ of *Rid of Me*. Decked out in glamorous 1950s dresses with feather boas, leopard skin prints, gold lamé pumps, enormous sunglasses and drag-queen make-up, she appeared to be a woman in control. But underneath the gaudy façade she was on the brink, consumed with self-loathing and driven to the point of collapse with her desire for perfection. As her records were charting and fans were queuing to get into her gigs, PJ was working on how she could become less successful, more invisible.

As the tour progressed across America, she began to crumble. Her manic controlling ways began to affect her relationship with Ellis and Vaughan and the tension between the trio mounted.

PJ roughed up her voice with wine and cigarettes and enlisted the help of two retired opera singers to give her singing lessons

Within a month of singing the praises of her fellow band members — the two people she could rely on when the going got tough, she claimed — the pair had stopped talking to PJ. After a disastrous show in New Orleans in which it was obvious how pissed off the boys were, PJ said she never wanted to play with them again. Later she would concede that it was her control fixation that drove the boys away.

PJ took herself out of the music circus at the end of the 1993 tour, returning to her new home in Dorset. She spent much of the next year working on new songs, putting together another band and focusing on her voice. She concentrated on roughing it up with wine and too many cigarettes and enlisted the help of two retired opera singers in her village who gave her singing lessons.

She left her hideaway several times to work on other projects. She recorded 'The Ballad of a Soldier's Wife' for a Kurt Weill tribute film *September Songs*, sang the Rolling Stone's 'Satisfaction' with Bjork at the Brit awards, appeared on Moonshake's album *The Sound Your Eyes Can Follow* and on the soundtrack to the indie film *Strange Days*.

By the end of 1994 she was back in the studio recording her next album, which featured considerably higher production values than the stripped bare *Rid of Me*. PJ co-produced the album with U2's producer Flood. A more emotionally

mature album, *To Bring You My Love* featured old friend John Parrish, also in the role of co-producer.

As a solo artist PJ now had the freedom to bring in various musicians to fulfill her creative vision. She enlisted the talents of ex-Tom Waits band member Joe Gore (guitar), Joe Dilworth (drums), Jean-Marc Butty (drums, percussion) and Mick Harvey, known for his work with Nick Cave, on organ and bass. Parrish also contributed on guitar, organ, drums and percussion.

To Bring You My Love was more blues oriented, yet still carried PJ's trademark of deeply primal, haunting licks around her favourite subject, sex. Her voice was at times almost a growl. This was the blues in its truest form, raw and at times brutal, prompting comparisons to Robert Johnson, the great southern blues man of the 1930s, and to John Lee Hooker, Jagger and Hendrix.

The album showed off PJ's talents as a musician — she played guitar, piano, organ, vibraphone, marimba, percussion, chimes and bell. The songs were heavily laced with biblical references. God, Jesus, Lazarus, Adam, Eve and the Devil all made appearances as PJ sang about sexual subjugation, carnal knowledge and sacrificing one's soul for love.

Once again she had delivered an album that challenged her own musical boundaries and brought the critics to their knees in adoration. The album won her 1995 artist of the year from *Rolling Stone* and *Spin* magazines. 'Down by the Water' was the first of her songs to make it into the Billboard modern rock chart, reaching number two.

For much of 1995 PJ toured with a new band: John Parrish, Eric Drew Feldman from Captain Beefheart, Joe Gore, Jean-Marc Butty and Nick Bagnall. She left many concert-goers gobsmacked with her rock chick attitude. She wore a hot pink catsuit or a bikini bra and low-slung pants with bananas protruding from the pockets.

By the end of 1995 she was back in Britain and back in intensive therapy.

She reverted to a quieter pace and spent much of the following year at home working on several independent projects. She worked with John Parrish writing lyrics to his music — a first for PJ and yet another avenue for her creative exploration. The outcome was the album *Dance Hall at Louse Point*, a collection of songs not dissimilar to those on *To Bring You My Love*. The album was part of a larger project with choreographer Mark Bruce. In 1997 PJ and Parrish appeared in several shows with the Mark Bruce Dance Company performing songs from the album. The record executives at Island were less than thrilled with this

her union with Nick Cave became all-consuming — 'we loved each other so intensely that it turned out to be quite damaging for both of us,' PJ said

digression, but they had never been successful in trying to tell PJ what to do creatively. She was a law unto herself and a tremendous drawcard for the label.

She also hooked up with Nick Cave, both creatively and romantically. For the first time in her life PJ felt she had found a soulmate. The two fell deeply in love. However the fervour of their union became all-consuming — 'we loved each other so intensely that it actually turned out to be quite damaging for both of us,' PJ said. Their duet 'Henry Lee' appeared on the Nick Cave and the Bad Seeds' *Murder Ballads* album in 1996.

By the following year the two were back to being friends, Cave reportedly heartbroken and pouring his soul out in *The Boatman's Call*. PJ was also emotionally devastated, but she had ended the tryst, the intensity pulling her focus from what she was born to do — create music.

In September 1998 her album *Is this Desire?* was released. Recorded over a twelve-month period, it was more experimental than her previous efforts and, according to PJ, contained more of her true self than any of her other albums. 'I finally feel comfortable … I am allowing myself to be myself for the first time ever,' she said. *Is this Desire?* was heavily influenced by electronic/techno sounds. The album's first single 'A Perfect Day Elise' became PJ's highest charting success in Britain.

Although *Is this Desire?* didn't have the commercial success of her previous album, critics were satisfied she was still the creative genius.

From PJ's perspective, it was just a simple case of growing up and out of the image and labels that had been handed her in the early days — she was no longer the lady of darkness, pain and sacrifice. She had moved on.

PJ's first experience of producing another's work was on Tiffany Anders' debut 2000 album *Funny Cry Happy Gift*, on which she also sang, played guitar, bass and organ.

In March 2000 PJ went into the studio to put down tracks for her own album, *Stories from the City, Stories from the Sea*, a collection of twelve songs that reflected her experiences in both New York and by the English seaside. PJ had finally created an album that didn't 'make you want to run screaming and crying from the room,' as she said. There was still plenty of rock'n'roll grunt, but it had quieter, almost melodic moments also. The album featured a duet with Radiohead's Thom Yorke, 'This Mess We're In'. Yorke also sang on other tracks and played keyboard.

Her previous albums had a minimalist quality. But *Stories* had all the bells and whistles — acoustic and electric pianos, harpsichord, keyboards, synthesiser, drums, bells, tambourine, E-bow, djembe, maracas and, of course, guitars and bass. The result was a record that PJ described as beautiful. The critics agreed, many surmising that perhaps Ms Harvey was in love not only with New

'I finally feel comfortable ... I am allowing myself to be myself for the first time ever,' she said about *Is this Desire?*

York, where she had written much of the new material, but also with a certain someone who was rumoured to be actor/musician/model Vincent Gallo. No one had heard her this happy, almost contented.

Always ready to try something new, in 2003 PJ took up an invitation from Josh Homme, Queen of the Stone Age's frontman, to play on his pet project, *Desert Sessions 9 & 10*. Homme has been working on *Desert Sessions* for years. It is a collaborative project in which he and his buddies spend a couple of weeks at Rancho De La Luna studio in the Mohave Desert, USA, and record whatever comes into their collective heads. The previous *Desert Sessions* albums (one to eight) were relatively obscure independent releases. But with Island's star performer on the record, *Desert Sessions 9 & 10* was elevated to new heights and the label put its muscle behind the release.

PJ became the first rock artist to perform at the Tate Modern in London. The concert, with Rob Ellis and Mick Harvey, featured PJ in a white fringed catsuit playing guitar and bellowing expletives as the audience of rock fans and art lovers circled uncomfortably. She also found the time to write and produce five songs for *Before the Poison*, the Marianne Faithfull album.

By the time *Uh Huh Her* was released in 2004 PJ was back to her old angst-ridden form, prompting rumours the love affair that had inspired *Stories* four years earlier had crashed and burned. Assumptions that a song like 'Who the Fuck' was a rant against an ex-lover prompted PJ to set the record straight, something she wasn't fond of doing. The song was about having a bad hair day, she explained.

Uh Huh Her was recorded over a two-year period, with the majority of the tracks put down at her home studio in Dorset using four- and eight-track systems. PJ played every instrument except drums, and produced the album. She strove to capture ugly, distressed sounds with guitars tuned low and played through poor quality amps. But distressed and depressed are two completely different states — PJ has said this was one of her most uplifting and hopeful records. *Uh Huh Her* was a slow mover, but still turned in a respectable performance on the charts. However success is not PJ's motivation. She has said that if she didn't perform, write, sing or play music she would die.

PJ continues to work, often with Flood and Parrish, on new music. Whatever she produces next, it is certain to introduce a new chapter in the life of this ever-evolving rock chick.

MELISSa ETHERIDGE

The Boss-ess

Often referred to as the female Bruce Springsteen, a compliment she relishes since the Boss is one of her greatest influences, Melissa Etheridge first hit the scene in 1988 with her impressive self-titled debut album.

Melissa was born in 1961 in the conservative prison town of Leavenworth, Kansas, in America's Mid West. Her love affair with music began early in life. She picked up her first guitar at eight and was songwriting by the time she was in high school. During her teenage years she played acoustically at local venues, performing her own material as well as covers of those who inspired her — her musical influences extend from Springsteen, to Bob Dylan, Led Zeppelin and Janis Joplin, with whom she has been compared.

Escaping Leavenworth for Boston, Melissa spent a year at Berklee College of Music before dropping out in the early 1980s to try her luck in LA. After several years playing acoustic gigs and developing a loyal following, she signed to Island Records.

Melissa's guitar playing and deeply personal lyrics created a melodic blues-infused, folk-rock sound that was a welcome antidote to the manufactured music that was filling the airwaves. Her hit single from her debut album, 'Bring Me Some Water', was nominated for a Grammy in 1989 but it wasn't until 1993, after four nominations, that she picked up her first award — for 'Ain't It Heavy' from her third album *Never Enough*, released in 1992.

An outspoken supporter of gay rights, Melissa 'came out' in 1993 at the Gay and Lesbian Ball held as part of President Clinton's inauguration celebrations. She announced to the 2000-strong crowd she was a lesbian. Fears that her sexuality would encumber her reputation were unfounded with the release of her fourth album, 1993's multi-platinum *Yes I Am*, which elevated her to the rock hierarchy on a global scale.

Yes I Am featured the singles 'Come to My Window', 'If I Wanted to' and 'I'm the Only One', all of which made it into the US top ten. 'Come to My Window' delivered Melissa her second Grammy in 1995. Having toured continuously since 1988 and released five albums in seven years, she took a break between 1995's *Your Little Secret* and 1999's *Breakdown*.

Melissa's trademark is her introspective and personal lyrics. When her relationship to filmmaker Julie Cypher ended after twelve years and two children, she poured her anguish into a collection of songs which became *Skin*, another top ten album. In 2004 Melissa was diagnosed with breast cancer — the same year she released her album *Lucky*. Sporting a bald head, the result of chemotherapy, she took to the stage at the 2005 Grammys to pay homage to Janis Joplin.

In 2006 Melissa and her partner Tammy Lynn Michaels celebrated the birth of twins. The next year she was awarded an Oscar for the song 'I Need to Wake Up' from Al Gore's documentary *An Inconvenient Truth*.

SHERYL crow

No mistake

When Sheryl Crow made her debut in 1993 many assumed she was another overnight sensation. The reality was less glamorous. Crow had slogged it out for the best part of a decade battling depression and earning a living as a backing singer before her lucky break.

Born in 1962 in the bible belt of the American South in the small town of Kennett, Missouri, Sheryl was brought up by liberal parents in an environment surrounded by music. Her lawyer father played trumpet and her mother, a piano teacher, sang in a local swing band. At home Sheryl listened to the eclectic record collections of her parents and older siblings. James Taylor, Bessie Smith, Stan Kenton, Billie Holiday, Rod Stewart, Joe Cocker and the Beatles were among her favourites. Sheryl learned the piano from the age of six and studied classical music at university. She made her living teaching music to handicapped children and singing advertising jingles.

Taking a gamble, in 1986 she headed to LA to try her luck in the music industry. She landed a job as the back-up singer on Michael Jackson's Bad tour. It was a role that seemed a great stepping stone for the young singer, but in reality she was burdened by constant sexual harassment. She channelled her experiences into songs, penning lyrics while she picked out tunes on her bass guitar.

Coming off the eighteen-month world tour, Sheryl fell into a deep depression that lasted months. She has said that the thought of suicide kept her company every day for years. Finally she found a therapist who helped her through the mire. She dragged her body out of bed and back to work as a session singer. It was at one of these gigs that she met Hugh Padgham, a producer who led her to A&M Records.

Signing to the label, she headed into the studio, but her first album didn't have the cut-through the record company was looking for. It was shelved and A&M sent Sheryl back into the studio to try again.

The result was *Tuesday Night Music Club*. The album took nearly twelve months to gain traction, but ended up turning multi-platinum — its success largely due to the single 'All I Wanna Do', which became an international number one hit. On the strength of the album, Sheryl picked up three Grammys in 1995, including record of the year.

Tuesday Night Music Club came out of a collaborative forum that involved Sheryl and a few of her musician buddies. Meeting once a week to smoke, get drunk and jam, they wanted to create music in a relaxed and informal environment. Sheryl has said it took her as long to physically recover from the recording sessions as it did to make the record. They played hard, but it was great fun and the relaxed vibe translated to the album, on which Sheryl plays guitar and piano.

Success propelled Sheryl into a realm where she associated with the likes of Bob Dylan and Joe Cocker. She sang on stage with Mick Jagger and toured with the

Eagles on their massive US comeback tour. It was a total headspin for the singer who was as much a fan as a rising star.

S heryl's musical style spans country, pop and rock — an eclectic collection of sounds that reflect her varied tastes and make her music universally accessible. She is a powerful songwriter and, although much of her material is autobiographical, it follows familiar themes.

So far Sheryl has collected nine Grammys, released five studio albums — all of which have sold platinum or more — and clocked up numerous top ten hits, including 'If It Makes You Happy', 'A Change Would Do You Good' and 'My Favourite Mistake'. She has produced much of her own material as well as tracks for Stevie Nicks, and collaborated with Kid Rock — their single 'Picture' was a number one hit in the US in 2003.

After a string of unsuccessful romances with musicians — one of the downsides of being in rock music, she has said ——Sheryl embarked on a relationship with champion cyclist Lance Armstrong. The pair intended to marry, but split up in 2006 after three years together.

Not long after Sheryl was diagnosed with breast cancer, which forced her to cancel plans to tour that year. Having recovered from the illness, she has began a new phase in her life, adopting a two-week-old boy, whom she named Wyatt after her father.

COURTNEY LOVE

Through the Looking Glass

Watching

Courtney Love

play out her life
in the tabloids and on TV
it is easy to write her off as a

self-indulgent, self-centred pain in the ass

whose limited talents are
only surpassed by her capacity
for excess.

B rush aside the publicity froth that surrounds her though and a much more complex picture unfolds. She is all of the above, and more — calculated, manipulative, obsessive and dangerous.

Courtney Love is born of a twisted personality that is clearly crying for help. Anyone else would have been locked up and the key thrown away. But she became known at a time when fascination with celebrities

Linda later said her daughter was bipolar, but it hadn't been diagnosed. Courtney was just known as strange

was hitting fever pitch. She was obscene, loud, lewd and opinionated, flashing her large breasts and sneering profanities through a lipstick-smudged mouth. The public lapped up every fall from grace, and there were many — arrests, child custody battles, drugs, booze, brawls, even accusation of murder.

She was riveting to watch and at the same time made your eyes bleed.

Born in 1964 in San Francisco, Love Michelle Harrison had an unorthodox upbringing. Her parents split when she was around five. Her mother Linda Carroll renamed her daughter Courtney and gained custody after accusing husband Hank Harrison of giving the child LSD. The charge was unproven but mud sticks.

In the era of peace, love and stoned hippies, Courtney's mother — a marriage guidance counsellor who has been married four times — moved from one relationship to another, shifting her growing brood (Courtney has four step-siblings) around various hippy communes in Oregon.

There was something different about Courtney from the start. Linda took Courtney to a therapist at age two. 'The first therapist I consulted said, "I don't know what's wrong, but I have a feeling it's going to get worse and there's not anything we can do".' In later years Courtney's mother would say her daughter was bipolar, but when she was a tot the psychiatric profession hadn't diagnosed it. She was just known as strange and hopelessly spoiled.

Her mother's transient lifestyle meant Courtney was in and out of different schools, homes, cities, even countries. In New Zealand at the age of ten she had her first encounter with prescription drugs. Because she was finding it hard to sleep and her behaviour was disrupting the entire household, Linda took her off to a doctor, who prescribed sedatives.

Courtney was a wild child, constantly in trouble at school. Although academically very bright, her antics got her expelled and in trouble with the law for shoplifting. By the time she was around fifteen she was in reform school, where she was in constant strife for fighting, smashing doors and being her unruly self. Of her stint there, Courtney said, 'I was semiotic about my delinquency. I studied it. I learned a lot. I'd grown up with no discipline and I learned a lot about denial. It did not have an adverse affect on me.'

When Courtney was sixteen, Linda Carroll 'emancipated' her — a clever way of telling her she wasn't welcome at home anymore.

For the next couple of years Courtney moved from one foster family to another in between staying in state facilities. One family, the Rodriguezs, are still a part of her life. She doesn't speak to either parent. 'There's actually a list in an American magazine of the worst celebrity parents ... two was my mother and number three was my father. I really got a raw deal.'

Once she was of legal age Courtney took off to travel the world. She survived on a small trust fund from her grandparents and supplemented her income by stripping.

She arrived in London around 1982. When masquerading as a music journalist to get into gigs, she came upon Julian Cope from Teardrop Explodes. Hanging out with Cope and his buddies, Courtney began to get a taste for the rock'n'roll life. But she was sending Cope nuts. At his wit's end, he ran an advertisement in a London newspaper: 'Free us from Nancy Spungen-fixated heroin A-holes who cling to our greatest rock groups and suck out their brains.' Even Courtney knew when she had worn out her welcome. She headed back to the States.

She landed in Portland, Oregon, later that year. She hung out with various bands and occasionally wrote for the street press. She hooked up with Rozz Rezabek, the singer in pop group Theatre of Sheep, and the two embarked on an unhealthy, drug-fuelled relationship.

Courtney's musical aspirations began to surface, but she was unable to say what she wanted other than to be a rock star. She knew she could sing and she owned a guitar, which she carted around with her but didn't play.

Tired of being treated like a hanger-on by Rezabek, she took off for San Francisco at the invitation of Jennifer Finch, who would later turn up in riot grrrl band L7. Finch and Courtney prowled the traps, checking out the live music scene. But it wasn't long before she grew restless again. Over the next few months she changed locations frequently — Taiwan, Hong Kong, Portland — before returning to San Francisco.

In 1983 she made a conscious effort to get her musical act together, fronting the hardcore rock band Faith No More — an odd choice for someone into the new romantics and a fan of Duran Duran, Soft Cell and Spandau Ballet. Still, she threw herself into the role of hard-ass rocker, setting her hair on fire on stage and smashing bottles. But that stint only lasted about twelve months and, despondent, she returned to Portland.

she threw herself into the role of hard-ass rocker, setting her hair on fire on stage and smashing bottles

There she met Kat Bjelland who played guitar. They headed to San Francisco. With Jennifer Finch, the three formed Sugar Baby Doll in 1985. But infighting between Bjelland and Courtney ended the party before it began. The band folded long before they'd even thought about playing a gig.

she was
unable to
articulate
what she
wanted to
achieve other
than to be a
rock star

Bored with San Francisco, Courtney took off for LA where Finch was working as a TV extra. Courtney went back to stripping, and began to entertain the idea of becoming an actress. Fixated with Nancy Spungen, the girlfriend and murder victim of Sid Vicious, she was ecstatic when she learned there was a film to be made about the pair. She auditioned for *Sid & Nancy*, reportedly breaking a painting over director Alex Cox's head in order to stand out. She was given a bit part as Nancy's best friend. During shooting in New York,

Courtney spent time at the Chelsea Hotel where Spungen was murdered, absorbing every macabre piece of the tale and revelling in the tragedy of it all

Courtney spent time at the Chelsea Hotel where Spungen was murdered, absorbing every macabre piece of the tale and revelling in the tragedy of it all.

Returning to San Francisco, Courtney mended fences with Bjelland. Bjelland wanted to move to Minneapolis where her family was living. That suited Courtney, who had no ties. Babes in Toyland became their next band. But it wasn't long before old tensions resurfaced and within months Courtney was ousted.

Sid & Nancy was followed in 1987 by another Cox film, the forgettable *Straight to Hell*, a western comedy shot in Spain with Courtney in the lead. She focused on acting, forgetting about music while she tried to make her mark in LA. But there were prettier starlets, and much thinner ones. By her own admission, she was overweight and unattractive. She was a nobody in Tinseltown. For a consummate attention-seeker like Courtney that was an untenable position. She shelved the acting idea.

For the next two years Courtney flitted around — to Minneapolis, where she and Bjelland had one more attempt at playing music together, Alaska, where she went to strip for three months, San Francisco and Seattle.

Then she headed back to Portland and met Kurt Cobain after a Nirvana gig. No sparks flew between the two and she pushed him from her mind until Nirvana became demigods two years later.

Back in LA, Jennifer Finch was now playing in L7. Courtney hung around, watching Finch live the life that she coveted, playing gigs around LA. To make ends meet, she went back to what she knew best — taking off her clothes. But she wasn't the best stripper in town and was relegated to the day shift which the less attractive girls worked.

Directionless and out of control, Courtney was all about pushing the limits. After getting wasted one night she ran off to Vegas to marry a friend of Finch's, transvestite Falling James Moreland of the alternate band the Leaving Trains. The marriage was annulled shortly after.

Finch's success spurred Courtney on. She went back to her plan to be a rock star, running an ad in a local music rag for musicians to form a band. Courtney busied herself learning guitar while she waited for the responses to flood in. Guitarist Eric Erlandson answered the call. He and Courtney hit it off, professionally and personally. They formed Hole. It took a few months for the line-up to settle, with Jill Emery coming in on bass and Caroline Rue on drums.

Hole had its first gig as a support to L7, after which they set about playing any club that would have them. In early 1990 Hole recorded the

Courtney admitted she set her sights on Cobain. She pursued him relentlessly

single, 'Retard Girl', on independent label Sympathy for the Record Industry. To promote the single they hit the road, playing in clubs across the US.

The next year, Hole's second single, 'Dicknail'/'Burn Black' was released on Sub Pop Records. It was followed by the album, *Pretty on the Inside*, on Caroline Records, a strange mix of punk rock and wrist-slashing lyrics delivered in Courtney's acid vocals that miraculously held a tune despite the angst and anger of her delivery. Produced by Sonic Youth's bassist Kim Gordon and Don Fleming, the songs were raw, at times ranting, and full of rage against everyone and everything.

Although the album wasn't a hit in the States, the British lapped up this large —she's nearly 178 centimetres — grossly made-up woman. She was like a giant baby doll with all the tragic self-indulgence of Bette Davis's character in *Whatever Happened to Baby Jane*. When Hole toured Britain as the support for Mudhoney, glowing reviews fuelled interest in the band. *Melody Maker*'s Everett True went into raptures over a Hole gig he'd seen in LA.

On stage Courtney was a dynamo, capturing the audience's attention and holding it in a vice-like grip for the duration. Dressed in baby-doll mini dresses that were strategically torn, exposing flesh and underwear, her tights ripped and tottering on heels, Courtney screamed her pain and the listener received her message in a series of blows to the brain. Her rouge-painted mouth sucked the audience in, her face a contorted river of sweating foundation and running mascara. She sang of rage and hate, angry sex and consuming self-interest. She was riveting, if painful, to watch.

Back in the US the media were more interested in her flirtation with Kurt Cobain than in her music. Nirvana's album *Nevermind* was released around the same time as *Pretty*. Whereas Hole's effort hadn't even made a blimp on the charts, *Nevermind* went on to sell in the millions. The attention around Nirvana catapulted Cobain, a shy, introspective songwriting genius, into the rock stratosphere, creating a new musical genre — grunge — in the process.

Courtney has admitted she set her sights on Cobain once she realised he was important. She pursued him relentlessly. By the end of 1991 she was officially his girlfriend, enjoying all the hype and status that it brought. The other members of Nirvana hated her. She didn't care comparing herself to Yoko Ono.

she was way more dangerous than him. Deep in his soul Cobain was a musician — that's all he wanted. He wanted to play his music

Cobain 'went on TV and said she was the best fuck in the world.' Hot sex would explain the whirlwind pace of the romance. They started dating in October 1991. Four months later they were married and by August parents. What a headspin. Photos of Cobain at that time show a man in complete shock.

Their relationship was one long cycle of arguments and escalating drug consumption. She relished the darker moments when she and Cobain would dress in disguise and hit the streets in order to score. She was way more dangerous than he. Deep in his soul Cobain was a musician — that's all he wanted. He didn't want the fame and the fortune. He wanted to play his music.

Courtney was all about the fame and the fortune. In those heady Nirvana days there was no shortage of money. Money for drugs, cigarettes, booze, whatever cravings the pregnant Courtney had. She had child protection services on her ass after a *Vanity Fair* article implied she was using heroin when pregnant. Frances was removed from her parents for a short time while her safety was assessed.

Mrs Cobain was a slimmed-down version of the *Pretty on the Inside* Courtney. She wanted to stay skinny — and drugs and cigarettes help you do that. She appeared naked on the cover of *Vogue*, pregnant with cigarette in hand. 'I want my anger to be valid and the only way to do that is to be fairly attractive.'

Her attachment to Nirvana gave Courtney the leverage to get her band off the indie label and into the mainstream. Suddenly she was all over the media, talking up her ambitions and her love for the skinny, permanently exhausted-looking lead singer of Nirvana. Industry notables started to look at Hole in a different light. Maybe some of Nirvana's magic would rub off.

her association with Nirvana gave Courtney the leverage to get her band into the mainstream. The power of association was clear

Madonna's company Maverick was among those showing an interest in signing Hole. Courtney found herself the centre of attention, just where she liked to be, and in a bidding war. The power of association was clear. She chose to go with Nirvana's label, and Hole began work on their second album, *Live Through This*. Many believe Cobain wrote much of the material on that album — and certainly it was a quantum leap over *Pretty on the Inside*.

Live Through This, released in 1994, went multi-platinum and its first single, 'Doll Parts', reached number four on the Billboard charts. The album introduced changes to Hole's line-up. Emery and Cue had been replaced by Kristen Pfaff and Patty Schemel. Sean Slade and Paul Q Kolderie co-produced, giving the album an edge that had the music media salivating. *Live Through This* won year-end critics polls at *Spin*, *Rolling Stone* and the *Village*

Voice, but it also drew its detractors. According to *Stylus*, 'Ms. Love … tunelessly croons the verses, predictably bellows the choruses.'

Live Through This was a week away from being released when Cobain, stoned to the eyeballs on heroin and Valium, killed himself with a shotgun in the lakefront home he shared with Courtney and Frances in Seattle.

When Cobain died, Courtney was in rehab in LA after being arrested for possession of a controlled substance and stolen property. Like the rest of the world, she heard of his death three days after the event. Cobain had

Cobain, stoned to the eyeballs on heroin and Valium, killed himself with a shotgun in the lakefront home he shared with Courtney and Frances

also been in rehab, but had absconded after two days. No one was with him when he died.

Cobain's suicide turned Courtney's world upside down. It also put her on centre stage. Her behaviour — lying in his blood, reading his suicide note at the funeral throughout which she interjected her own recriminations — was her finest performance, proving she was indeed a skilled actress.

The bad press she had received around the time she was carrying Frances was nothing compared with how the media treated her following Cobain's death. Her money-grubbing ways and parody of the grieving widow incited an anti-Courtney stance that would last for more than a decade, completely overshadowing her musical career.

Courtney put on a stiff upper lip and went on the road later that year to promote her album. 'My goals keep me alive … and no personal issue is going to interfere with that,' she said. Only two months after Cobain's death, Hole bassist Kristen Pfaff died from a heroin overdose. Courtney gritted her teeth and pushed on. Melissa Auf Der Maur replaced Pfaff in the band.

Hole toured to Britain later that year, performing at the Reading Festival. The show was more like a Herculean effort rather than entertainment, the band hanging together by a thread, Courtney so wasted that she found it hard to stand, let alone perform.

The next year they went on the road in the US as the support act to Nine Inch Nails. Death threats escalated. A bullet shell was thrown on stage in Pittsburgh. She picked it up, showed the audience then the band left the stage. Courtney wasn't going to take that kind of treatment from anyone. She became violent, throwing her guitar at a heckling audience member who was taunting her with 'who's your next victim?' Nirvana fans were showing up at Hole concerts just to abuse Courtney. 'They abuse me and I abuse them,' she said matter-of-factly.

Fellow musicians were at the end of her fists. She and Bikini Kill vocalist Kathleen Hanna came to blows at the Lollapalooza Music Festival in 1995, the same year that an inebriated Courtney crashed an MTV interview with Madonna and threw a make-up mirror at the mega-star. A judge ordered Courtney to undertake anger management classes.

In the 1996 film *The People vs. Larry Flint*, she played a character not unlike herself — a former stripper who indulged in the seedier side of life and was hopelessly addicted to excess. Her performance gained her a Golden Globe nomination.

While filming *Larry Flint* she was dating one of its stars, Edward Norton. Their relationship lasted for three years and was surprisingly low key, one she didn't play out in the media. She has said of her relationship with Norton, 'I've either had the very good guys or the bad. I left Ed Norton, who was good and wonderful, for an average bad man. It's upsetting.' While the two were dating, Norton played guitar on stage at two Hole shows in LA.

Hole's next studio effort was the 1998 release *Celebrity Skin*. The album was contentious from the start, with drummer Patty Schemel quitting shortly after its release because 'what the band has become I don't want to be part of anymore.' The critics disliked the album, which Kurt Loder of MTV likened to a 'Bangles record without the tunes'. Billy Corgon of the Smashing Pumpkins had co-written five tracks for the album — Courtney liked to collaborate with her lovers and she and Corgon had been an off-and-on item before she'd hooked up with Cobain.

Produced by Erlandson, *Celebrity Skin* introduced a new sound. Gone was the mindless anger and torturous angst of Courtney's lyrics. In their

'I've either had the very good guys or the bad. I left Ed Norton, who was good and wonderful, for an average bad man. It's upsetting,' Courtney said

place was music that could almost be termed pop rock, but definitely not grunge and not punk. The album lacked the originality and energy of *Live Through This*, but its material did capture a new audience. The title single went to number one on the Billboard modern rock chart and four on the mainstream rock chart, and the single 'Malibu' made it to number three.

The band hit the road to promote the new album, touring solidly throughout 1999. In the USA they performed with Marilyn Manson, although Hole pulled out of the forty-date tour after only nine shows. Hole also toured to Australia and New Zealand that year, hit the road in Canada on the Edgefest tour and crammed in dates in Europe.

As is often the case with Courtney, her art took a back seat in 2000. When she waltzed down the Golden Globes red carpet that year the media were astonished at the new-look Courtney — new nose, pert boobs and a svelte body clad in an elegant gown. She was transformed into a starlet right before our eyes. Courtney brushed it off with her usual finesse.

'Women want to wear nice fucking clothes,' she said.

But it wasn't long before she was back in the land of dope. She admitted that, even though she thinks heroin is a revolting drug, it hadn't stopped her hitting up subsequent to Cobain's death. But pills are really her thing. Percodan, Valium, OxyContin, Vicodin. Pills washed down with booze.

Growing bored with Hole, Courtney briefly formed another band, Bastard, in 2001, a super-punk all-female group. But it fell apart after recording a demo because of personality conflicts. The diversion into Bastard was a way of denying that Hole was in a free fall. But by 2002 the band had disintegrated and officially announced it was over.

Courtney was seemingly out of control — breaking into an ex-lover's home when stoned on cocaine, hitting a woman over the head with a bottle, turning up to court five hours late.

She lost custody of her daughter, the final straw being a suicide attempt while the little girl was home. Courtney said she tried to make it fun for Frances while they waited for the ambulance to arrive.

In 2004 she released her first solo album, *America's Sweetheart*. Patty Schemel was back playing drums and also contributing to several songs co-written with Courtney and Linda Perry. The album's two singles, 'Mono' and 'Hold onto Me', both made it into the Billboard top forty, but the album failed to fly.

Its failure hit Courtney hard. *Rolling Stone* said of Courtney's solo effort, 'For people who enjoy watching celebrities fall apart, *America's Sweetheart* should be more fun than an Osbournes marathon.'

When she appeared on David Letterman's show, she flashd the poor man

the new-look Courtney — new nose, pert boobs and a svelte body clad in an elegant gown — was transformed into a starlet right before our eyes

no less than six times. Later that night she put in an impromptu performance on stage at a New York club and threw a mike stand into the crowd — it decked one of the audience members and resulted in a charge of disorderly conduct. By 2005 she was under house arrest as part of her rehabilitation program which spanned eighteen months.

Courtney Love may have had moments of artistic brilliance. But she is living proof that the notion of celebrity is nothing more than the fabrication of a hungry media — working with great raw material — and the guilibility of a voyeuristic public.

ALANIS MORISSETTE

emotional overdrive

A child star in her native Canada, Alanis Morissette became an international sensation with her hit album *Jagged Little Pill* in 1995. But the pressure to be 'little Miss Perfect' almost destroyed this petite performer.

Born in 1974 in Ottawa, by the age of ten Alanis was playing piano, writing songs and starring in a TV series. In her teens she released two pop albums, but her success came at a high personal price — a struggle with anorexia and bulimia, panic attacks and low self-esteem fuelled by constant remarks about her weight. Her troubles drove her into therapy.

The young Alanis listened to music by Olivia Newton-John, Abba and George Michael. Gradually her musical taste matured to Radiohead, Tori Amos, the Pretenders, Annie Lennox and Sinead O'Connor and she rediscovered Bob Dylan, who had been a favourite of her parents.

Leaving Canada in the early 1990s, she made the trek to LA. There she met Glen Ballard who became her songwriting soulmate. Ballard was well connected, having worked with numerous name acts, including Michael Jackson and Aerosmith. They worked together in his studio, furiously writing songs, which Alanis recorded with the likes of Benmont Tench from Tom Petty's Hearbreakers, and Flea and Dave Navarro from the Red Hot Chili Peppers. After hearing the completed tracks Maverick, Madonna's label, cut her a deal.

Jagged Little Pill was released in 1995. Its smash hit single 'You Oughta Know' took Alanis from child star to rock superstar. 'You Oughta Know'

convoluted
tales of love,
revenge,
anger and
personal
misery
became her
hallmark

set expectations that Alanis was a hard-core rock chick, but the rest of the album didn't support the theory. *Jagged Little Pill* spawned no less than five number one singles in the US and delivered Alanis four Grammys in 1996, including album of the year.

The songs on the album were deeply personal — Alanis has said she uses songwriting to exorcise her demons. Convoluted tales of love, revenge, anger and personal misery became her hallmark. *Jagged Little Pill* has sold upwards of thirty million copies.

It took three years before her follow-up, *Supposed Former Infatuation Junkie*, was released. During this period, Alanis, fed up with the pressures of touring, had seriously questioned her future in music. *Junkie* was influenced by Eastern sounds, reflective of a sojourn to India to regain a sense of perspective.

On this album she collaborated with Ballard once again, took on producing and played flute, piano and harmonica. Although another number one multi-platinum hit, sales were disappointing in comparison with *Jagged Little Pill*. The record's only number one single, 'Thank U', caused something of a stir — Alanis appeared naked in the video. The album's long meandering

lyrics, which some termed psychobabble, had critics claiming it was self-indulgent. Alanis agreed, saying that was what art was about, self-obsession.

There were more Grammys in 1999 and 2000. Alanis went back to acting, appearing as God in the film *Dogma* and onstage in *The Vagina Monologues* on Broadway. She also toured with Tori Amos and performed for Amnesty International in Paris along with Radiohead, Bruce Springsteen, and Tracy Chapman. She is a committed activist.

Her next album, *Under Rug Swept*, was released in 2002. She had severed her ties with Ballard and wrote and produced all the songs herself. Sounding closer to *Jagged Little Pill*, it didn't contain the hit material of that album. Two years later it was followed by *So-Called Chaos*, an intensely emotional album filled with tales of joy and love reflecting Alanis's own personal state — she was engaged to actor Ryan Reynolds (*Smokin' Aces*). The album was Alanis's most up-vibed offering and featured dance and pop tunes, including the top five hit 'Everything'.

In 2007 Alanis and Reynolds split after three years. Once again she turned to songwriting to express her emotions, filling journal upon journal.

GWEN STEFANI

Sweet escapee

G wen Stefani, your classic 'accidental rock star', was more interested in getting married and having babies than making music.

Born in 1969, Gwen grew up in Orange County, California, dancing to Duran Duran, Depeche Mode, the Cure, Prince and early Madonna. She spent her days sewing, daydreaming about her boyfriend and watching TV, giving little thought to what she would do when she left school.

Gwen's older brother Eric encouraged her to sing with him as he bashed out tunes on the family piano. Eric's passion for ska music rubbed off on his unfocused sister, who left behind the new romantics and threw herself headlong into the music of British ska band Madness.

In 1987, when Eric formed No Doubt with singer John Spence, he dragged Gwen along to provide backing vocals. Spence committed suicide a year later and she became lead singer. Over the next few years Gwen juggled study for an arts degree and playing gigs at clubs, college events and parties.

A couple of times it looked like the band would take off, with gigs supporting Red Hot Chili Peppers and Ziggy Marley. But it took nine years before No Doubt made the big time.

Signed in 1991 to new label Interscope Records,

as a
teenager
she spent
her days
daydreaming
about her
boyfriend
and watching
TV

headed up by producer Jimmy Iovine, No Doubt issued their eponymous first album in 1992. Radio refused to pick it up and MTV rejected the video. The band pushed on.

In 1995 they released *Tragic Kingdom*, which featured their first hit song 'Just a Girl', transporting Gwen and her platinum blonde hair, washboard abs and kooky little-girl voice on to the world stage. Many of the songs express Gwen's grief over her break-up with boyfriend of seven years, No Doubt's bassist Tony Kanal. Fourteen months after its release, *Tragic Kingdom* reached number one around the world.

The common theme in interviews was Gwen's desire to start a family. In 1998, she fell in love with Bush's lead singer Gavin Rossdale. They have married and had their first child.

Return of Saturn, released in 2000, was influenced by new wave, rock, pop and reggae. Gwen also teamed up with rapper Eve on 'Let Me Blow Ya Mind', delivering the pair a Grammy. The following year No Doubt released *Rock Steady* and headed off on another world tour.

Gwen's first solo album *Love Angel Music Baby* (*L.A.M.B.*) drew on the dance music of the 1980s. An instant success, it included collaborations with Dr Dre, Linda Perry and Outkast's Andre 3000.

The Harajuku Girls were created for *Love Angel Music Baby*. The

four Japanese girls appeared with Gwen on stage and in videos. The geisha-doll fantasy drew her first real criticism, with accusations of racism and power tripping.

Gwen made her movie debut in 2004, appearing as Jean Harlow in Martin Scorsese's *The Aviator*. The next year she released her second solo album, *The Sweet Escape*, which was even more dance-oriented.

With MTV awards, three Grammys and multi-platinum albums to her name, plus the hubby and babies she always wanted, Gwen has proven she's not just any girl from Orange County.

'Just a Girl' transported Gwen and her platinum blonde hair, washboard abs and kooky little-girl voice on to the world stage

2000

Hip
Hop
&
Pole Dancers

As Heart's Nancy Wilson said, now is the music of the pole dancer. Music videos border on soft porn. Just about every female singer is a scantily clad, writhing seductress singing about getting her man — by stealing, cajoling or sexual temptation, or all three for good measure.

Perhaps the proliferation of women singing about their 'baby' reflects the desire of millions of single women out there hoping to find someone to love. In the 2000s more people are living on their own than at any other time in history. By the turn of the new millennium, technology had driven us to form friendships over the internet. The online chat rooms of the 1990s grew into full blown online dating services used by millions to find that special someone — or a bit on the side.

A perfect pout, turned-up nose, cellulite-free skin and bleached blonde hair became the prerequisites for female pop singers. And so did enhanced cleavages. Kids as young as sixteen are having breast implant surgery, graduation gifts from parents desperate to see their babies succeed in the plastic world.

The 2000s will become known as the decade of fear, the decade when governments of all colours used terrorism to erode civil rights. The so-called War on Terror has spurned such aberrations as Guantanomo Bay and Abu Graib. A fertile subject, artists of all types have explored terrorism and the attendant human and civil rights abuses in movies, ficton, art and music.

But the boy bands kept on creaming it, with 'N Sync selling millions of copies of its singles and the Backstreet Boys continuing to chart. Marc Anthony, who later in the decade would marry Jennifer Lopez, had numerous hits too. Madonna's new album *Music* delivered the singer more number one singles in the year she married British film director Guy Ritchie in an elaborate Scottish wedding.

After the tragedy of September 11, 2001, Paul McCartney called his entertainment mates together to put on the Concert for New York City the following month at Madison Square Garden. The Who, David Bowie, Eric Clapton, Mick Jagger, Keith Richards, Billy Joel, Melissa Etheridge, Five for Fighting, Bon Jovi, Kid Rock and the Goo Goo Dolls all played. Another concert featuring Bette Midler, Destiny's Child, Mariah Carey, Rod Stewart, Michael Jackson, P Diddy, Backstreet Boys, 'N Sync and Aerosmith, was held in Washington the next day.

When 'N Sync split up, Justin Timberlake went solo and sold records in the millions. Other multi-platinum chartbusters were Usher, Christina

Aguilera, Beyonce and Alicia Keys, demonstrating that R&B was still a predominant force in popular music.

Hip-hop music continued in popularity, with Eminem's single 'Lose Yourself' from the soundtrack of the film *8 Mile* picking up an Oscar in 2002 and 50 Cent sweeping the charts in 2003. In many ways hip-hop had replaced rock'n'roll for America's youth, although rock legends like Aerosmith, U2, Guns'n'Roses, the Rolling Stones, Metallica and Bon Jovi were still making noise.

The first half of the decade saw a mixed bag of female performers in the charts. Beyonce became a solo artist performing with her boyfriend Jay Z and independently from Destiny's Child. The country band the Dixie Chicks had a mainstream hit with the Stevie Nicks song 'Landslide' and copped a ban from the neo-cons for speaking out against George Bush's war in Iraq. Canadian teenager Avril Lavigne hit the airwaves with one of 2002's biggest selling albums *Let Go* and *American Idol* winner Kelly Clarkson kept racking up the hits. In New York Karen O made her mark with Yeah Yeah Yeahs.

In the USA a new rock chick emerged, one who had a unique take on the world around her — many thought Pink would settle into the pop category along with Gwen Stefani, Christina Aguilera and J Lo. But she has rock in her heart and by the release of her second album *M!ssundaztood* in 2002 she was topping the charts.

Pink reintroduced us to the female singer who writes and sings about things that aren't the most comfortable topics — the impact of warring parents on children, the entertainment industry's fixation on thin surgery-enhanced women, and internal conflict. It was the first time for a long while that a woman in rock was singing about something other than losing her man.

Other bands were taking up the protest song again. New wave punk rockers Green Day's 2004 album *American Idiot* debuted in the top spot on the Billboard charts, its lyrics expressing the sentiments of a disgruntled generation and seeding this previously alternate band in the mainstream consciousness.

New music was being made in New York with the formation of the Yeah Yeah Yeahs headed up by punk rocker Karen O. The Yeah Yeah Yeahs — Karen with Brian Chase and Nick Zinner — released their first album in 2003, *Fever to Tell*. The punk-oriented sound and O's voice showed leanings towards the same stripped-back rock of the early PJ Harvey.

On Boxing Day 2004 the largest recorded tsunami hit Asia killing more than 200,000 and wiping out communities across nations. British musicians came to the aid of the displaced people with the biggest benefit concert since Live Aid. Tsunami Relief Cardiff, held in Wales in January 2005, raised over a million pounds for the relief effort.

The rock sound known as nu-metal, which appeared at the end of the 1990s, continued to be popular on the alternate charts, but as the decade rolled on the public lost interest in this narrow stream fed by bands like Linkin Park, Limp Bizkit, Good Charlotte and the Vines. Another group of indie musicians moved into the punk-rock space including the White Stripes and the Killers.

In July 2005 the Live8 series of concerts were held simultaneously across ten different cities, including London, Philadelphia, Paris, Berlin, Johannesburg, Rome and Moscow. Bob Geldof, who had masterminded Live Aid, was once again in the organiser's seat. The concerts featured more than a thousand musicians. In London U2, Madonna, Coldplay, Sting, Pink Floyd, the Who, Paul McCartney and Elton John entertained the thousands who poured into Hyde Park.

As the year rolled around to 2006 female pop singers began to dominate the charts — Ashlee Simpson and her sister Jessica, Kelly Clarkson, Michelle Branch, Vanessa Carlton and Britney Spears. In 2007 the Pussycat

Dolls became the next band to enter the reality TV realm, holding auditions in the search for a new 'doll'.

The Idol shows swept the globe, with national TV competitions to find a star. *American Idol* winner Kelly Clarkson was the show's real success story, clocking up multiple international hits.

At the time of writing, the USA was trying to wind up its involvement in Iraq, but was deeper into Afghanistan. The conflict between Israel and Palestine was no closer to resolution, North Korea and Iran were flexing their nuclear muscles and China and India were becoming major powers. Global warming was accepted as a reality and governments were scrambling to make up for lost time.

We are living in a material world where credit card debt is at an all-time high. And in a culture that is fixated with celebrities. Reality shows have redefined TV entertainment, taking it back to ancient Rome and the games of the Coliseum. The only difference is you don't have to leave your living room and no one is mauled to death by a lion — death in reality TV land is of the metaphoric kind.

The only rock chick consistently figuring in the charts is Pink.

So where have all the rock chicks gone?

KELLY
CLARKSON

Million-dollar babe

Kelly Clarkson's rise to fame reads like a fairytale. The first winner of *American Idol* in 2002, Kelly walked away with a million dollars in prize money and a recording contract with RCA. But she has proved that her musicianship extends far beyond the manufactured environment of TV's hottest talent contest.

Born in 1982 in Burleson, Texas, a small Christian community near Fort Worth, Kelly grew up in a sheltered part of the USA that until recently was one of the last

remaining bastions of prohibition. Kelly gained a broad musical education. Her parents' diametrically opposed musical tastes — Billie Holiday and Etta James could often be heard along with Guns'n'Roses — provided an inspirational environment for the young singer who sang with the school choir.

Wanting to spread her wings, in her late teens Kelly headed to Los Angeles where she tried her hand at acting. She landed a few bit parts in TV shows like *Sabrina the Teenage Witch*. But her curvy figure wasn't what Hollywood was looking for and it wasn't long before Kelly was back in Burleson working as a cocktail waitress. Friends encouraged her to audition for *American Idol*. The rest, as they say, is history.

Following her win, Kelly threw herself headlong into the world of rock'n'roll. Her first album, *Thankful*, was released in 2003, hitting the top spot on the charts and putting in a double platinum performance. Its number one single, 'Miss Independent', was co-written by Kelly and Christina Aguilera. The album was a mixture of pop, R&B, gospel and country, Kelly handling the range with ease.

She hit the road for the first time to support the release of *Thankful*. And she performed on the *American Idol* tour and competed in *World Idol* in 2004 — she came second. That year her next album, *Breakaway*, was released. This multi-platinum selling album cemented Kelly's position as an international artist and not just a competition winner. It launched no less than four hit singles, including the chart topper 'Since U Been Gone'.

On *Breakaway* Kelly demonstrated her prowess as a songwriter, co-writing six tracks, including the ballad 'Because of You', which was about the breakdown of her parents' marriage. The album's title single was co-written with Avril Lavigne, who Kelly says is an incredible songwriter. *Breakaway* was more rock oriented, a deliberate decision on Kelly's part. It reflects the energy and tone of her live performances. *Breakaway* topped the Billboard hot adult contemporary songs for 2005 and 'Since U Been Gone' spent thirty-three weeks in the weekly top forty, making it the longest charting single for that year.

Success hasn't altered the values of this deeply religious singer. Kelly has chosen to live in Texas rather than take up digs in LA. She isn't interested in buying into the hype around being a rock star, including the pressure to be thin — she likes her curves and has refused to join the ranks of the size zero.

Since she stepped on to the world musical stage, Kelly has picked up two Grammys, MTV awards, and several American Music Awards, including 2005 artist of the year. In 2006 Kelly headlined a massive world tour before heading back into the studio. Her latest album is *My December*. She continues to be the only *American Idol* winner to date to prosper.

P!NK

A Rockin' Tomboy

When **Pink** hit the charts in 2000, the music press anticipated she would be another stereotypical pop girl — lots of attitude, exposed flesh and catchy dance tunes. **On first glimpse that's exactly what Pink was.** But as the singer found her feet the **rock chick within was unleashed,** positioning her apart from the rest of her peers.

Another Christina Aguilera or Britney Spears *she was not.*

Pink was born Alecia Beth Moore in 1979. She grew up in a working-class neighbourhood of Doylestown in Pennsylvania, an hour north of Philadelphia. Doylestown was a typical north-eastern American city. Downtown was like a demolition zone, its empty buildings, vandalised shops and dilapidated warehouses a grim reminder of the sweep of progress and the shopping mall mentality that had killed off many lively town centres.

Her father Jim Moore, a Vietnam vet, was an insurance broker who loved to play guitar, write songs and sing. The Moores played an eclectic mix of music. Pink's father favoured Dylan, Joplin, the Mamas and Papas and Billy Joel. Her mother Judy, who worked as a nurse, loved to listen to R&B and soul sisters, including Dionne Warwick, Donna Hathaway and Aretha Franklin.

Jim regularly sang his baby daughter to sleep. When she was older he would play the guitar while the little girl sang along. She remembered telling him she was going to be a rock'n'roll star — and he believed her. Even as a youngster she had a powerful voice and a steely determination.

As an infant, Pink suffered from a collapsed lung, the ongoing effects of which manifested themselves in various bronchial conditions, including asthma, which plagued her throughout childhood. To combat her breathing difficulties, she undertook singing lessons to teach her how to expand her lung capacity.

Home life was anything but happy. The Moores may have loved their offspring but the same couldn't be said for each other. There were constant screaming

by her mid-teens, she had pretty much worn out the desire to trash herself with narcotics

matches, often in front of the children, and tempers ran hot. Pink captured the domestic turmoil of her childhood in her video for the 2002 song 'Family Portrait', which she says is an honest portrayal of the way life was in the Moore household when she was a kid. Apparently the video seriously distressed her parents, who were unaware of the impact their arguments had on their children.

Her parents divorced when she was seven years old and Pink, with her older brother Jason, lived with their mother until she was fifteen. Her fondest memories of her childhood are centred on being outdoors, rough-housing in the woods with Jason, playing sports and camping.

There are two stories about how Pink got her moniker. One suggests that it was a result of her embarrassment at a schoolmate's discovery she had no knickers on under her trousers. The other refers to the colour of her vagina and was in answer to an African-American friend wanting to know what white girls looked like. Her friends began calling her Pink from the time she was about fifteen. It stuck.

A tomboy in both physicality and attitude, in her youth Pink would be out skateboarding with her mates, playing pool or hanging at local gay clubs, places where she wouldn't get hassled by men. She wasn't a lesbian but has many gay female friends. When she did go to straight clubs she occasionally toted a handgun. Philadelphia could be pretty rough at night and she learned how to read the street earlier than most.

As a child she was wild and unruly, smoking a packet of cigarettes a day from the age of nine, despite her lousy lungs. The young teenager stayed out to all hours, dropping acid and any other illicit drugs she could get her hands on, except heroin. Having read up on the different effects of drugs and how much you could take before killing yourself, she steered clear of smack — it was too unpredictable.

She'd lost friends to drug overdoses. The closest she came to becoming a statistic was one Thanksgiving when she nearly OD-ed on a cocktail of cocaine, ecstasy, angel dust and booze.

Music became her salvation. At thirteen she was singing in gospel choirs, usually the only white face. But her voice could easily have been mistaken for that of an African-American. By fourteen she was a back-up vocalist with local hip-hop group Schools of Thought, trying to get a rock band off the ground and doing a solo stint at dance joint Club Fever. The DJ let her sing a song one night a week. If she wasn't singing, she was busting moves as a break dancer.

Pink was full of rage against the establishment and stuck her finger up at any figures of authority — teachers, police, her mother. She had her fair share of trouble with the police for typical teenage acts like running away from home and shoplifting.

At her wit's end, and struggling to cope as a single mom, Judy Moore took Pink to a therapist at the age of fourteen. Pink used the sessions to spin fantastic tales about the things she'd like to do to those who made her mad. The therapist gave up after a few visits. It wasn't long before her mother showed her the door. Pink moved in with her father.

She dropped out of school and took whatever work came her way — at fast-food outlets and gas stations. When she was too wasted to go home, she'd crash at friends' houses. By the time she was in her mid-teens, she had pretty much worn out the desire to trash herself with narcotics. She let the drugs slide, although booze and cigarettes would remain constant companions.

the songs she wrote focus on her frustration at the injustices that life hands out

Her father was stricter with her and tried to give his daughter guidance. But she was headstrong and didn't like to be told. There were frequent clashes, but Pink knew how far she could push her father before she hit the point of no return. The hostility existing between mother and daughter wasn't present. Slowly Pink began to channel her energies into more positive areas.

Jim Moore tried to impart his own values on his daughter, encouraging her to base her life on honesty. She took the lesson to heart — as is evidenced by the shoot-from-the-hip frankness which is as much her trademark as her cropped hair and commanding voice.

Songwriting became a new form of therapy for the angst-ridden teen, who was living a life that was far older than her years. At fifteen she was in a relationship with a man who had a three-year-old daughter. The affair lasted six years, with Pink playing mother for part of that time. The songs she wrote during this period focus on her frustration at the injustices life hands out — not only to her. She was full of anger.

297

At fifteen she was spotted at Club Fever by an executive from MCA, who enlisted Pink for R&B girl group Basic Instinct. But it was a short-lived venture. Then came another R&B group, Choice, a trio with Chrissy Conway and Sharon Flanagan. Choice was signed to LaFace Records on the basis of a demo tape. LaFace, which was distributed through Arista, was headed by Antonio 'LA' Reid and Kenneth 'Babyface' Edmonds, both of whom had been in the 1980s' R&B band the Deele before starting their own label.

Pink remembered how daunting it was when Choice was asked to fly down to Atlanta to sing for LA Reid. They were confronted with an audience of dozens — it seems that Reid was so impressed with the demo that he had called in all his staff to witness the birth of his new superstars.

Despite having a record contract, Choice split up before they made it into the studio. The girls couldn't agree on the group's musical direction. Conway would go on to make her name as a Christian singer in ZOEgirls. Both Conway and Flanagan appeared on Pink's first album as back-up vocalists.

By 1997 Pink was signed to LaFace as a solo artist. While she waited for the label to make a decision on her future, she sang back-up vocals for various artists, including Diana Ross and Kenny Lattimore. The session work kept the wolf from the door and meant that Pink could concentrate on her songwriting.

LaFace had an impressive stable, including Toni Braxton, Outkast, TLC, Dido and Usher. Pink was suitably awestruck, but she also realised that in such high-calibre company she needed to get serious. Gone were the late nights and crippling hangovers. She threw herself into training. She spent hours in the gym and pounded the pavement getting her body into shape. And she worked on her voice.

Wanting to be recognised for her songwriting skills as well as her powerful soprano vocals, Pink busied herself writing. The label put together a slew of producers to work on her first album *Can't Take Me Home*, which was recorded in Atlanta. LA Reid and Babyface headed the team as executive producers.

Pink has said working on the album was akin to being on a conveyor belt in a music factory — in the studio with one producer, record the song, then move on to the next studio, next producer, next song. It was less that satisfying, but she knew she had to toe the line first time around.

On first hearing Pink's powerful voice, many assumed she was an African-American. There was a rumble in the music world when it was discovered she was a tattooed white girl with a shock of pink hair, rock hard abs and a mouth that would make a truck driver blush. But that didn't take away from the fact she had an amazing R&B voice.

Released in 2000, *Can't Take Me Home* drew positive reviews from the music press, which was surprised at the maturity of the newcomer's work. Likened to R&B darlings TLC, the album shot her into the spotlight. Pink co-wrote seven tracks on the album, including the US top ten hit 'There U Go'. Its other singles, 'Most Girls' and 'You Make Me Sick', also became top ten hits. The album clocked up double platinum sales.

Before LaFace unleashed its new star on the media, it had suggested she take etiquette classes. Pink flatly refused. Media training was also part of the new-star package, but she had no intention of

Pink was a refreshing antidote to the cute-as-pie girl singers populating the charts

playing ball. Pink was a refreshing antidote to the cute-as-pie girl singers populating the charts. The media applauded her frankness.

She hit the road for the first time, undertaking a massive stadium tour as the support act for 'N Sync on their Celebrity tour. Performing in front of tens of thousands of people was daunting even for someone with the amount of attitude Pink displays. The experience left her feeling disconnected with the audience. She was determined to play smaller venues when next she had the chance.

Now living in LA, Pink set up house in a two-bedroom apartment in Venice Beach, a place she'd always wanted to live. Venice Beach didn't disappoint her. She felt at home in this bohemian, seedy beachside northern LA suburb. During the day, its streets are crowded with artists and hustlers vying for the tourist dollar. After sundown it isn't the safest place to hang out. For a time Pink kept a gun just in case of unwanted attention. Her apartment was decorated with her collection of ornamental frogs — she has a frog tattooed on her foot — and her pet rats Thelma and Louise. Her Jack Russell terrier also lived with her for a time before her father adopted him. Pink named the dog Fucker so she could shock passers-by when she had to call him. At twenty-one she was still the rebellious teen.

The following year she teamed up with Christina Aguilera, Mya and Lil' Kim to record a cover of La Belle's 'Lady Marmalade' which

for a time Pink kept a gun in her apartment just in case of unwanted attention

was included on the *Moulin Rouge* soundtrack. The song hit number one in the USA and Britian and took out two MTV awards and a Grammy.

A massive fan of extreme sports, in 2001 Pink met motorcross rider Carey Hart at the X Games in Philadelphia shortly before he tried a jump that resulted in two broken arms. Horrified, Pink recalled telling a friend that there was no way she could ever fall for someone like that. Famous last words. Three months later they were a couple. In the coming months, Pink and Hart would discover the difficulties of conducting a long-distance love affair.

Not wanting to lose the momentum around their new star, in 2001 LaFace sent Pink back into the studio to record her second album.

Refusing to be lumped in with other pop divas, Pink, a self-confirmed control freak, took advantage of being in the executive producer's seat (along with LA Reid) and set about making a rock album.

Pink wanted to work with Linda Perry, who had enjoyed brief success as lead singer with 4 Non Blondes, which had been one of Pink's favourite bands as a child. The pair embarked on an intensive songwriting session that lasted three months, Pink camping out at Perry's home in LA for the duration.

The end result was *M!ssundaztood*, which undeniably rocked. It positioned Pink in a category all her own and delivered her a slew of hits — and new fans who had previously dismissed her as fluff. The album also featured rockers Steve Tyler of Aerosmith and Bon Jovi's Richie Sambora, giving it further rock cred. In 2002 Pink was named the number one top Billboard album female artist and *M!ssundaztood* came in at number four for the year.

Pink took advantage of being in the executive producer's seat and set about recording a rock album

Pink undertook her first headlining tour of the US in May 2002 — the Party tour. Those expecting the R&B artist of *Can't Take Me Home* were in for a shock. Flexing her new rock chick muscles, Pink introduced songs from her new album and performed covers of hits by Aerosmith and Guns'n'Roses and songs by Janis Joplin and 4 Non Blondes. The thirty-five date tour was a roaring success.

That summer she also toured with Lenny Kravitz as his support act, getting her name on the bill after calling him directly. But after headlining her own show, it seemed a step down. Exhausted from the gruelling schedule, missing her boy Carey

Pink did much of her growing up in the pages of the music press and tabloids

and suffering from chronic insomnia, Pink became sullen and un-cooperative.

As her fame grew so it seemed did her ego. Pink did much of her growing up in the pages of the musical press and tabloids. One moment she was giving up alcohol because of stomach ulcers, the next she was recovering from a tequila bender. She pledged her dislike of firearms, then was seen firing rounds at a pin-up of Saddam Hussein while swigging beer. There were so many stories of her downing Corona that it was reminiscent of Janis Joplin's affair with Southern Comfort.

The multi-platinum success of *M!ssundaztood* — sixteen million and counting — was putting enormous pressure on her to deliver again.

Reinventing herself once more, Pink took a new stance on her third studio album *Try This*, introducing a more punk-oriented style. It drew comments that perhaps Pink was the natural successor to the queen of reinvention, Madonna.

On *Try This*, Pink teamed with Tim Armstrong, lead singer of punk band Rancid, who co-wrote eight of the thirteen songs. Perry also appeared on the album as did bad-girl rapper Peaches. Many of the tracks Armstrong produced were recorded on his tour bus while on the road with his side project the Transplants. Pink enjoyed hanging with the boys and the experience of recording in a non-traditional studio environment.

Try This wasn't as commercially successful in the States as her previous album, but the single 'Trouble' won Pink her second Grammy. The album was released at a time when Arista was in free-fall, causing many to speculate that it would have had a better run had the label been able to support it. By the time Pink came to record her next album, Arista had folded, LA Reid had been given the bullet and Pink was part of the Zomba Music Group through Sony/BMG.

By 2004 Pink had moved out of her Venice Beach digs and was living in LA with her dogs Nanny and Bailey in a house formerly owned by ex-Van Halen drummer Alex Van Halen. She had also broken up with Hart.

Rumours abounded that she was locking lips with the likes of Tommy Lee. Others suggested she was a lesbian after smooching with Kristanna Loken of Terminator 3 at the World Music Awards. The media had long tried to drop the lesbian label on Pink because of her tough attitude. But as she has said several times, she likes the male physique too much.

After her responsibilities for promoting *Try This* were over, Pink took time off. Over the next year she busied herself writing songs. She consumed books of all genres and read film scripts in her search for the right acting role. She had been living life at a manic pace. Now at the age of twenty-six she had time to reflect on

Pink took a more punk-oriented style for *Try This*. It led some to comment that perhaps she was the natural successor to the queen of reinvention, Madonna

her life and determine what was important to her. Hart appeared on the top of the list and during her hiatus the two reconciled.

By the time her next album was released, Pink was a married woman. She had popped the question while Hart had been racing, holding up a sign as he'd zoomed past. Sporting matching tattoos saying 'tru luv', they married in Costa Rica in a barefoot beach ceremony in January 2006 and spent their honeymoon snowboarding. Now retired from freestyle racing, Hart owns a tattoo parlour and is also a regular reality TV star.

Pink's next release hit the market in April 2006. *I'm Not Dead* was her most political record to date, expressing her opinion on a range of issues from the entertainment industry's manipulation of women ('Stupid Girls') to the serial failures of the Bush administration ('Dear Mr. President'). On the album Pink teamed with Billy Mann, who had previously worked with her on *Try This* and is credited with co-writing 'God is DJ'. Her father contributed a song, 'I Have Seen the Rain', which he had written when he was in Vietnam during the war. He also sings on the song.

'Stupid Girls', a fantastic send-up of the world of celebrity and its obsession with painfully thin, compliant dolly girls, became a massive hit worldwide. The sentiment behind the song was brilliantly executed in the video, with Pink parodying various dumb female celebrity stereotypes — carrying the latest fashion accessory, a tiny dog, in her handbag, squirming semi-naked in foam and water atop a car, and in an hilarious bulimic moment featuring a toothbrush. The song moved talk-show queen Oprah Winfrey to dedicate an entire show to the topic.

I'm Not Dead entered the US charts at number six and sent an unequivocal and fans alike that this rock chick wasn't anyone's patsy. Pink began her I'm Not Dead tour in mid-2006, playing twenty shows in the USA before heading to Europe where she wowed crowds with her aerial acrobatics and highly choreographed performance.

In 2007 she was on the road again with Justin Timberlake, whom she'd come to know on her first tour supporting 'N Sync. As the opening act for Timberlake's Future Sex/Love Show tour, Pink performed in front of massive audiences at American stadiums. Suspended from scaffolding and twisting herself into head-spinning routines while belting out her hits, it was an impressive performance. Many wondered if Pink had been a circus performer in another life.

Focusing on her celluloid ambitions, Pink co-starred in the horror flick *Catacombs* with Shannyn Sossamon. She had been suggested for the role of Janis Joplin in *The Gospel According to Janis*, but she lost out to Zooey Deschanel.

'Stupid Girls', a fantastic send-up of the world of celebrity and its obsession with painfully thin, compliant, dolly

When Pink took a break from Carey Hart in the year following their marriage, she said she knew he was the man she wanted to have babies with. It just wasn't the right time. In 2009 the pair had reconciled and Hart joined Pink on the Funhouse Tour. But there is no patter of tiny 'pink feet yet'.

Funhouse, released in 2008, was Pink's break-up album. She described its songs as about 'fun', 'drunkenness', 'debauchery', 'silliness' and 'heartbreak'. She said originally she wanted to name it *Heartbreak is a Motherfucker*, because it was about love gone wrong. But 'Walmart wouldn't take it'. The album rocketed into the Billboard Top 200 charts at number two and topped the charts around the world. The single 'So What' took out the top spot in the USA, her first number one single on the Billboard Top 100. On the Funhouse Tour, Pink showed off her acrobatic skills twirling high above the audience without missing a beat, her voice clear and strong. The tour played Britain and Europe with USA dates added later as the album gained traction. By 2010, Pink's worldwide records sales had passed the thirty million mark.

AVRIL LAVIGNE

The best bratty thing

Canadian Avril Lavigne was discovered by Arista Records boss LA Reid when she was sixteen. A year later she skyrocketed to international stardom. Her tomboy attitude was hailed as a breath of fresh air among the scantily clad teenagers led by Britney Spears.

Born in 1984 in the tiny Ontario town of Napanee, Avril was raised in a strict Christian environment. Her mother kept a close eye on what her offspring listened to — Avril grew up with a steady diet of gospel and country music. Her early influences included artists like Faith Hill.

Avril sang with the church choir from a young age. In her early teens she performed at shopping malls and fairs. She learned guitar and began writing songs. At fourteen she won a competition to sing a Shania Twain song at that artist's concert in Ottawa. Five years later she sold out the same stadium as headliner.

Signed to Arista Records in 2000, Avril moved to New York with her older brother as chaperon and began working on songs for her debut album. Progress was slow until the record company moved her to LA. There she was assigned to

the songwriting team known as the Matrix, who took her raw material and turned it into chart-topping hits.

Avril's first album *Let Go* was released in 2002. She instantly became the darling of MTV's tweeny-bopper hour *TRL*, her skater-chic outfits and bratty attitude resonating with thousands of young fans. The album, a mix of rock numbers and catchy pop tunes, was an international hit spawning three number one singles — 'Complicated', 'Sk8er Boi' and 'I'm with You'.

Avril hit the road to promote *Let Go* and surprised many reviewers with her assured stage presence and captivating, if slightly thin, voice. Avril loved performing for her fans, but she didn't enjoy the promotional grind. In interview the petite teen didn't bother concealing her boredom and contempt for the whole process.

When it was time to record her second album she chose to take more control over the songwriting process, wielding her multi-platinum selling power. *Under My Skin*, released in 2004, had a slightly edgier tone and its songs were more concerned with the anguish of teenage love gone wrong and navel-gazing. It prompted reviewers to compare her to Alanis Morissette, although Avril's material wasn't as angst-ridden and contemplative.

In 2004 Avril started dating Sum 41 frontman Deryck Whibley. She moved out of her apartment in Toronto and the pair bought a house in LA. They tied the knot in 2006 in a traditional white wedding.

Her third album, *The Best Damn Thing*, was released in 2007 and topped the charts. Its first single 'Girlfriend', a classic pop song with catchy hooks and a chorus that gets stuck in your head, put Avril firmly back in the number one position for weeks. *The Best Damn Thing* is Avril at her bratty best. Even though she's now in her early twenties, her slight frame and girlie voice let her get away with material that is pitched directly to the tween-age market. On this album she uses profanity with gay abandon. It's classic bubblegum anarchy that lacks any substance, but would be great to sing along to if you're nine.

KAREN O

Fever Pitch

Karen O is the dynamic, charismatic and eccentric lead singer of the New York punk/avant-garde/pop/rock trio the Yeah Yeah Yeahs.

Formed in 2000, the band crashed onto the New York club scene. It was a time when garage rock was enjoying a resurgence led by the Strokes, who were at their peak. Just three years later, the tables would turn with the Yeah Yeah Yeahs leading the pack and the Strokes claiming them as their 'favourite band of the moment'.

Karen's onstage antics and idiosyncratic fashion style have almost eclipsed her musical abilities. Almost. During performances she douses herself and her adoring fans in beer, stomps, shouts, throws gear (sometimes hitting audience members), shoves microphones down her throat and frequently grabs her crotch.

Her fashion sense is courtesy of best friend, fashion designer Christian Joy. It involves lots of torn clothing — ripped fishnets, T-shirts with holes, tatty mini skirts and spandex. With a mop of black hair and a Chrissie Hynde fringe, a porcelain complexion, red lips and kohl-rimmed dark eyes, Karen is a fashion icon for hoards of pre-pubescent girls.

But Karen O is much more than a caricature. An accomplished songwriter for both the Yeah Yeah Yeahs and for film soundtracks, Karen O has become a rock icon of the new millennium, with one journalist calling her the first woman of rock for the twenty-first century. She's been likened to everyone from Pat Benatar to Patti Smith and been called the female Iggy Pop. She has a magnetic appeal on stage and a voice that ranges from an orgasmic yowl to melodic tones, and everything in between. She is a performance artist and uses the stage — and the audience — as her canvas.

Karen O's creator Karen Orzolek said the 'Karen O persona' was designed to be outrageous, to see what 'I could get away with … manipulative, deceptive'. And designed to dance. Karen O, she said, was born on the dance floor. In fact, Karen Orzolek was born in South Korea in 1978, to a Korean mother and Polish father. She grew up in a middle-class town of Englewood in Bergen County, New Jersey, with her parents and younger brother.

In her teens her musical tastes were broad. She loved dancing to Michael Jackson and listening to the melodies of Simon and Garfunkel and Cat Stevens. She also got into artists like Neil Young in her 'hippie phase', a period when she clashed frequently with her mother, once a fashion designer, who couldn't understand her daughter's tattered clothing choices.

After graduating from high school Karen attended Oberlin College in Ohio for two years before transferring to New York to complete her studies at New York University's Tisch School of the Arts. At Oberlin she met Brian Chase, who would later become the Yeah Yeah Yeahs' drummer.

Karen hadn't been in New York long before she met guitarist Nick Zinner in a seedy East Village bar one night. Too drunk to recall the meeting in any great detail, Karen ran into Nick again shortly after and the pair decided to form a band.

In 2000, under the name Unitard, the pair wrote a number of acoustic folk songs. But Karen quickly grew bored. She wanted to amp it up. Inspired by Ohio's avant-garde punk scene, they added electric guitar and microphones to their musical compositions. At first Zinner was skeptical about forming a rock band, but Karen's enthusiasm was infectious. Chase came in on drums and the Yeah Yeah Yeahs was born.

Their early gigs included supporting the Strokes and the White Stripes, bands they had been influenced by. They played underground clubs, bars and galleries to small crowds. And they played random illegal venues in Brooklyn at shows put on by promoters the Twisted Ones. They were 'exciting … crazy times … it was madness,' said Karen. Except the night they played their first gig at CBGBs. The Yeah Yeah Yeahs were fillers between the metal bands. Karen said it was the most 'depressing' show, with the audience all but ignoring them. But their live performances got tongues wagging and the excitement around the Yeah Yeah Yeahs, and Karen's exuberant and at times totally outlandish onstage actions, attracted a groundswell of support.

Prolific songwriters, Zinner and Karen soon had enough material to put down their first EP and by early 2001 their debut recording was on the streets. The EP was produced independently on their own label, Shifty, with Jerry Teel of punk blues band Boss Hog. The eponymous EP drew attention to the trio and in 2002 NME awarded the song 'Bang!' the number two position on its annual Tracks of the Year list. 'Bang!' was the band's attempt to 'emulate the sassafrass and aloof cool of ESGs leading ladies'. The band is on record saying ESG's album *A South Bronx Story* (2000) was the 'single most influential record for us at the very start, even though we had no bass player!' Zinner plays through two amps, supplanting the need for a bass guitar.

Perversion, sex and violence are the three things Karen has said she wanted to get out of her system through music. Chorus lyrics to 'Bang!' — 'As a fuck son, you sucked' — escaped the notice of the censors in Britain, where the song was given airplay and introduced the band to a new audience.

In early gigs Karen used olive oil all over her face and body so she looked sweaty. It was messy and stung her eyes. Beer seemed a better option and she began to spray herself and the audience. She'd fire up before the show with tequila or champagne using the alcohol to fuel her onstage persona — in retrospect, her wild performances shocked even herself.

In March 2002 they performed at the annual South by Southwest Music Festival in Austin, Texas, where they were the hottest band on the bill. In June they toured Britain as a supporting act, along with the Liars, for the Jon Spencer Blues Explosion and performed their debut headline show at the Metro on Oxford Street in London. Karen credits Jon Spencer, and his wife Cristina, lead singer of Boss Hog, with bringing 'us into this whole mess'.

Late in 2002 the new offering from the Yeah Yeah Yeahs, *Machine* was released. The EP's title single was crowned Single of the Week by *Kerrang Magazine*. And *Rolling Stone* added the band to its Artists to Watch list. Eminent music journalist Reverend Al Friston claimed the Yeah Yeah Yeahs were the new White Stripes. Karen didn't take kindly to being pigeonholed into any particular music genre: the Yeah Yeah Yeahs were making a new sound all of their own.

The following year the band signed with Interscope who, Karen believed, was 'more risk taking' and also bred 'fine rock star personas'. In the stable were Eminem, Marilyn Manson and No Doubt.

Their debut album, *Fever To Tell*, was produced by Alan Moulder (Eurythmics, Smashing Pumpkins) in 2003 in London and it became an instant hit. 'Maps', the first single from the album, was a stirring love ballad about Karen's romance with Angus Andrew from the Liars. After the video was put online, radio play followed and MTV2 put the video on rotation. Fans and critics lapped up Karen's emotional video performance for 'Maps', which was complete with real tears thanks to her emotional state about her boyfriend Andrew, who she was leaving to go on tour. She has said one of the reasons she dislikes touring so much is its impact on her personal life. 'Maps' showed a vulnerable, soft side to this wild woman as well as her versatility as a musician.

She has said being the front woman of a band that plays 'hard and noisy' is exciting for fans, particularly the girls. Of course being a rock chick has drawn other attention also. Karen doesn't subscribe to claims she's a sex symbol. She told *Playboy* when she turned down an invitation from them in 2003 that Karen O wouldn't be showing 'any t**ies, d**ks, or f**nies!'

The success of 'Maps' was followed by the band's first hit, 'Fever To Tell', which reached gold record status. In 2003 the band went back to Europe and Britain, where they performed on Top of the Pops along with a couple of the Spice Girls, Marilyn Manson and Kelly Clarkson. Karen has said it was 'strange company … but fun'. In 2006 she called Clarkson a 'poisonous varmint' for using a guitar break from 'Maps' in her smash hit 'Since U Been Gone'.

In 2003 the band also toured to Japan and Australia, where they were part of the Livid Festival. Slightly overenthusiastic in her performance at the Metro in Sydney, one night Karen danced off the stage and injured herself. When it came time for the band to take the Triple J Big Top stage at the festival, Karen was confined to a wheelchair and pushed onto the stage by Andrew. By the following year the pair had split and Karen moved to Los Angeles.

The draw in LA was new lover, the film director Spike Jonze who had directed the band's earlier video *Y Control*. And it offered the chance for anonymity. In New York Karen O was a recognised celebrity, but in LA there were more famous faces for the paparazzi to focus on. And she was craving some downtime.

Jonze's brother Squeak E Clean, aka Sam Spiegel, produced the band's second album, *Show Your Bones*.

The accolades and awards continued. *SPIN* magazine gave Karen her second Sex Goddess award. Blender ranked her one of the Rock's Hottest Women and in 2007 Spinner.com placed her at number three on its Women Who Rock Right Now list. And rock icon Lee Ranaldo, famed guitarist with Sonic Youth, said Karen was the 'kind of frontperson who comes along once in a decade'.

A three-year hiatus between albums gave Karen time to regroup. *Show Your Bones* was released in Spring 2006 and charted at number eleven on the Billboard 200. The album featured a range of musical styles — 'Gold Lion', the first single from the album, was reminiscent of a pure rock song, other tracks took their cues from Nirvana, Sonic Youth and R.E.M. Dark and brooding were two words frequently associated with this offering.

In 2007 the band released another EP, *Is Is*, which hit number seven on the Billboard Top Independent Albums. That year Karen performed on the collaborative Dylan piece 'Highway 61 Revisited' for the soundtrack of the movie *I'm Not There*, which also featured Lee Ranaldo, Steve Shelly (both Sonic Youth), Tom Verlaine (Television) and Dylan band bassist Tony Garnier.

Perversion, sex and violence are the three things Karen has said she wanted to get out of her system through music

Karen performed a one-off show under the name Native Korean Rock & the Fishnets in 2008. She has said as a teen she was ashamed of her Asian background, but since then she has visited relatives in South Korea several times and developed a deeper understanding of her mother's culture. The musical style she chose for this experiment was reminiscent of her and Zinner in Unitard.

Karen's love of dancing and disco tunes influenced the band's 2009 album *It's Blitz*, which peaked at twenty-two on the Billboard 200. Zinner's signature guitar sounds were replaced with electronic synthesisers and keyboards. Karen wanted no guitars on this album and Zinner, who frequently clashed with her, acquiesced. Recorded at El Paso's Sonic Ranch studio and also on a farm in Massachusetts, *It's Blitz* was produced by Dave Sitek and Nick Launay (INXS, Talking Heads). She collaborated on the soundtrack of ex-flame Spike Jonze's film *Where the Wild Things Are* and its single, 'All is Love', was nominated for a Grammy in 2010.

The Yeah Yeah Yeahs still pull crowds around the globe, headlining festivals such as All Points West and Lollapalooza and are adored by the media — London's *Evening Standard* calling them 'one of the most important bands of the decade'.

Karen hasn't lost any of the enthusiasm and energy that drove the band's success. She's still bawling, screaming and grinning maniacally at the audience, secure in her place in rock history as one of the genre's most outrageous — and talented — women.

Discography

In some cases, these are not complete listings, but selected works from a large oeuvre.

Chrissy Amphlett
Divinyls
- *Monkey Grip* EP (1982)
- *Desperate* (1983)
- *What a Life!* (1985)
- *Temperamental* (1988)
- *Divinyls* (1991)
- *Underworld* (1996)

Pat Benatar
- *In the Heat of the Night* (1979)
- *Crimes of Passion* (1980)
- *Precious Time* (1981)
- *Get Nervous* (1982)
- *Live from Earth* (1983)
- *Tropico* (1984)
- *Seven the Hard Way* (1985)
- *Wide Awake in Dreamland* (1988)
- *True Love* (1991)
- *Gravity's Rainbow* (1993)
- *Innamorata* (1997)
- *Go* (2003)

Kim Deal
The Pixies
- *Surfer Rosa* (1988)
- *Doolittle* (1989)
- *Bossanova* (1990)
- *Trompe Le Monde* (1991)

The Breeders
- *Pod* (1990)
- *Last Splash* (1993)
- *Title TK* (2002)
- *Mountain Blues* (2008)
- *Fate to Fatal* (EP) (2009)

Marianne Faithfull
- *Come My Way* (1965)
- *North Country Maid* (1966)
- *Love in a Mist* (1967)
- *Dreamin' My Dreams (1976)*
- *Broken English* (1979)
- *Dangerous Acquaintances* (1981)
- *A Child's Adventure* (1983)
- *Strange Weather* (1987)
- *Blazing Away* (1990)
- *A Secret Life* (1995)
- *20th Century Blues* (1996)
- *Seven Deadly Sins* (1998)
- *Vagabond Ways* (1999)
- *Kissin' Time* (2002)
- *Before the Poison* (2004)
- *Easy Come Easy Go* (2008)

Kim Gordon
Sonic Youth
- *Confusion is Sex* (1983)
- *EVOL* (1986)
- *Sister* (1987)
- *Daydream Nation* (1988)
- *Goo (1990)*
- *Dirty* (1992)
- *Washing Machine* (1995)
- *A Thousand Leaves* (1998)
- *SYR4: Goodbye 20th Century* (1999)
- *Murray Street* (2002)
- *Sonic Nurse* (2004)
- *The Eternal* (2009)

Debbie Harry

Blondie

Blondie (1976)

Plastic Letters (1977)

Parallel Lines (1978)

Eat to the Beat (1979)

Autoamerican (1980)

The Hunter (1982)

No Exit (1999)

The Curse of Blondie (2004)

Solo

Koo Koo (1981)

Rockbird (1986)

Once More into the Bleach (1988)

Def, Dumb & Blonde (1989)

Debravation (1993)

Necessary Evil (2007)

PJ Harvey

Dry (1992)

Rid of Me (1993)

To Bring You My Love (1995)

Dance Hall at Louse Point (1996)

Is This Desire? (1998)

Stories from the City, Stories from the Sea (2000)

Uh Huh Her (2004)

The Peel Sessions 1991–2004 (2006)

White Chalk (2007)

A Woman A Man Walked By (2009)

Heart

Dreamboat Annie (1976)

Little Queen (1977)

Magazine (1978)

Dog and Butterfly (1978)

Bebe Le Strange (1980)

Private Audition (1982)

Passionworks (1983)

Heart (1985)

Bad Animals (1987)

Brigade (1990)

Rock the House Live (1991)

Desire Walks On (1993)

The Road Home (1995)

Alive in Seattle (2003)

Jupiter's Darling (2004)

Chrissie Hynde

The Pretenders

Pretenders (1980)

Pretenders II (1981)

Learning to Crawl (1984)

Get Close (1986)

The Singles (1987)

Packed! (1990)

Last of the Independents (1994)

The Isle of View (1995)

Viva el Amor! (1999)

Loose Screw (2002)

Pirate Radio (2006)

Break Up the Concrete (2008)

Joan Jett and the Blackhearts

Bad Reputation (1981)

I Love Rock'n'Roll (1981)

Album (1983)

Glorious Results of a Misspent Youth (1984)

Good Music (1986)

Up Your Alley (1988)

The Hit List (1990)

Notorious (1991)

Flashback (1993)

Pure and Simple (1994)

Fetish (1999)

Sinner (2006)

Janis Joplin

Big Brother and the Holding Company
   (1967)
Cheap Thrills (1968)
I Got Dem Ol's Kozmic Blues Again
   Mama (1969)
Pearl (1971)

Annie Lennox

The Tourists
   The Tourists (1979)
   Reality Effect (1979)
   Luminous Basement (1980)
Eurythmics
   In the Garden (1981)
   Sweet Dreams (1983)
   Touch (1983)
   Be Yourself Tonight (1985)
   Revenge (1986)
   Savage (1987)
   We Too are One (1989)
   Peace (1999)
Solo
   Diva (1992)
   Medusa (1995)
   Bare (2003)
   Songs of Mass Destruction (2007)
   Annie Lennox Collection (2010)

Courtney Love

Hole
   Pretty on the Inside (1991)
   Live Through This (1994)
   Celebrity Skin (1998)
Solo
   America's Sweetheart (2004)
   Nobody's Daughter (2010)

Madonna

Madonna (1983)
Like a Virgin (1984)
True Blue (1986)
You Can Dance (1987)
Like a Prayer (1989)
I'm Breathless (1990)
The Immaculate Collection (1990)
Erotica (1992)
Bedtime Stories (1994)
Ray of Light (1998)
Music (2000)
American Life (2003)
Confessions on a Dance Floor (2005)
Hard Candy (2008)

Stevie Nicks

Fleetwood Mac
   Fleetwood Mac (1975)
   Rumours (1977)
   Tusk (1979)
   Mirage (1982)
   Tango in the Night (1987)
   Behind the Mask (1990)
   Time (1995)
   The Dance (1997)
Solo
   Bella Donna (1981)
   The Wild Heart (1983)
   Rock a Little (1985)
   The Other Side of the Mirror (1989)
   Timespace: The Best of Stevie Nicks
     (1991)
   Street Angel (1994)
   Enchanted (1998)
   Trouble in Shangri-La (2001)
   The Divine: Stevie Nicks (2002)
   Crystal Visions: The Very Best of Stevie
     Nicks (2007)

Karen O

Yeah Yeah Yeahs

Yeah Yeah Yeahs (EP) (2001)

Machine (EP) (2002)

Fever to Tell (2003)

Show Your Bones (2006)

Is Is (EP) (2007)

It's Blitz (2009)

Pink

Can't Take Me Home (2000)

M!ssundaztood (2001)

Try This (2003)

I'm Not Dead (2006)

Funhouse (2008)

Suzi Quatro

Quatro (1974)

Your Mama Won't Like Me (1975)

Aggrophobia (1976)

If You Knew Suzi (1978)

Suzi and Other Four Letter Words ... (1979)

Rock Hard (1981)

Main Attraction (1983)

Oh Suzi Q (1990)

What Goes Around (1996)

Unreleased Emotion (1998)

Back to the Drive (2006)

Patti Smith

Horses (1975)

Radio Ethiopia (1976)

Easter (1978)

Wave (1979)

Dreams of Life (1988)

Gone Again (1996)

Peace and Noise (1997)

Gung Ho (2000)

Trampin' (2004)

Twelve (2007)

Tina Turner

Solo

Tina Turns the Country On (1974)

Acid Queen (1975)

Rough (1978)

Love Explosion (1979)

Private Dancer (1984)

Break Every Rule (1986)

Foreign Affair (1989)

Wildest Dreams (1996)

Twenty Four Seven (1999)

Acknowledgements

Thanks to Jenni Lans for her honesty and support; Vicki Giordano for picking her brains; my sons Jackson and Lewis who provided a steady supply of hot tea and hugs; my fantastic and dear friends Nina, Angela B, Tasj, Sandy, Sally P-R, Karen, Meredith, Rowena — all great chicks; AB for keeping the faith; Tony Mott for his awesome photographs; Nicole Moore for helping with the photo research; my publishers Lisa Hanrahan and Mark Byrne for giving me the chance to write the book of my dreams; editor Mary Trewby for her eye for detail; David Dalton for giving his time and sharing his experiences with Janis Joplin; and, most importantly, to the rock chicks who appear in this book who inspire with their talent, passion, commitment and sheer determination to do it their way.

Photographs

All black & white photographs by Tony Mott, except the following: Getty Images — pages 17, 21, 22, 23, 25, 26, 31, 33, 34, 35, 38, 41, 42, 52, 67 (Blondie, Joan Jett), 70, 71, 75, 78, 81, 82, 84, 85, 88, 93, 94, 96, 98, 99, 102, 105, 106, 109, 115, 116, 134, 135, 139, 146, 149, 151 (Madonna, Chrissie Hynde), 153, 155, 168, 169, 171, 173, 180, 184, 189, 200, 209, 283 (Kelly Clarkson), 289, 290.

Tony Mott's personal selection: page 11 — Adilta of Magic Dirt; page 12 — Marianne Faithfull (top), Kim Gordon of Sonic Youth (bottom); page 13 — Patti Smith; pages 14–15 —(clockwise, from top left) Alanis Morissette, Adilta of Magic Dirt, Chrissy Amphlett, Johnette Napolitano of Concrete Blonde, Adilta of Magic Dirt.

Colour photographs between pages 64–65:
1st page — Tina Turner, photo: Tony Mott. 2nd page — Patti Smith, photo: Getty Images;

3rd page — Blondie, photo: Tony Mott; 4th p. — Susie Quatro, photo: Getty Images.

Colour photographs between pages 80–81:
1st page — (top left) Debbie Harry, photo: Getty Images; (top right) Patti Smith, photo: Getty Images; (bottom left) Ann and Nancy Wilson, photo: Getty Images; 2nd page — Joan Jett, photo: Getty Images; 3rd page — (top lef Fleetwood Mac, photo: Tony Mott; (top right) Deborah Harry, photo: Tony Mott; (bottom) Joan Jett, photo: Getty Images; 4th page — (tc Pat Benatar, photo: Getty Images; (bottom) Eurythmics, photo: Tony Mott.

Colour photographs between pages 192–193:
1st page — Chrissie Hynde, photo: Getty Images; 2nd page — Chrissy Amphlett, photo: Tony Mott; 3rd page — Annie Lennox, photo: Tony Mott; 4th page — Courtney Love, photo: Tony Mott.

Colour photographs between pages 208–209:
1st page — (top) Sheryl Crow, photo: Tony Mott; (bottom) Melissa Etheridge, photo: Tony Mott; 2nd page — PJ Harvey, photo: Tony Mott; 3rd page — Gwen Stefani, photo: Tony Mott; 4th page — Pink, photo: Tony Mott;

The author

Alison Stieven-Taylor, a freelance journalist for over twenty years, has written for a wide variety of magazines, from *Rolling Stone* through to *Cleo*. Alison started her working life as a rock'n'roll publicist. Today she is the director of a successful PR consultancy working with leading global brands. She has studied documentary film, narrative form in literature and film and is an accomplished researcher. She is the author of *The Price of Love* and a photographic artist.